Schematron 2025

A language for validating XML

Erik Siegel

XML PRESS

Schematron 2025

A language for validating XML

Disclaimer

Credits

Schematroll mascot image:	Cody Chang
Author photo:	Maaike Siegel

Trademarks

XML Press
Denver, CO
https://xmlpress.net

Second Edition
978-1-937434-93-9 (print)
978-1-937434-94-6 (ebook)

Table of Contents

CHAPTER 1

Preface

Computer systems process, read, exchange, and spit out data like the contents of this book, your tax form, electronic health records, social media messages, and much more. All such computer data must be in some kind of well-defined format, so it can be understood and processed correctly.

Computer data formats can be organized into families, according to the ground rules they follow. This is analogous to natural languages. In the western world we have a limited character set (A–Z, sometimes a few more), and we write from left to right. Other language families, for example Chinese, have a much more extended character set and a different writing orientation. If you speak a western language but don't understand French, you can't comprehend text in French, but you can still recognize constructs from the Western language family, such as characters, words, sentences, and paragraphs. For Chinese that will be much more difficult.

Computer data format families work the same way. Examples of data format families include EDI, CSV, JSON, and XML. Each has its own syntax rules, application domains, pros, cons, and fan club. And just as a French person and a Swedish person cannot easily communicate, even though their languages are in the same family, a computer system that talks XML language A cannot understand XML language B. Both people and computers can perceive familiar language constructs, but they cannot understand what the other person/computer is saying unless they know the specific language being used.

In the natural language world we can sometimes partly solve that communication problem with a little improvisation, such as sign language or gestures. However, for computers that's not so easy. What goes in and what comes out must be correct and understandable. The process of establishing this correctness for computer data is called *validation*.

Validation is usually done in phases:

- First the data is checked to see whether it follows the language-family ground rules.
- Then checks are done to determine whether it's in the correct language and follows the grammar of that language.
- And, optionally, additional rules (sometimes called business rules) are checked to determine whether the data makes sense.

Table 1.1 compares these phases for natural and computer languages:

Table 1.1 – Comparison of natural versus computer language validation

Check	Natural language	Computer language
Language family ground rules	Does it use only allowed characters? Are these characters organized into words? Is punctuation used correctly? Are sentences organized into paragraphs, etc.?	Does it uses only allowed characters? Are data elements delimited correctly? Are things grouped correctly, etc.?
Language grammar check	Are the words spelled correctly? Are the verbs conjugated correctly? Is the word order as expected for this language, etc.?	Is the data recognizable? Are all data elements there? Are numbers written as numbers, dates as dates, etc. Are all required data elements present, etc.?
Additional rules check	Does it have an introductory paragraph? Do numbers, if any, make sense? Is the author's name spelled correctly, etc.?	Is this date before that date? Is the sum of this set of numbers not more than some threshold? Is the value of this data element present in that external database table, etc.?

The rules for computer data checks can be expressed in special formal computer languages called *validation languages*. Validation languages allow the computer system to validate whether the data it consumes or produces is correct and *valid*. Schematron, the subject of this book, is about validating XML, so let's focus on that.

- For XML, checking the ground rules of the language family is an absolute precondition for any subsequent checks. An XML document that passes this stage is called *well-formed*.
- To check grammar you can choose from several XML validation languages. The most common ones are DTD, W3C XML Schema, and RELAX NG. If this stage is passed, an XML document is called *valid*.
- Schematron is a validation language that checks additional rules. A set of checks written in the Schematron language is called a *Schematron schema*. There's no official name for a document that passes this stage, but let's call it *Schematron valid*.

This process of validating XML documents is explained in much more detail in Chapter 3.

A Schematron schema consists (mostly) of assertions. A simple example would be that, somewhere in an XML document, a given start date must always be before a given end date. You can write such an assertion in the Schematron language and then validate that it's true for your data. If it's not true, an error message is produced.

This book explains how to create Schematron schemas and use them to check XML data for compliance with your additional/business rules.

Schematron 2025, its predecessor, and this book

In September 2025, a new edition (or version if you prefer) of Schematron was published, called, no surprise, *Schematron edition 2025*.[1] It is a major upgrade over its predecessor, the 2020 edition, with many new features and improvements. This book is about the 2025 edition.

However, the 2020 edition will continue to be used for a long time to come. Switching to the new edition may be technically or business-wise unnecessary. And even though the 2025 edition was designed to be backwards compatible, moving to a new version is always a technical challenge.

To get the most out of this book, you need to consider which edition of Schematron you're using, or planning to use:

- If you're new to Schematron, don't know which edition to use, or are not yet committed to a specific edition, my advice would be to use the 2025 edition. Why not use the latest and greatest? This book will teach you all about it.
- If you're already using, or planning to use, the 2025 edition, this is the book for you.
- If you're (still) using the 2020 edition, you can also use this book. The 2025 edition did not fundamentally change the language, and lots of constructs and language features stayed the same. Wherever there's a change between the editions, you'll find a note explaining this (see below for an example of such a note).
- That said, if you are just interested in the 2020 edition, you might be better off using the previous edition of this book, by the same author, called *Schematron: A Language for Validating XML* (XML Press, 2022). It is available at https://xmlpress.net/publications/schematron/.

[1] In this book, I shorten this to *Schematron 2025*.

To help you with the changes the 2025 edition introduced, this book does two things:

- Appendix G contains an overview of all changes introduced in the 2025 edition (based on the 2020 edition). This will be especially useful if you are accustomed to edition 2020 and want to know what changes edition 2025 introduced.
- Wherever this book describes or mentions something that does not exist in, or is different from, the 2020 edition, there is a note, like the one below, describing the difference:

> **Schematron 2020 note**
>
> This is an example of a note describing a change between Schematron 2020 and Schematron 2025. You will find them scattered throughout this book.

Who is this book for?

This book is for anyone who wants to learn Schematron 2025 or expand their existing knowledge of the language.

I assume you have at least a basic knowledge of XML. That is, you know roughly what documents, elements, and attributes are, and you have seen data formatted like Example 1.1 and Example 1.2:

Example 1.1 – An example XML document (`schematron-book-code-2025/data/invoices.xml`)

```
<invoices date="2020-11-11" total="10101.33">
  <invoice date="2020-10-04" total="10000.50" id="12345"/>
  <invoice date="2020-10-16" total="100.83" id="56789"/>
</invoices>
```

Example 1.2 – Another example XML document (`schematron-book-code-2025/data/text.xml`)

```
<body>
  <p class="greeting">Hello <b>Schematron</b>!</p>
</body>
```

If the examples above look like complete gibberish, this book is probably not for you. But if you know your way around XML at this level, read on.

In writing this book, I assumed that Schematron is used by a wide variety of people with a broad range of backgrounds. Some will be XSLT or XQuery programmers. Some will previously have written schemas in other languages like W3C XML Schema, or RELAX NG. Others will be less tech-savvy or newer to the XML world. This book tries to explain Schematron for both XML aficionados and people who are less experienced. I assume a basic familiarity with XML. A little programming experience helps but is not strictly necessary. If your experience fits this profile, basic Schematron should be no problem.

For those that want to go beyond basics, there's also a lot to be gained. Schematron schemas can do amazing things, like combining data from many sources or even digging into databases. You can mix it with programming languages like XSLT, unleashing all the power these languages provide. This book will teach you how to do this.

If, after reading the above, you think Schematron might be interesting but are still a little unsure, please jump ahead to the section titled "An illustrative example" (p. 12), which contains an example of basic Schematron usage. Hopefully it will give you a good picture of what Schematron can do.

How to use this book

There are several ways you can use this book. Here are a few suggestions:

- For those that are new to the XML world or have limited programming experience, this book contains two introductions on important topics:
  - To create Schematron schemas, you need at least a basic knowledge of *XPath*. If you don't know what this is and expressions like `/data/entry` or `//invoice[1]/@id` don't make sense to you, please read the technology primer, Appendix A, first.
  - Appendix B introduces another tricky subject in the XML world: *namespaces*. Even if you have never used Schematron, there's a good chance you need to know something about namespaces when working with XML.
- If you already use Schematron 2020 and are interested in the changes introduced in Schematron 2025, start with Appendix G.
- If you want to know more about validating documents in general, using Schematron and other languages, read Chapter 2 and Chapter 3.
- If you want to know how to apply Schematron and how to set a Schematron schema to work, read Chapter 4.
- Chapter 5 explains the basics of Schematron. This will provide you with enough information to get going and write simple, but nonetheless useful, Schematron schemas.

- Chapter 6, Chapter 7, and Chapter 8 go beyond the basics to teach you to create reusable schema components, integrate other programming languages, and use other nifty features.
- Chapter 9 contains more advanced examples and recipes.
- For those that need to see the nitty-gritty details of the language, please refer to the references in Appendix C and Appendix D.
- Schematron QuickFix (SQF), a not widely supported but nonetheless valuable extension to Schematron, is explained in Appendix E.

Finding and using the code examples

The code examples in this book are at https://github.com/xatapult/schematron-book-code-2025, a public GitHub repository. Feel free to download or clone the repository and use the code and data in any way you like. You can find the path to any example that comes from this repository underneath the title, as shown in Example 1.3.

Example 1.3 – Example document from the book code repository (`schematron-book-code-2025/data/parcels-valid.xml`)

```
<parcels max-weight="100" delivery-date="2021-10-10">
  <parcel weight="50" date="2021-09-29">
    <contents>A large quantity of mouth masks</contents>
  </parcel>
  <parcel weight="45" date="2021-09-12">
    <contents>Toys for children</contents>
  </parcel>
</parcels>
```

For example, if you've cloned the repository into `/work/data`, you can find Example 1.3 in the file `/work/data/schematron-book-code-2025/data/parcels-valid.xml`.

Schematron 2020 note

The previous version of this book also had an example code repository, which is still available at: https://github.com/xatapult/schematron-book-code.

IDE support for Schematron

Applying Schematron, especially when you're just beginning, is easiest using an IDE (Integrated Development Environment) that natively supports Schematron. Such an IDE helps you write schemas. You can run validations interactively and see the results in the user interface. How to do this, including examples, is handled in the section titled "IDE-based Schematron validation" (p. 37). Unfortunately, at the time this book was written and finalized (early 2026), the IDE support for Schematron 2025 was still limited. However, by the time you're reading this it will most probably be available.

The most commonly used XML IDE that supports Schematron is oXygen.[2] oXygen has committed to supporting Schematron 2025 starting version 29, scheduled for somewhere second half of 2026. See the section titled "Schematron validation using oXygen" (p. 38) for more information.

I know of only one other IDE that supports Schematron validation natively, XMLBlueprint.[3] It is currently not widely used, and I have only limited experience with it. However, given its very fast adoption of Schematron 2025, it's definitely worth a try. See the section titled "Schematron validation using XMLBlueprint" (p. 40) for more information.

If you can't or don't want to use an IDE, you can also perform Schematron validations "raw." What this means and how to do this is explained in the section titled "Raw Schematron validation" (p. 42). **Beware:** this does require some technical skills.

Contact information

This book was written by Erik Siegel (Xatapult, http://www.xatapult.com). You can reach me at erik@xatapult.nl.

I would definitely like to hear from you. Whatever you have to say about this book, please drop me an email. Knowing that there are people who use what I have written keeps me motivated.

---

2 https://www.oxygenxml.com
3 https://www.xmlblueprint.com/

Acknowledgments

I would like to thank all people that reviewed (parts of) this book and provided me with valuable feedback.

For the previous edition of this book (most of it carried over to this one), these were (in alphabetical order): Paul van Aalstede (†), Jennifer Flint, Tony Graham, Rick Jelliffe, Pieter Lamers, Pieter Masereeuw, Birgit Orthofer, and Andrew Sales.

For this edition specifically (in alphabetical order): David Maus and Andrew Sales.

Also, many thanks to my editor and publisher, Richard Hamilton. His attention to detail, both technical and editorial, made this a much better book.

Thanks to all of you for your time and effort!

CHAPTER 2
Introduction to Schematron

This chapter provides a high-level overview of Schematron. The last section, the section titled "An illustrative example" (p. 12), contains an example of Schematron usage to introduce you to the language itself.

What is Schematron?

Here's an overview of Schematron's main high-level characteristics:

- Schematron is a formal schema language in which you can express rules for XML documents.
- There are two types of rules:
  - **Assertions:** when the condition for an assertion fails, an error message is issued.
  - **Reports:** when the condition for a report holds, a report message is issued.

  In practice, you will use assertions more often than reports.
- In Schematron you define all the error and report messages in your own words.
- Schematron is expressed in XML: a Schematron schema is an XML document.
- Schematron allows you to specify the underlying language for its expressions. In practice, XPath is the only language supported.
- Schematron can, by design, incorporate constructs from other programming languages. Currently support for XSLT and XQuery is available.

Why Schematron?

There are a number of reasons why Schematron is such a useful tool in the XML toolbox. Here are the most important ones:

- Schematron is a relatively simple but powerful validation language. Basic Schematron (covered in Chapter 5) already has a wide field of application and is relatively easy to master.
- Schematron can go way beyond the validations of the "classic" validation languages like DTD, W3C XML Schema, and RELAX NG. It allows you to do extensive checks on XML structures and data that are not possible in other languages. Anything you can express as an XPath test can be used for validation purposes. More experienced users can take advantage of XSLT features such as keys and functions.

- In Schematron you define all the error or report messages. For other validation languages you're at the mercy of the validation processor's implementer, and this often results in technically correct but obscure messages. In Schematron this is under your control. You can enrich messages using XPath expressions to compute text from or about the validated document.
- Since the messages are under your control, Schematron is often used to partially take over validations normally done by other validation languages. Messages can be tailored to the user's knowledge level or context. So instead of:

  ```
  The content of element 'section' is not complete. One of '{para}' is expected
  ```

  You could tell the user:

  ```
  A section in a report must have at least one paragraph of text
  ```

The history of Schematron in a nutshell

Schematron came to life in 1999 in Taiwan with a presentation called "From Grammars to Schematron" by Rick Jelliffe.[1] This resulted, in 2001, in Schematron 1.5, which is based on XSLT 1.0. To use it, you only needed an XSLT processor, which was one reason it succeeded.

After this, ISO (International Organization for Standardization) took over standardization and in 2006 released ISO Schematron, which added new features such as variables and abstract patterns.

Development continued and newer versions of XPath and XSLT were incorporated. Through a succession of editions we arrived at the 2020 edition, officially called *ISO/IEC 19757-3, Third edition, 2020-06: Information technology - Document Schema Definition Languages (DSDL) - Part 3: Rule-based validation using Schematron*. This is the version used for the previous edition of this book (see https://xmlpress.net/publications/schematron/).

There was still room for improvements. A group of Schematron enthusiasts (Tony Graham, David Maus, Andrew Sales, and me) started the "Schematron enhancement proposals" initiative: a list of points for improvement.[2] ISO re-opened the standardization process, and in 2025 they released *ISO/IEC 19757-3 Information technology - Document Schema Definition Languages (DSDL) - Part 3: Rule-based validation using Schematron*, which this book is based on.

---

[1] This and many other background stories are still available at https://www.schematron.com. The initial presentation can be found at https://schematron.com/download/hints/schematron.pdf.

[2] https://github.com/Schematron/schematron-enhancement-proposals

The Schematron standard

The Schematron 2025 official standard can be obtained from ISO.[3] In 2026 it cost 204 Swiss francs. If you buy it you'll get a PDF of 51 pages, describing the Schematron standard.[4] This includes many pages with listings of RELAX NG and other schemas for Schematron itself and its reporting language SVRL. See the section titled "Validating a Schematron schema" (p. 161) for a description of how to obtain these schemas.

Schematron 2020 note

The 2020 edition of Schematron is also still for sale on the ISO website. You can find it at https://www.iso.org/standard/74515.html

Is it necessary to buy this standard for writing Schematron schemas? My advice would be not to spend your money on it. This book and/or what you can find on the web will give you more than enough information and examples to get going. The standard itself is a formal and terse document that doesn't add any value for most users.

The only reason I can think of to buy it is if you plan to write a new Schematron processor (or, of course, another Schematron book), in which case you need access to all the minor details of the language definition. But for day-to-day use, don't bother.

The Schematroll

What would a standard be without a mascot? And for Schematron, that's Schematroll:[5]

Figure 2.1 – The notorious Schematroll

[3] https://www.iso.org/standard/85625.html

[4] When this book talks about "the standard" or "the specification," it's referring to this document.

[5] Schematroll was drawn by Cody Chang. It's a cross between two marsupials, the Bilby and the Bettong. You can use it for free on any Schematron-related product. It has its own GitHub repository: https://github.com/Schematron/schematroll.

An illustrative example

This section contains the first illustrative example of Schematron. The example is a simple Schematron schema that checks an inventory list in an XML document for errors.

Schematron lets you specify a language for its expressions. In practice, only XPath is supported. There is nothing overly complex here, but to understand the examples, you need a basic understanding of XPath. If you are new to XPath (or think your XPath knowledge needs a booster), please read Appendix A first. Another tricky subject I touch upon is namespaces, to which you can find an introduction in Appendix B.

Schematron 2020 note

To keep this first set of examples general, most of it is compatible with both the 2025 and 2020 editions of Schematron. To run them with a 2020-edition-only processor, simply remove the `schematronEdition="2025"` attribute from the root element. If an example schema in this section is not compatible with the 2020 edition, a note like this will tell you why.

The example document

Schematron is about validating XML documents. This set of Schematron examples is based on the following inventory list example document:

Example 2.1 – An example inventory list XML document (`schematron-book-code-2025/data/example-1.xml`)

```
<inventory-list depcode="IMP">
  <article code="IMP0001">
    <name>Bolts</name>
    <description>Nuts to secure things with</description>
  </article>
  <article code="IMP0002">
    <name>Nuts</name>
    <description>Bolts to turn on the nuts</description>
  </article>
  <article code="EXP0234">
    <name>Bananas</name>
    <description>Delicious ripe bananas</description>
  </article>
</inventory-list>
```

The rule imposed on this type of document is that the `code` attribute on an `<article>` element must start with the department code. This department code can be found in the `depcode` attribute on the root element. So the first two articles are valid, but the third one isn't.

Of course, this example is small, and you could easily validate it by hand. But what if it contained thousands of articles instead of just three? Or if you had many documents instead of just one. That is when you need automated validation, which is where Schematron comes to the rescue.

Running the examples

If you want you can follow along and try the example Schematron schemas yourself. To do this:

- Download the example code as described in the section titled "Finding and using the code examples" (p. 6).
- You need some means to actually run the schemas:
  - By the time you read this, Schematron 2025 support should be available in the oXygen IDE. See the section titled "Schematron validation using oXygen" (p. 38) for more information on using oXygen for Schematron validation.
  - XMLBlueprint is a lesser known XML IDE, but it already supports Schematron 2025. See the section titled "Schematron validation using XMLBlueprint" (p. 40) for more information on using XMLBlueprint for Schematron validation.
  - You can run Schematron from the command-line. See the section titled "Raw Schematron validation" (p. 42) for more information.

Checking the value of the `code` attribute

Let's start by checking the value of the `code` attribute on the `<article>` elements in Example 2.1. The root element of the inventory list has an attribute for its department code called `depcode`.

We need to verify that the value of each `code` attribute begins with this department code. For Example 2.1, the first two articles are valid, but the third one isn't. Example 2.2 validates this.

Example 2.2 – A Schematron schema for checking the code attributes of Example 2.1 (schematron-book-code-2025/examples/introduction/example-1.sch)

```
<schema xmlns="http://purl.oclc.org/dsdl/schematron" schematronEdition="2025"
  queryBinding="xslt3">

  <pattern>
    <rule context="article">
      <assert test="starts-with(@code, /inventory-list/@depcode)">
        The article code must start with the right prefix
      </assert>
    </rule>

  </pattern>

</schema>
```

In a nutshell:

- All <article> elements in the document are checked, one by one:

  ```
  <rule context="article">
  ```

- The assertion that their code attributes start with the correct prefix is verified:

  ```
  <assert test="starts-with(@code, /inventory-list/@depcode)">
  ```

- If so, nothing happens, but if this isn't the case this message is issued:

  ```
  The article code must start with the right prefix
  ```

When validating Example 2.1 against the Schematron schema in Example 2.2, the third <article> element will raise an error, as expected:

```
The article code must start with the right prefix
```

This immediately illustrates one of the major benefits of Schematron validations: the message is in the code, it is part of the schema, and you specify the text.

Let's examine how Example 2.2 is constructed in more detail. References to where you can find more information are at the end of this section.

- The root element of a Schematron schema is always `<schema>`.
- This, and all other Schematron elements, must be in the Schematron namespace. This is taken care of by the `xmlns="http://purl.oclc.org/dsdl/schematron"` "attribute"[6] that defines this as the default namespace.
- The `queryBinding="xslt3"` attribute tells the Schematron processor what underlying programming language(s) you can use. It's called the "query language binding." The value `xslt3` means you can use certain XSLT 3.0 constructs (though this example doesn't), but also, more importantly, you can use XPath 3.1 expressions.

  For instance, the `context` and `test` attributes in Example 2.2 contain XPath expressions. Setting the query binding to `xslt3` lets you use the most current version of XPath (as of 2025).

Other query language bindings

When trying this example, your Schematron processor might complain about the `xslt3` query language binding. Here are some ways around this:

- If you're using XQS (see the section titled "The XQS Schematron processor" (p. 49)), use `xquery31`. Be aware that for XQS you'll also have to change the value of the `context` attributes of the `<rule>` elements in the examples, as explained in the section titled "XQS and context" (p. 50). For example, the `context` attribute in Example 2.2 would become `context="//article"` (or `context="/*/article"` or `context="/inventory-list/article"`).
- Change the value of the `queryBinding` attribute to `xslt2`. If that still doesn't work, try `xpath31`, `xpath3`, or `xpath2`.
- In the unlikely case that none of this works in your environment (maybe you're using a proprietary Schematron processor), it will be difficult to follow and try the examples. You will need to find out which query language(s) work with your processor or use one of the processors suggested in this book. You can find more information about query language binding in Chapter 7.

6 Although it looks like one, it's not really an attribute but a namespace declaration. See Appendix B for details.

- A Schematron schema always consists of (one or more) patterns or groups in <pattern> or <group> elements.

> **Schematron 2020 note**
>
> The 2020 edition does not have <group> elements, only <pattern> elements.

- A pattern or group consists of rules in <rule> elements. A rule has a context attribute that defines where this rule applies. For Example 2.2 this is the <article> element:

  ```
  context="article"
  ```

  The effect here is that this rule will be held against all <article> elements in the document.
- The most common constructs in rules are assertions, which are contained in <assert> elements. An assertion checks something, as expressed in its test attribute. In Example 2.2 it checks whether the value of the article's code attribute starts with the value of the depcode attribute on the root element:

  ```
  starts-with(@code, /inventory-list/@depcode)
  ```

  If so, this expression returns true, the assertion holds, all is fine, and no message is issued. However, if the assertion fails, the expression returns false and the text in the <assert> element is issued as an error message.

For more information:

- XPath in general: Appendix A.
- Namespaces in general: Appendix B.
- Basic schemas: the section titled "Setting up a Schematron schema" (p. 51).
- Patterns, rules, and asserts: the section titled "Patterns, groups, rules, assertions, and reports" (p. 53).
- Query language binding: Chapter 7.

Improving the message

The message issued by Example 2.2 can be improved. For instance, it would be nice if it would tell us what article it is about. For this, Schematron allows you to insert values from your document into your messages, using the <value-of> element (see Example 2.3).

Example 2.3 – Using the name of the article in the messages (schematron-book-code-2025/examples/introduction/example-2.sch)

```
<schema xmlns="http://purl.oclc.org/dsdl/schematron" schematronEdition="2025"
  queryBinding="xslt3">

  <pattern>
    <rule context="article">
      <assert test="starts-with(@code, /inventory-list/@depcode)">
        The article code must start with the right prefix
        for <value-of select="name"/>
      </assert>
    </rule>
  </pattern>

</schema>
```

The `<value-of select="name">` element inserts the value of the article's `<name>` element in the message, resulting in:

```
The article code must start with the right prefix for Bananas
```

There's no limit to how far you can go dressing up your messages. For instance, Example 2.4 tries to make the error absolutely clear.

Example 2.4 – Using even more information in the message (schematron-book-code-2025/examples/introduction/example-2b.sch)

```
<schema xmlns="http://purl.oclc.org/dsdl/schematron" schematronEdition="2025"
  queryBinding="xslt3">

  <pattern>
    <rule context="article">
      <assert test="starts-with(@code, /inventory-list/@depcode)">
        The article code (<value-of select="@code"/>) must start with the
        right prefix (<value-of select="/inventory-list/@depcode"/>)
        for <value-of select="name"/>
      </assert>
    </rule>
  </pattern>

</schema>
```

This will result in:

```
The article code (EXP0234) must start with the right prefix (IMP) for Bananas
```

For more information: the section titled "More meaningful messages: inserting values" (p. 65).

Using variables

The last subject for this first example is variables. A variable allows you to compute a value once, store it using a name, and then use the name to retrieve the value in subsequent expressions. Variables are useful for efficiency reasons,[7] but they can also improve code readability and maintainability.

We use the value of the root's `depcode` attribute (`/inventory-list/@depcode`) in the assertion. But assertions are checked against all `article` elements, so this value is retrieved multiple times. For our simple input document in Example 2.1 there are only three of these, but what if these documents get bigger? It seems more efficient to retrieve the department code only once.

To do this, define a variable that holds the department code and then use it later in the assertion, as shown in Example 2.5.

Example 2.5 – Using a variable to store the department code (`schematron-book-code-2025/examples/introduction/example-3.sch`)

```
<schema xmlns="http://purl.oclc.org/dsdl/schematron" schematronEdition="2025"
  queryBinding="xslt3">

  <let name="department-code" value="/inventory-list/@depcode"/>

  <pattern>
    <rule context="article">
      <assert test="starts-with(@code, $department-code)">
        The article code (<value-of select="@code"/>) must start with the
        right prefix (<value-of select="$department-code"/>)
        for <value-of select="name"/>
      </assert>
    </rule>
  </pattern>

</schema>
```

[7] Code efficiency is a bit of a tricky subject. Modern compilers are very good in optimizing code and might already do the work for you. Nonetheless, it certainly doesn't hurt to optimize code yourself if you can.

The `<let>` element defines a variable called `department-code` and fills it with the value of the `depcode` attribute of the root element.[8] Whenever you need this value you can reference it using the name of the variable prefixed with a `$` character: `$department-code`.

You can define and use variables on almost any level in a Schematron schema. For instance, you could create a variable for the `code` attribute. This is not strictly necessary, but you might consider it to increase code comprehensibility, as shown in Example 2.6.

Example 2.6 – Using a second variable to store the article code (schematron-book-code-2025/examples/introduction/example-3b.sch)

```
<schema xmlns="http://purl.oclc.org/dsdl/schematron" schematronEdition="2025"
  queryBinding="xslt3">

  <let name="department-code" value="/inventory-list/@depcode"/>

  <pattern>
    <rule context="article">

      <let name="article-code" value="@code"/>

      <assert test="starts-with($article-code, $department-code)">
        The article code (<value-of select="$article-code"/>) must start with
        the right prefix (<value-of select="$department-code"/>)
        for <value-of select="name"/>
      </assert>
    </rule>
  </pattern>

</schema>
```

For more information see the section titled "Declaring and using variables: `<let>` " (p. 70).

[8] Strictly speaking, this example doesn't store the attribute's value; it creates a variable with the attribute as its value. I will discuss how to improve this later.

CHAPTER 3

Schematron in context

Schematron is an XML validation language. It expresses rules and limitations for the contents of XML documents. But Schematron is not the only way to validate XML, and to fully understand and appreciate it, it's important to know about the world surrounding it. This chapter dives into the broader world of XML document validation: what it is, why we need it, what kinds there are, and what to use when.

Validating XML documents

This section serves as an introduction to the general subject of validating XML documents: Why do we need to validate anyway? How can we do this?

Restricting XML freedom

The XML language specification sets a number of general syntax rules for its documents. Here are some (informal) examples:

- The main building blocks for XML documents are elements (`<para>`, `<bank-account>`, `<MeasurementArea>`, etc.). They're written using angled brackets.
- Elements must be properly opened and closed (`<para>...</para>`, `<Empty/>`, etc.).
- Elements must be properly nested (`<p>...<b>...</b>...</p>`, not `<p>...<b>...</p>...</b>`).
- Elements can have attributes (`<p class="header">`, `<Measurement unit="cm" value="12.45">`, etc.).
- An XML document must have a single root element.
- The character set for element and attribute names is defined: letters, digits, dots, hyphens, and underscores. Names must start with a letter or underscore.
- The names of elements and attributes are case-sensitive (`<email>` is not the same element as `<EMail>` or `<EMAIL>`).

However, within these rules you have complete freedom. When creating an XML document from scratch, you can call some element `<business-email>`, `<businessEMail>`, `<BusinessEMail>`, or just `<BE>`. It's up to you. You can choose which elements appear inside which elements (nesting), whether to use attributes, and so on. That's a lot of freedom!

Assume two separate developers have been asked to create XML documents that contain customer information. One developer comes up with Example 3.1.

Example 3.1 – One way to convert customer information into XML

```
<CUSTOMER ID="12345" NAME="Johnny Coder" EMAIL="jc@acme.com" COMPANY="ACME"/>
```

The other, with clearly more verbose preferences, encodes the same information as Example 3.2.

Example 3.2 – Another way to convert customer information into XML

```
<customer>
  <identification-code>12345</identification-code>
  <full-person-name>Johnny Coder</full-person-name>
  <business-email-address>jc@acme.com</business-email-address>
  <company-working-for>ACME</company-working-for>
</customer>
```

We can bicker about what is the right approach (which XML designers do), but it's obvious that systems written for Example 3.1 won't communicate with systems designed for Example 3.2. Even though the information carried is the same and they're both XML, the formats used are different and therefore incompatible.

When systems are isolated, for instance when they're only used in-company, these differences don't matter. But as soon as the format is used for communicating information outside of system or company boundaries, it becomes important that all systems involved use the same definition, the same format. Therefore, we need a way to define an XML format so it can be widely used.

This same situation, on a larger scale, occurs with official XML standards. After long and detailed discussions, committees establish the names, meaning, and usage of elements and attributes. For example, DocBook (the standard used to write this book) defines that a paragraph is surrounded by a `<para>` element—not `<Para>`, `<PARA>`, or `<p>`. Another example is the Schematron standard, which defines that a Schematron schema starts with the `<schema>` element—not `<schematron>` or `<SCHEMA>`. If these rules were not there, nobody would know what was meant, and it would be impossible to process the XML the way it was intended.

So XML design gives freedom, but to make it usable we have to restrict that freedom. That's what XML schema languages are about.

How to define XML formats

To align our non-communicating developers of Example 3.1 and Example 3.2 or the users of any important XML standard, we need to define the XML format. There are several approaches:

- **Informal:** Provide one or more examples and maybe a little written documentation. This happens a lot and is usually good enough for situations where the document format is simple, the user community small, and conformance not very critical. But as soon as one of these preconditions goes away, it becomes a different story.
- **Less informal:** Document, for humans, exactly how the XML must be formatted. This is already considerably better, but it has several drawbacks:
  - You need to find a documentation format that communicates the intent. For XML, with its elements, attributes, nesting, and so on, this is not particularly easy. There's no agreed upon common way to do this.
  - You need to write the documentation, maintain it, and keep it up to date as changes occur. This is a chore not to be underestimated.
  - Most importantly, there's no way to automate checking whether a document conforms to the specification. Manually checking that a long document conforms to the specification or checking a document against a complex specification is impossible—too much detail.

  Still, XML formats are often defined in prose, but mostly for documentation purposes. For instance, this book contains appendices detailing XML formats, including Schematron itself (Appendix C). When documentation (the passing of intent and meaning from one human to the other) is important enough, it's a good idea to provide it.
- **Formal:** Write a specification in a formal language that a computer can use to establish whether an XML document conforms or not. This process is called *validation*. There are several validation languages, Schematron being one of them.

Validating XML documents

Validation can be defined as: formally establishing whether an XML document conforms to the set of rules for its document type, which can include the following:

- Are all element and attribute names correct?
- Are elements nested correctly?
- Is all necessary information there?
- Is there any unexpected information?
- Does the information conform to any additional rules?

Every document type that needs to undergo validation has its own rule set. The XML contents for a book are different from, let's say, a tax form, or a patient record. We should be able to verify, in an automated way, whether documents conform to the rules for their intended document type.

Validation of XML documents is usually done in two or three stages (Figure 3.1).

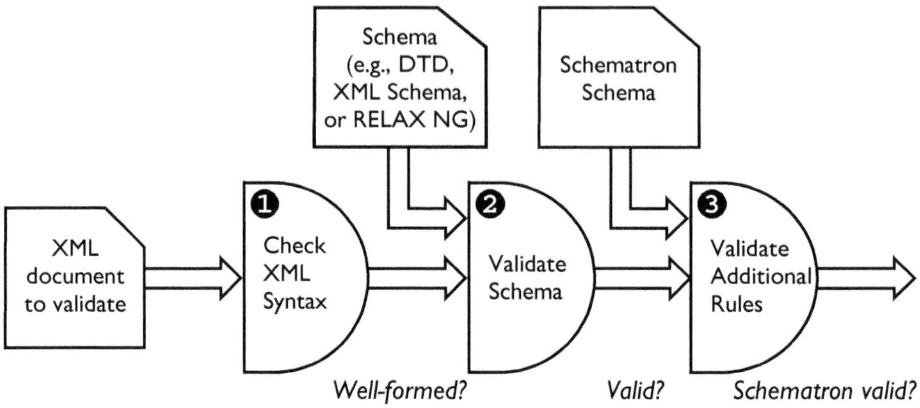

Figure 3.1 – The three stages for a full XML document validation

1. The first threshold is: does the document conform to the basic syntax rules of XML? Are the angle brackets, the element and attribute names, the nesting, and so on, OK? If not, you won't get far because no XML processing software will be able to parse and use it.

   When a document passes this stage, it's called *well-formed*. Well-formedness is a requirement for all XML document types, regardless of their meaning.

2. Once a document passes stage 1, and is therefore well-formed, you can check it against the rule-set for its document type. A formalized version of such a rule-set is called a *schema*.

   When a document passes all checks prescribed by the schema, it is called *valid*.

   There are several flavors for schemas. The most important ones are DTD, XML Schema, and RELAX NG. More about this in the section titled "The main schema languages" (p. 26).

   Schemas check things like element and attribute names, nesting, whether required elements and attributes are there, etc. They have limited support for checking more complicated rules.

3. Once a document passes stage 1 and 2, you can check it against the additional rules for this type of document. For example, this date must be before that one, the sum of the weights of the parcels must not exceed some threshold, etc.

The main language for defining additional rules is *Schematron*. A rule-set expressed in the Schematron language is called a *Schematron schema*. There's no official term for a document that passes Schematron defined checks, but in this book it is called *Schematron valid*.

Now if only the world would be as structured as suggested by the neatly numbered validation stages of Figure 3.1. Stage 1 will always be there but there are many possible variations in applying stage 2 and stage 3:

- You don't necessarily need to pass stage 2 before doing a Schematron validation in stage 3. They're more or less independent. However, in most applications, a document is first confirmed valid (stage 2) before Schematron validation (stage 3) is performed.

  The reason for performing stage 2 before stage 3 is that Schematron schemas often rely on documents being valid. For instance, suppose two dates you need to compare are in required attributes. The schema (stage 2) checks whether these attributes are there and are formatted as valid dates. The Schematron schema (stage 3) can then compare them, knowing they're present and formatted correctly.

- You could create a Schematron schema that partly takes on the role of a schema. Most schema checks can be expressed in a Schematron schema. An example of this can be found in the section titled "Using Schematron for schema validation" (p. 166).

  The main reason to do this is to control messages. Schematron lets you completely control messages, so you can make them as user-friendly and informative as required. With schema validation, you have to live with whatever messages the schema processor gives you.

- With the advent of W3C XML Schema version 1.1, you can add limited additional-rules checking to schemas, although this capability is not widely used. For instance, the "this date must be before that one" test can be validated using a version 1.1 W3C XML Schema. You can see an example of this in the section titled "W3C XML Schema version 1.1" (p. 29).

  A good reason to avoid this feature, and use Schematron instead, is the rather user-unfriendly set of messages produced by the currently available W3C XML Schema validators.

- There are a large number of things that can be checked almost equally well by schemas or Schematron schemas. For instance, both can check the following:
  - References from one element to another using identifiers.
  - Uniqueness of values (for example, identifiers).
  - Whether values of elements and attributes conform to specific rules (like enumerations, regular expressions, length, minimums and maximums, etc.).

Again, a very good reason to use Schematron for this is that you can define your own messages. However, if you don't Schematron (yet), getting better messages might not be worth the cost of adding such a stage. What's best here depends on your circumstances.

The main schema languages

For those that are new to the world of validation, this section contains a short introduction to the main languages: DTD, W3C XML Schema, RELAX NG, and, of course, Schematron. Apart from Schematron, I don't teach these languages; I provide an overview and show a few examples. Appendix F lists additional resources if you want to dive further into any of these languages.

I use the XML document in Example 3.3 as an example of a document to validate. It contains data about parcels, their weights, and shipment dates:

Example 3.3 – Valid example document used for introducing the main Schema languages (`schematron-book-code-2025/data/parcels-valid.xml`)

```
<parcels max-weight="100" delivery-date="2021-10-10">
  <parcel weight="50" date="2021-09-29">
    <contents>A large quantity of mouth masks</contents>
  </parcel>
  <parcel weight="45" date="2021-09-12">
    <contents>Toys for children</contents>
  </parcel>
</parcels>
```

Here is an informal description of some rules you could apply to documents like the one shown in Example 3.3:

1. Must have a structure as in Example 3.3, and all attributes in the example are required.
2. There must be one or more `<parcel>` elements.
3. The content description (in the `<contents>` element) must be at least five characters long.
4. The sum of the weights of the separate parcels (in the `weight` attributes) must not exceed the maximum weight, as specified on the root element in the `<max-weight>` attribute.
5. The date as set on a parcel (in the `date` attribute) must be at least 10 days before the delivery date specified on the root element in the `delivery-date` attribute.

Rules 1 through 3 are examples of rules that can be checked by regular schemas. Rules 4 and 5 are additional rules, which can be checked using Schematron.

To try out the examples, you need validation software. It's easiest to use an IDE that has these validation methods built in, for instance oXygen (see the section titled "IDE support for Schematron" (p. 7)).

Document Type Definition (DTD)

DTD, Document Type Definition, is an ancient validation language that goes way back to the previous century and XML's predecessor, SGML. DTDs are not written in XML but in a language of its own that looks a little bit like XML but isn't. Example 3.4 shows the structural rules for Example 3.3, expressed as a DTD.

Example 3.4 – A DTD for validating Example 3.3
(`schematron-book-code-2025/examples/context/parcels.dtd`)

```
<!ELEMENT parcels (parcel)+>
<!ATTLIST parcels
  xmlns CDATA #FIXED ''
  delivery-date CDATA #REQUIRED
  max-weight CDATA #REQUIRED>
<!ELEMENT parcel (contents)>
<!ATTLIST parcel
  xmlns CDATA #FIXED ''
  date CDATA #REQUIRED
  weight CDATA #REQUIRED>
<!ELEMENT contents (#PCDATA)>
<!ATTLIST contents
  xmlns CDATA #FIXED ''>
```

DTDs have several drawbacks, including their non-XML format, no support for namespaces, no data type support, and more. However, they are still used a lot.

More background information and examples can be found on the Wikipedia page for DTD: https://en.wikipedia.org/wiki/Document_type_definition.

W3C XML Schema

A much more modern approach to schema validation is the W3C XML Schema language. This language is expressed in XML and contains features to support namespaces, data types, reusable components, and more. Example 3.5 shows the structural rules for Example 3.3, expressed as a W3C XML Schema.

Example 3.5 – The W3C XML Schema for validating Example 3.3
(schematron-book-code-2025/examples/context/parcels.xsd)

```
<xs:schema xmlns:xs="http://www.w3.org/2001/XMLSchema"
  elementFormDefault="qualified">
  <xs:element name="parcels">
    <xs:complexType>
      <xs:sequence>
        <xs:element maxOccurs="unbounded" name="parcel">
          <xs:complexType>
            <xs:sequence>
              <xs:element name="contents">
                <xs:simpleType>
                  <xs:restriction base="xs:string">
                    <xs:minLength value="5"/>
                  </xs:restriction>
                </xs:simpleType>
              </xs:element>
            </xs:sequence>
            <xs:attribute name="weight" type="xs:positiveInteger"
              use="required"/>
            <xs:attribute name="date" type="xs:date" use="required"/>
          </xs:complexType>
        </xs:element>
      </xs:sequence>
      <xs:attribute name="max-weight" type="xs:positiveInteger"
        use="required"/>
      <xs:attribute name="delivery-date" type="xs:date" use="required"/>
    </xs:complexType>
  </xs:element>
</xs:schema>
```

Example 3.5 also highlights a frequent criticism of XML Schema: it's a very complicated language. It's difficult to create and maintain XML Schemas without some kind of user interface support. For instance, oXygen allows you to draw W3C XML Schemas as a diagram and translates this into the underlying XML. Figure 3.2 shows how the user interface in oXygen represents the XML Schema in Example 3.5.

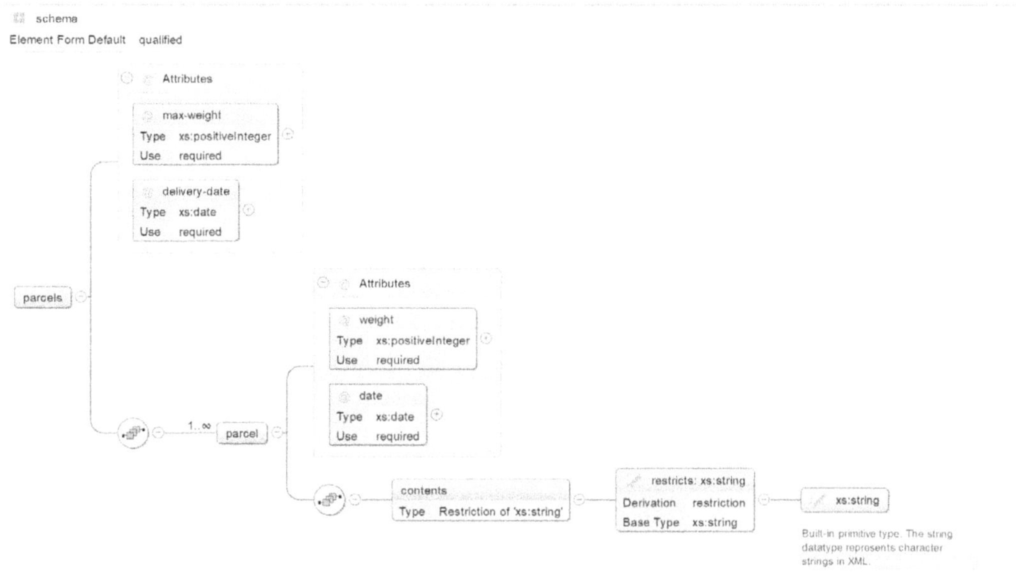

Figure 3.2 – The W3C XML Schema for Example 3.3 in oXygen's XML Schema design view

More background information and examples can be found on the XML Schema Wikipedia page: https://en.wikipedia.org/wiki/XML_Schema_(W3C).

W3C XML Schema version 1.1

Example 3.5 uses W3C XML Schema version 1.0, which is currently (2026) the most commonly used version of the standard. The newer version 1.1 has limited support for additional rule checking. For instance, Example 3.6 shows a version 1.1 XML Schema that adds a rule about total weight to Example 3.5.

Example 3.6 – The W3C XML Schema version 1.1 for validating Example 3.3 (schematron-book-code-2025/examples/context/parcels-v1.1.xsd)

```
<xs:schema xmlns:xs="http://www.w3.org/2001/XMLSchema"
  xmlns:vc="http://www.w3.org/2007/XMLSchema-versioning"
  elementFormDefault="qualified"
  vc:minVersion="1.1">
  <xs:element name="parcels">
    <xs:complexType>
      <xs:sequence>
        <xs:element maxOccurs="unbounded" name="parcel">
          <xs:complexType>
            <xs:sequence>
              <xs:element name="contents">
                <xs:simpleType>
                  <xs:restriction base="xs:string">
                    <xs:minLength value="5"/>
                  </xs:restriction>
                </xs:simpleType>
              </xs:element>
            </xs:sequence>
            <xs:attribute name="weight" type="xs:positiveInteger"
              use="required"/>
            <xs:attribute name="date" type="xs:date" use="required"/>
          </xs:complexType>
        </xs:element>
      </xs:sequence>
      <xs:attribute name="max-weight" type="xs:positiveInteger"
        use="required"/>
      <xs:attribute name="delivery-date" type="xs:date" use="required"/>

      <!-- The sum of all parcels weights must not exceed maximum weight: -->
      <xs:assert test="sum(parcel/@weight) le xs:double(@max-weight)"/>

    </xs:complexType>
  </xs:element>
</xs:schema>
```

Let's validate an invalid version of Example 3.3 against this schema. For instance, in Example 3.7 the total weight of the parcels exceeds the maximum weight (as specified by the `max-weight` attribute on the `<parcels>` element). Validating Example 3.7 against the schema in Example 3.6 results in the error message shown in Example 3.8.

Example 3.7 – Invalid version of Example 3.3 (schematron-book-code-2025/data/parcels-invalid.xml)

```
<parcels max-weight="100" delivery-date="2021-10-10">
  <parcel weight="50" date="2021-09-29">
    <contents>A large quantity of mouth masks</contents>
  </parcel>
  <parcel weight="55" date="2021-10-05">
    <contents>Toys for children</contents>
  </parcel>
</parcels>
```

Example 3.8 – The error message when validating Example 3.7 with the schema of Example 3.6

```
Assertion evaluation ('sum(parcel/@weight) le xs:double(@max-weight)')
for element 'parcels' on schema type '#AnonType_parcels' did not succeed.
```

I hope you agree with me that that's not a particularly user-friendly message.[1] Most users, with the exception of the schema designer, wouldn't be able to make much sense of it.

RELAX NG

RELAX NG was developed in response to the complexity of XML Schema. It also tries to fix some of its shortcomings. RELAX NG has two notations: a non-XML compact syntax (Example 3.9), and an XML syntax (Example 3.10). The two examples show the same set of rules for Example 3.3.

Example 3.9 – The RELAX NG Compact Syntax schema for validating Example 3.3 (schematron-book-code-2025/examples/context/parcels.rnc)

```
default namespace = ""
namespace doc = "http://relaxng.org/ns/compatibility/annotations/1.0"
namespace xsi = "http://www.w3.org/2001/XMLSchema-instance"
start =
  element parcels {
    attribute delivery-date { xsd:date },
    attribute max-weight { xsd:positiveInteger },
    element parcel {
      attribute date { xsd:date },
      attribute weight { xsd:positiveInteger },
      element contents { text }
    }+
  }
```

[1] The exact message depends on the validation software you're using; this one was produced by Xerces.

Example 3.10 – The RELAX NG Schema for validating Example 3.3 (`schematron-book-code-2025/examples/context/parcels.rng`)

```
<grammar ns="" xmlns:xsi="http://www.w3.org/2001/XMLSchema-instance"
  xmlns="http://relaxng.org/ns/structure/1.0"
  xmlns:doc="http://relaxng.org/ns/compatibility/annotations/1.0"
  datatypeLibrary="http://www.w3.org/2001/XMLSchema-datatypes">
  <start>
    <element name="parcels">
      <attribute name="delivery-date">
        <data type="date"/>
      </attribute>
      <attribute name="max-weight">
        <data type="positiveInteger"/>
      </attribute>
      <oneOrMore>
        <element name="parcel">
          <attribute name="date">
            <data type="date"/>
          </attribute>
          <attribute name="weight">
            <data type="positiveInteger"/>
          </attribute>
          <element name="contents">
            <text/>
          </element>
        </element>
      </oneOrMore>
    </element>
  </start>
</grammar>
```

I think we can agree that both examples are easier to understand than their W3C XML Schema counterpart. Even if you don't know any RELAX NG, the basics are easy to understand. The compact and XML notations for RELAX NG are functionally equivalent and can be mechanically translated in either direction.

You can find more background information and examples on the RELAX NG Wikipedia page: https://en.wikipedia.org/wiki/RELAX_NG or at https://relaxng.org/.

Schematron

This overview of the main schema languages concludes with the subject of this book: Schematron. As I described earlier, Schematron is a language for checking the additional rules for an XML document. Let's assume our XML survived the scrutiny of a validation, whether against a DTD, W3C XML Schema, or RELAX NG schema. What's left to check is:

- The sum of the weights of the separate parcels (in the `weight` attributes) must not exceed the maximum weight, as specified on the root element in the `max-weight` attribute.
- The date as set on a parcel (in the `date` attribute) must be at least 10 days before the delivery date, as specified on the root element in the `delivery-date` attribute.

Example 3.11 shows a Schematron schema for checking these rules. Note that it also defines the exact messages an end user will see—a key strength of Schematron.

Example 3.11 – The Schematron schema for validating Example 3.3
(`schematron-book-code-2025/examples/context/parcels.sch`)

```
<schema xmlns="http://purl.oclc.org/dsdl/schematron" schematronEdition="2025"
  queryBinding="xslt3">

  <ns uri="http://www.w3.org/2001/XMLSchema" prefix="xs"/>

  <group>
    <rule context="/*">
      <assert test="sum(parcel/@weight) le xs:double(@max-weight)">The total
        weight is too high</assert>
    </rule>
    <rule context="parcel">
      <assert test="(xs:date(/*/@delivery-date) - xs:date(@date)) gt
        xs:dayTimeDuration('P10D')">The parcel's date must be more than
        10 days before the delivery date</assert>
    </rule>
  </group>

</schema>
```

Schematron 2020 note

Example 3.11 will not work using a Schematron 2020 processor: the 2020 edition only has patterns (`<pattern>` elements), not groups (`<group>` elements). You can find an edition 2020 version of Example 3.11 in `parcels-2020.sch` (in the same directory as `parcels.sch` from Example 3.11).

CHAPTER 4

Applying Schematron

This chapter is about applying Schematron. Given an XML document and corresponding Schematron schema, how do you perform a Schematron validation? How do you get it singing and dancing? As you'll learn, there are several ways to go about this.

This chapter starts simple but gets increasingly more complicated and technical. If you're just interested in applying Schematron, you can stop at the section titled "Raw Schematron validation" (p. 42) and continue with Chapter 5.

The examples here use the parcel document introduced in Chapter 3 and the accompanying Schematron schema originally shown in Example 3.11. The schema is repeated in Example 4.1 and the parcel document is repeated in Example 4.2.

Example 4.1 – The Schematron schema to validate Example 4.2 with (a repeat of Example 3.11) (`schematron-book-code-2025/examples/context/parcels.sch`)

```
<schema xmlns="http://purl.oclc.org/dsdl/schematron" schematronEdition="2025"
  queryBinding="xslt3">

  <ns uri="http://www.w3.org/2001/XMLSchema" prefix="xs"/>

  <group>
    <rule context="/*">
      <assert test="sum(parcel/@weight) le xs:double(@max-weight)">The total
        weight is too high</assert>
    </rule>
    <rule context="parcel">
      <assert test="(xs:date(/*/@delivery-date) - xs:date(@date)) gt
        xs:dayTimeDuration('P10D')">The parcel's date must be more than
        10 days before the delivery date</assert>
    </rule>
  </group>

</schema>
```

Example 4.2 – Valid example document, used for explaining how to apply Schematron (a repeat of Example 3.3) (`schematron-book-code-2025/data/parcels-valid.xml`)

```
<parcels max-weight="100" delivery-date="2021-10-10">
  <parcel weight="50" date="2021-09-29">
    <contents>A large quantity of mouth masks</contents>
  </parcel>
  <parcel weight="45" date="2021-09-12">
    <contents>Toys for children</contents>
  </parcel>
</parcels>
```

Creating Schematron schemas

Creating a Schematron schema is just like creating any other XML document: you open a new document in your favorite editor and start typing. Use Notepad, Emacs, VI, Visual Studio Code, oXygen, Eclipse, or whatever you like: an XML document is basically just a text file with lots of angle brackets. Having said that, it is nice to get at least some support on the XML level and preferably also the Schematron level:

- XML-aware editors help you create well-formed documents. They can help you keep open and close tags aligned and make sure your document follows XML syntax rules.
- XML-schema-aware editors also validate documents against a particular XML schema. They can tell you what elements and attributes are valid at any point in your document to make it easier to create a valid XML document.
- A Schematron-aware editor can do everything a schema-aware editor can do and, at the same time, validate your document against a Schematron schema. See the section titled "IDE support for Schematron" (p. 7) for more information about this.

If you don't have (or want) the luxury of a Schematron-aware editor, I would advise you to start by using a template file, for instance Example 4.3 or Example 4.4.

Example 4.3 – Empty Schematron schema template with a single empty group (`schematron-book-code-2025/templates/empty-schema-group.sch`)

```
<schema xmlns="http://purl.oclc.org/dsdl/schematron" schematronEdition="2025"
  queryBinding="xslt3">
  <group/>
</schema>
```

Example 4.4 – Empty Schematron schema template with a single empty pattern (`schematron-book-code-2025/templates/empty-schema-pattern.sch`)

```
<schema xmlns="http://purl.oclc.org/dsdl/schematron" schematronEdition="2025"
  queryBinding="xslt3">
  <pattern/>
</schema>
```

Using a template will, at least, save you the effort of correctly typing the namespace URI and the root element. Depending on your environment and Schematron processor you might need a different value for the `queryBinding` attribute. More about this in Chapter 7.

Since Schematron schemas are XML documents, it's entirely possible to validate these themselves. More about this in the section titled "Validating a Schematron schema" (p. 161).

IDE-based Schematron validation

Suppose you have a Schematron schema (either written yourself or acquired) and some XML document(s) you want to validate. The easiest way to do this is by using an IDE (Integrated Development Environment) that supports Schematron validation:

- oXygen (https://www.oxygenxml.com) is a well-known and commonly used IDE in the XML world. Schematron 2020 is very well supported, including the Schematron QuickFix (SQF) extension (see Appendix E). Unfortunately, at the time this book was finalized (early 2026), support for Schematron 2025 was not yet available.

  oXygen has committed to supporting Schematron 2025 starting with version 29, scheduled for somewhere in the second half of 2026. This comes too late to include any experiences about it in this book. However, by the time you read this, it will probably be there. Given their excellent support for the 2020 edition, I have high hopes for it.

  You can see an example of what using oXygen for validation for Schematron 2020 looks like in the section titled "Schematron validation using oXygen" (p. 38).
- XMLBlueprint (https://www.xmlblueprint.com/) is a lesser known XML IDE. However, it already supports Schematron 2025. In the section titled "Schematron validation using XML-Blueprint" (p. 40) I provide you with an example of what this looks like.

Both products are not free software, but both offer a trial license/period for testing things out.

Schematron validation using oXygen

> **Warning**
>
> Since this book was published before oXygen released Schematron 2025 support, this section shows how to use Schematron in the oXygen IDE for Schematron *2020*. I expect support for Schematron 2025 will look very similar.

The most commonly used XML IDE containing Schematron support is oXygen.[1] To show you what validating a document using Schematron in the oXygen IDE looks like, let's validate a Schematron-invalid version of the parcels document in Example 4.2 (see Example 4.5).

Example 4.5 – A Schematron-invalid version of the parcels document in Example 4.2 (`schematron-book-code-2025/data/parcels-schematron-invalid.xml`)

```
<parcels max-weight="100" delivery-date="2021-10-10">
  <parcel weight="50" date="2021-10-08">
    <contents>A large quantity of mouth masks</contents>
  </parcel>
  <parcel weight="55" date="2021-09-12">
    <contents>Toys for children</contents>
  </parcel>
</parcels>
```

Example 4.5 is invalid because:

- The sum of the parcel weights, in the `parcel/@weight` attributes, is `105`, which is more than the maximum weight of `100`, as specified in the `/parcels/@max-weight` attribute.
- The date of the first parcel in its `parcel/@date` attribute (`2021-10-08`) is less than 10 days before the delivery date in the `/parcels/@delivery-date` attribute (`2021-10-10`).

To validate this document using oXygen:[2]

- Open the Schematron schema (`schematron-book-code-2025/examples/context/parcels-2020.sch`).

---

[1] https://www.oxygenxml.com

[2] These instructions are for version 28.0 or older, the exact commands/behavior may change with newer versions. oXygen has more ways/commands for performing Schematron and other validations. Since this is not an oXygen tutorial these won't be covered here.

- Open the invalid document (`schematron-book-code-2025/data/parcels-schematron-invalid.xml`).
- With the document (not the schema!) having focus, from the menu choose: **Document > Validate > Validate with…**.
- Provide a reference to the Schematron schema in the **URL:** input box. Because this file is already open, you can easily select it by pressing the down arrow at the end of the input box. oXygen determines the schema type for you. On my machine the result looks like Figure 4.1.

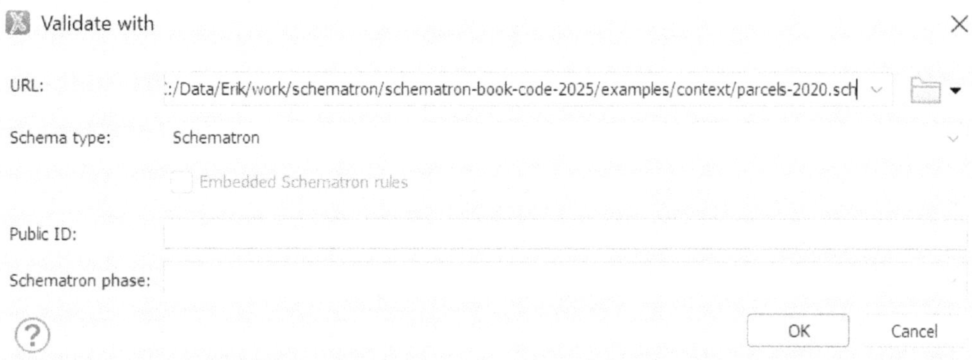

Figure 4.1 – Selecting a schema in oXygen

- Press **OK** and the validation starts. As both the document and the schema are very small, this won't take long.

oXygen underlines the places where there is an error according to the schema:

```
<parcels max-weight="100" delivery-date="2021-10-10">
  <parcel weight="50" date="2021-10-08">
    <contents>A large quantity of mouth masks</contents>
  </parcel>
  <parcel weight="55" date="2021-09-12">
    <contents>Toys for children</contents>
  </parcel>
</parcels>
```

Figure 4.2 – The invalid parcels document validated by oXygen

The oXygen results window (usually at the bottom of your screen) provides the error messages. Please notice that these messages come straight from the Schematron schema.

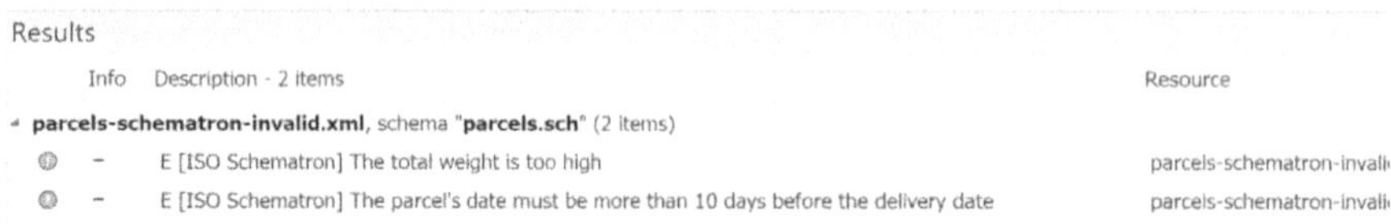

Figure 4.3 – The results window for Figure 4.2

Validation messages also appear when you move the cursor. For instance, if you position the cursor over the `max-weight="100"` attribute, the following message appears:

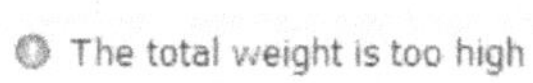

Figure 4.4 – Validation message in oXygen, shown at the bottom of the editing window

Schematron validation using XMLBlueprint

As far as I know there is only one other IDE that supports Schematron validation natively, called XMLBlueprint (https://www.xmlblueprint.com/). They adopted Schematron 2025 quickly: by the end of 2025, version 22 of their product supported it.

Let's perform the same validation as we did in the section titled "Schematron validation using oXygen" (p. 38) using XMLBlueprint:[3]

- Open the Schematron schema (`schematron-book-code-2025/examples/context/parcels.sch`).
- Open the invalid document (`schematron-book-code-2025/data/parcels-schematron-invalid.xml`).
- With the document (not the schema!) having focus, from the menu choose: **Schema > Associate DTD or Schema...**.

[3] These instructions are for version 22, the exact commands/behavior may change with newer versions. XMLBlueprint has more ways/commands for performing Schematron and other validations. Since this is not an XMLBlueprint tutorial these won't be covered here.

- Provide a reference to the Schematron schema in the **Choose a DTD or Schema (path or url):** input box. Because this file is already open, you can easily select it by pressing the **Choose** > button. XMLBlueprint determines the schema type for you. On my machine the result looks like Figure 4.5.

Figure 4.5 – Selecting a schema in XMLBlueprint

- Press **OK** and XMLBlueprint will associate the schema with the document by inserting an `xml-model` processing-instruction at the top of the document:

```
<?xml-model href="../examples/context/parcels.sch"
    schematypens="http://purl.oclc.org/dsdl/schematron"?>
```

  Using such a processing-instruction is the common way to include a reference to a Schematron schema in an XML document. Some more information and examples about this in the section titled "Validating a Schematron schema" (p. 161).

- The validation starts and continues running in the background while you edit the document.

XMLBlueprint underlines the places where there is an error according to the schema:

```
1 <?xml-model href="../examples/context/parcels.sch" schematypens="http://purl.oclc.org/dsdl/schematron"?>
2 <parcels max-weight="100" delivery-date="2021-10-10">
3   <parcel weight="50" date="2021-10-08">
4     <contents>A large quantity of mouth masks</contents>
5   </parcel>
6   <parcel weight="55" date="2021-09-12">
7     <contents>Toys for children</contents>
8   </parcel>
9 </parcels>
```

Figure 4.6 – The invalid parcels document validated by XMLBlueprint

Validation messages appear in the status bar at the bottom of the window when you move the cursor. For instance, if you position the cursor on line 3, the following message appears:

The parcel's date must be more than 10 days before the delivery date.

Figure 4.7 – Validation message in XMLBlueprint, shown at the bottom of the editing window

Raw Schematron validation

If you perform validation in an IDE, it shows you the validation results in a user-friendly way. However, the actual validation (the process that generates the validation results) is hidden from view. It's like driving a car and not looking under the hood: fine when you just need to drive from point A to point B, but sometimes you want to know a little more.

This section looks under the hood of Schematron validation and explains how it's actually done. It covers validation processors, XSLT transformations, and other more technical information. If you're not interested in this level of detail, you can skip this section and go straight to the next chapter, where I explain the basics of the Schematron language.

Schematron validation (or any type of XML validation) is performed by a processor that takes an XML document and a schema and produces a validation result (see Figure 4.8).

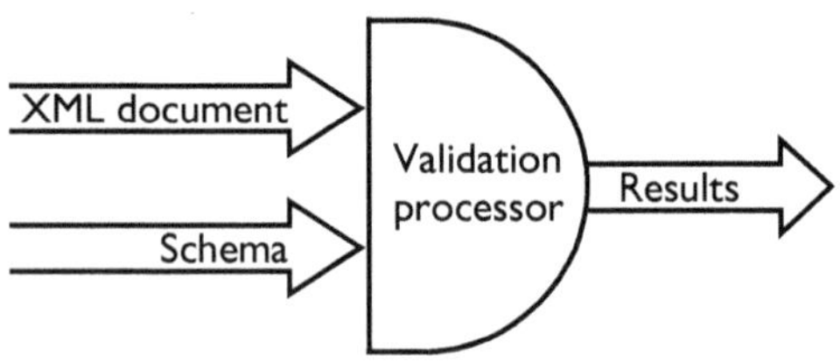

Figure 4.8 – A schematic representation of a validation processor

There are cases where you need or want to use this validation machinery directly. Maybe you're a seasoned command-line jockey and think clicking GUI menus is only for rookies. Or you need to incorporate validation as an automated step in a pipeline or other process. Or you have no IDE available and need to perform a validation directly.

Validation processors are often Java or .NET components, so they can be incorporated into bigger systems and tool chains. For instance, you can do W3C XML Schema validation from the command line or in a tool chain with the Saxon EE (Enterprise Edition)[4] processor (the commercial version, not the free Home Edition).

While there are processors that can validate Schematron, current (in 2026) processors are rather complicated and rely on pre-compilation and an underlying XSLT or XQuery processor. I'll dive into this, but first I need to discuss the results of a validation and how to represent them.

4 https://www.saxonica.com

Validation results

Let's take a closer look at the results of a validation. What could a validation tell us about the document it validated?

1. As a bare minimum, just "valid" or "invalid."
2. Since that's not very helpful, processors usually specify what's wrong and the location of the problem (line/column number).
3. A validation processor might also produce a machine-readable report, most likely another XML document, that you can use in a tool chain, for instance to produce a customized report.

An IDE can only give you result 1 and result 2. The messages are presented in a list and the problem locations are marked in some way (often with red squiggly lines).

When you use a raw validation processor, from the command line or otherwise, you usually see result 2 as output on your console. Result 1, valid or invalid, is often reflected as the tool's process execution status.

Result 3, the validation results in machine-readable format, is rarer. Schematron however has defined such a format. It's called SVRL (Schematron Validation Reporting Language), an XML vocabulary for reporting the results of a Schematron validation. And although the part of the standard that describes SVRL is informative (meaning processor builders don't have to implement it), most existing Schematron validation processors produce SVRL.

SVRL

SVRL stands for Schematron Validation Reporting Language. It's an XML-based format that reports the results of a Schematron validation. You can find an SVRL reference in Appendix D.

For example, let's validate Example 4.5 again, using the SchXslt2 validation processor (see the section titled "The SchXslt2 Schematron processor" (p. 46)). Example 4.6 shows the result.[5]

[5] The SVRL output shown in Example 4.6 (and the SVRL examples to come) is somewhat sanitized: whitespace is trimmed and the file paths are shortened to an ellipsis (...).

Example 4.6 – The SVRL generated when validating the document in Example 4.5 with the schema from Example 3.11.

```
<schematron-output xmlns="http://purl.oclc.org/dsdl/svrl"
                   schematronEdition="2025"
                   phase="#ALL">
   <ns-prefix-in-attribute-values prefix="xs"
uri="http://www.w3.org/2001/XMLSchema"/>
   <active-group/>
   <fired-rule context="/*" document="…/parcels-schematron-invalid.xml"/>
   <failed-assert test="sum(parcel/@weight) le xs:double(@max-weight)"
                  location="/Q{}parcels[1]">
      <text>The total weight is too high</text>
   </failed-assert>
   <fired-rule context="parcel" document="…/parcels-schematron-invalid.xml"/>
   <failed-assert test="(xs:date(/*/@delivery-date) - xs:date(@date)) gt
xs:dayTimeDuration('P10D')"
                  location="/Q{}parcels[1]/Q{}parcel[1]">
      <text>The parcel's date must be more than 10 days before the delivery
date</text>
   </failed-assert>
   <fired-rule context="parcel" document="…/parcels-schematron-invalid.xml"/>
</schematron-output>
```

- An SVRL document uses the `http://purl.oclc.org/dsdl/svrl` XML namespace.
- An SVRL document is basically a linear list of what the Schematron processor did. A pattern that becomes active produces an `<active-pattern>` element, a rule that fires produces a `<fired-rule>` element (I'll get to what patterns and rules are in Chapter 5).
- Most interesting are the two `<failed-assert>` elements, which contain error messages.

You can post-process SVRL to format the validation results to your liking.

XVRL

Another standard for representing validation results in machine-readable format block is XVRL (eXtensible Validation Report Language). This format, introduced by the XProc 3.0[6] community group, is an attempt to create a unified vocabulary for validation reports for all validation languages. The validation types incorporated in XProc 3.0, including Schematron, can report their results in XVRL. Example 4.7 shows what Example 4.6 looks like, expressed in XVRL.

---

[6] XProc is an XML-based programming language for processing documents in pipelines: chaining conversions and other steps together to achieve the desired results. See https://xproc.org.

Example 4.7 – The XVRL equivalent of Example 4.6

```
<report xmlns="http://www.xproc.org/ns/xvrl">
  <metadata>
    <timestamp>…</timestamp>
    <document href="…/parcels-schematron-invalid.xml"/>
    <schema href="…/parcels.sch"
schematypens="http://purl.oclc.org/dsdl/schematron"/>
  </metadata>
  <detection severity="error">
    <location xpath="/Q{}parcels[1]"/>
    <message>The total weight is too high</message>
  </detection>
  <detection severity="error">
    <location xpath="/Q{}parcels[1]/Q{}parcel[1]"/>
    <message>The parcel's date must be more than 10 days before
      the delivery date</message>
  </detection>
</report>
```

Because XVRL is a new language, not specifically Schematron related, and currently implemented only by XProc 3.0, I won't say more about it here. See https://spec.xproc.org/master/head/xvrl/ or the XVRL Codeberg repository https://codeberg.org/XProc/xvrl for more information.

Schematron validation processors

There are several Schematron validation processors, but currently (2026) only two support Schematron 2025: SchXslt2 (which is used for this book) and XQS. I will also briefly discuss the older Schematron "skeleton" implementation, because it was (and sometimes still is) important for many applications.

If you're interested in other processors (for instance those written in Python or Java), see the software section in the README.md file at https://github.com/Schematron/awesome-schematron.

The "skeleton" XSLT Schematron processor

Until about 2020, the official Schematron processor was the "skeleton" XSLT implementation of Schematron. It was originally created by Rick Jelliffe, released in 2000, and maintained by a number of people. You can find it at https://github.com/Schematron/schematron.

However, its GitHub repository was archived and made read-only in October 2020. Maintenance has stopped: it doesn't (and will never) support Schematron 2025. Its home page advises you to use the SchXslt processor instead.

Nonetheless, this processor is still used a lot. If your software tool chain already contains this processor and you have no need for Schematron 2025 features, there is no urgent need to replace it. But if you have a choice, use the SchXslt2 or XQS processor.

The operation of the skeleton XSLT Schematron processor is roughly similar to that of the SchXslt2 processor: XSLT stylesheets are used to produce an XSLT version of the Schematron schema. You then use this generated stylesheet to validate the document(s) against the schema. This principle is discussed in more detail in the next section.

The SchXslt2 Schematron processor

At the XML Prague conference in 2019, David Maus introduced a different way of doing Schematron validation in his talk, "Ex-post rule match selection: A novel approach to XSLT-based Schematron validation." [7] This was the beginning of the rise of the SchXslt Schematron processor.

In 2020, SchXslt became the official Schematron processor and development/maintenance of the skeleton processor stopped. You can find SchXslt on Codeberg.[8] It supports query language bindings `xslt` and `xslt2` (see Chapter 7 for more about this). The SchXslt repository was archived in November 2025 and maintenance has stopped.

SchXslt was further developed and became SchXslt2. SchXslt2 supports the query language binding `xslt3` only and implements most of Schematron 2025. Therefore, we'll focus on SchXslt2.

SchXslt2 currently has a number of manifestations:

- You can use it directly from the command-line as explained in the section titled "SchXslt2 from the command-line" (p. 47).
- The core of SchXslt2 is a *transpiler*, which can also be used directly. This is explained in the section titled "The SchXslt2 transpiler" (p. 47).
- There is an implementation of SchXslt2 as a step in XProc 3. I won't go into it further, but those interested can find it here: https://codeberg.org/dmaus/mausotron-xproc.

---

[7] This talk is still online: https://www.youtube.com/watch?v=1xJ6F9M1k1k. The text version can be found in the 2019 conference proceedings (https://www.xmlprague.cz/archive/).

[8] https://codeberg.org/SchXslt/schxslt

SchXslt2 from the command-line

Running SchXslt2 directly from the command-line is possible using its Java-based implementation Mausotron CLI (a name no doubt inspired by that of its implementer David Maus). You can find it here: https://codeberg.org/dmaus/mausotron-cli.

To use the Mausotron CLI you need to have Java installed. Download the latest Mausotron CLI `.jar` file from the releases page (https://codeberg.org/dmaus/mausotron-cli/releases). Here are a few command examples for validating Example 4.5. The examples assume all files are in the same directory. The Mausotron CLI version number used (`1.1.2`, downloaded early 2026) may differ from your download.

- To get help about the Mausotron CLI command-line options:

  ```
  java -jar mausotron-1.1.2.jar help
  ```

  Or for help on validation:

  ```
  java -jar mausotron-1.1.2.jar validate help
  ```

- To simply validate a document against a Schematron schema:

  ```
  java -jar mausotron-1.1.2.jar validate parcels.sch
  parcels-schematron-invalid.xml
  ```

  This produces the simple but clear message: `Validation result: INVALID.`

- To get the SVRL result of the validation, use the `--report` option:

  ```
  java -jar mausotron-1.1.2.jar --report=svrl.xml validate parcels.sch
  parcels-schematron-invalid.xml
  ```

The SchXslt2 transpiler

The core of the SchXslt2 processor is a *transpiler*: it doesn't validate directly. Instead it produces an XSLT stylesheet to perform the actual validation. This was also the approach of the original skeleton processor, but SchXslt2 produces different, more efficient, code. You can find the SchXslt2 transpiler here: https://codeberg.org/SchXslt/schxslt2. Figure 4.9 shows how it works.

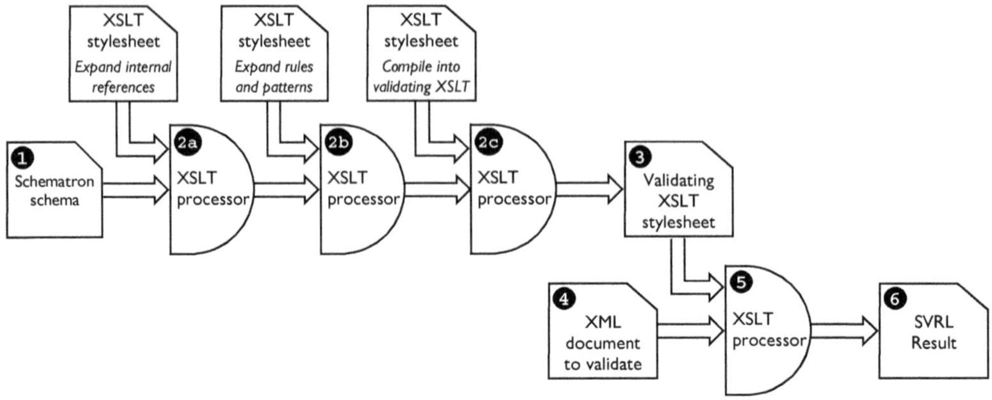

Figure 4.9 – Schematic representation of the operation of the SchXslt processor

1. The process starts with the Schematron schema.
2. This schema is transformed ("transpiled") by an XSLT transformation. This transformation is supplied by, and is part of, SchXslt2.[9]
3. The result of this transformation is a generated XSLT stylesheet.
4. The XML document we want to validate comes into play.
5. This document is transformed using the generated XSLT stylesheet.
6. The result of this transformation is the SVRL representation of the validation result.

The SchXslt2 transpiler, in its raw form, has a few limitations as of the beginning of 2026:

- The transpiler enforces some rules, but does not fully validate the schema.
- The transpiler does not support dynamic phase selection using the `phase/@when` attribute (see the section titled "Dynamic phase selection" (p. 96)). This is because the phase must be known at the time SchXslt2 generates ("transpiles") the stylesheet that performs the actual validation. In other words: a SchXslt2 generated stylesheet is for a single phase only.
- The transpiler does not implement proper scoping rules of pattern and phase variables. Schema, pattern, and phase variables are all implemented as global XSLT variables. Therefore, the name of a schema, pattern, or phase variable must be unique for the entire schema.

The command-line implementation of SchXslt2 (see the section titled "SchXslt2 from the command-line" (p. 47)) does implement full schema validation and dynamic phase selection.

[9] The skeleton processor and SchXslt implementations use multiple consecutive XSLT transformations to achieve this.

The XQS Schematron processor

XQS stands for "XQuery for Schematron" and is, as its name says, an XQuery implementation of Schematron. It was developed by Andrew Sales, the editor of the Schematron 2025 standard (and its previous version). It is a highly conformant implementation of Schematron 2025, supporting the query language bindings `xquery`, `xquery3`, and `xquery31`. You can find XQS on GitHub: https://github.com/AndrewSales/XQS.

XQS runs on the BaseX database engine (https://basex.org/, version 10 or higher). It operates using the same principle as SchXslt2: the Schematron schema is converted into an XQuery script. You can use this generated script with any conformant XQuery processor to perform the actual validation. Figure 4.10 shows how it works, which is similar to the way the SchXslt2 transpiler works (see the section titled "The SchXslt2 transpiler" (p. 47)).

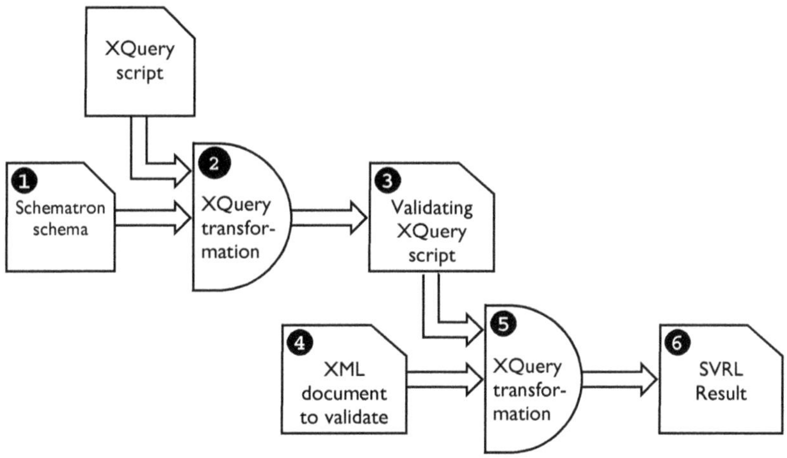

Figure 4.10 – Schematic representation of the operation of the XQS processor

1. The process starts with the Schematron schema.
2. This schema is transformed by an XQuery script. This script is part of XQS.
3. The result of this transformation is a generated XQuery script.
4. The XML document we want to validate comes into play.
5. This document is processed using the generated XQuery script.
6. The result of this is the SVRL representation of the validation result.

The XQS readme contains instructions on how to operate it. Don't let the requirement to use BaseX discourage you: once BaseX is properly installed (which is easy), using XQS is remarkably simple. No further knowledge of BaseX is required.

Be aware the XQS, because of its XQuery nature, does some things a little different than the usual XSLT based processors. Please read the section below, and the XQS readme Troubleshooting section, carefully.

XQS and context

Be aware that XQS introduces an important difference with the more usual XSLT based Schematron processors regarding the `<rule>` element `context` attribute:

- In XSLT based processors, this attribute is a so-called "XSLT match pattern". For instance, `context="book"` matches with *all* `<book>` elements in the input document, wherever they are.
- In contrast, in XQS theses attributes are always evaluated in the context of the document root. This means you'll have to write a full XPath expression to match.

This has several consequences:

- A `context="book"` in XQS will only match when `<book>` is the root element.
- If `<book>` is anywhere else in your document, you'll have to write a full XPath expression that selects it. For instance:
  - When `<book>` is always a child of the root element: `context="/your-root-element/book` or `context="/*/book"`.
  - When you want to match `<book>` wherever it is in your document (like what happens in an XSLT type binding with `context="book"`): use `context="//book"`.

CHAPTER 5
Schematron basics

In this chapter you will learn how to write a basic Schematron schema; how to use concepts like groups, patterns, rules, assertions, and reports; and how to tie these concepts together. I also describe the algorithm a Schematron processor follows to process a schema.

To get the most out of this chapter, you need a basic knowledge of XPath. Appendix A provides an overview of XPath that covers what you need to know.

I suggest that while you read this chapter, you try out some of these examples and run Schematron validations of your own or variations of the given examples.[1] Chapter 4 contains information on how to perform Schematron validations.

To experiment, it's easiest to use an IDE, for instance oXygen or XMLBlueprint (see the section titled "IDE-based Schematron validation" (p. 37)). But you can also perform "raw" validations from the command line (see the section titled "Raw Schematron validation" (p. 42)).

Schematron 2020 note

An important new building block of Schematron 2025 schemas is groups (`<group>` elements). The 2020 edition has no groups (only patterns, `<pattern>` elements). Please keep this in mind when using the information in this chapter for constructing Schematron 2020 schemas.

Setting up a Schematron schema

Let's start with two basic, but nonetheless valid, Schematron schemas that do absolutely nothing.

Example 5.1 – An empty Schematron schema with an empty pattern (schematron-book-code-2025/templates/empty-schema-pattern.sch)

```
<schema xmlns="http://purl.oclc.org/dsdl/schematron" schematronEdition="2025"
  queryBinding="xslt3">
  <pattern/>
</schema>
```

[1] the section titled "Finding and using the code examples" (p. 6) describes how to obtain the example code.

Example 5.2 – An empty Schematron schema with an empty group (schematron-book-code-2025/templates/empty-schema-group.sch)

```
<schema xmlns="http://purl.oclc.org/dsdl/schematron" schematronEdition="2025"
  queryBinding="xslt3">
  <group/>
</schema>
```

Here are a few things to consider when looking at Example 5.1 and Example 5.2:

- The root element of a Schematron schema is always `<schema>`, and there must be at least one `<pattern>` or one `<group>` element. More about patterns and groups in the next section.

> Although the Schematron specification says that an empty schema must have at least one `<pattern>` or `<group>` element, some environments accept an empty `<schema>` element. Of course, nothing happens when you apply such a schema.
>
> The only reason you need to be aware of this is if you create an empty `<schema>` element on purpose, for instance as a placeholder for future changes. A strict Schematron processor may reject this if it doesn't have at least a `<pattern>` or `<group>` element.

- The next thing to notice is that the XML vocabulary for Schematron is in a namespace (namespaces are explained in Appendix B): `http://purl.oclc.org/dsdl/schematron`

  You can usually forget about this, as long as you make sure all of your Schematron XML is in this namespace. Including `xmlns="http://purl.oclc.org/dsdl/schematron"` on the root element, as in Example 5.1 and Example 5.2, will take care of this.
- The root element has a `schematronEdition="2025"` attribute. This means this is a Schematron 2025 schema and should be treated as such.

> **Schematron 2020 note**
>
> For Schematron 2020 schemas, *do not use* the `schematronEdition` attribute. Schematron 2020 does not have this attribute, so `schematronEdition="2020"` will not work.

- There is also a `queryBinding="xslt3"` attribute on the `<schema>` root element. The Schematron language allows you to specify the language used to define expressions. This is called the "query language binding." The `queryBinding` attribute defines this.

  In Example 5.1 and Example 5.2, the value of the `queryBinding="xslt3"` attribute tells the Schematron processor to use XSLT 3.0 (and because of that XPath 3.1). You can forget about this for now, but if you who want to know more, Chapter 7 is devoted to this topic.

  The `queryBinding` attribute is optional, but if you omit it the default binding `xslt` is used. This means that your expressions are limited to what you can do in XSLT 1.0 (and because of that, XPath 1.0). Given the current (in 2025) state of the XML standards, which have advanced significantly from this version, that's severely limiting.

> **Using other query language bindings**
>
> Your Schematron processor might complain about the `xslt3` query binding. In that case try the value `xslt2` first. If that still doesn't work, try `xpath31`, `xpath3` or `xpath2`.
>
> If you're using XQS (see the section titled "The XQS Schematron processor" (p. 49)), use `xquery31`. Be aware that for XQS you'll also have to change the value of the `context` attributes of the `<rule>` elements in the examples, as explained in the section titled "XQS and context" (p. 50).
>
> If none of these values work in your environment,[2] it will be difficult to follow and try the examples in this book. I suggest you use one of the processors discussed in the book to learn Schematron. Afterwards, it should be easier for you transfer what you know to whatever query binding language your processor uses.

Patterns, groups, rules, assertions, and reports

The core parts of Schematron are patterns, groups, rules, assertions, and reports:

- A Schematron schema consists of patterns and/or groups: `<pattern>` and/or `<groups>` elements.

[2] Although this is unlikely, you might encounter a different query language with a proprietary Schematron processor.

- Each pattern or group consists of rules: `<rule>` elements. A rule contains a query (using the query language specified in the `queryBinding` attribute), and when that query matches something, for example an element or attribute in your XML instance, the rule is triggered.

  How rules are processed depends on whether they are part of a pattern or a group:

  - **Patterns:** For every node in the document being validated, if more than one rule in the pattern matches this node, only the first rule triggered is executed.

    Or, in other words: A rule within a pattern is triggered when its `context` attribute matches nodes in the document being validated, *unless* a previous rule in the same pattern has already matched those nodes. Rules within a pattern are evaluated in document order.

    This behavior sometimes causes a common pitfall when creating a schema. See the section titled "Rule processing in patterns" (p. 58) for more information.

  - **Groups:** For rules in a group it's much simpler: For every node in the document being validated, all rules triggered are executed.

- Each rule consists of assertions and/or reports: `<assert>` and/or `<report>` elements. When a rule is triggered, *all* assertions and reports in that rule are checked.

Let's illustrate this with a simple example. Suppose you need to validate XML documents in which there are `<ID>` elements that hold some identifier. These elements can occur in several places (see Example 5.3).

Example 5.3 – An XML document that contains `<ID>` elements (`schematron-book-code-2025/data/data-with-ids.xml`)

```
<DATA>
  <ARTICLE>
    <NAME>BOOK</NAME>
    <ID>ABC12345</ID>
  </ARTICLE>
  <ARTICLE>
    <NAME>TOY</NAME>
    <ID>XYZ123456</ID>
  </ARTICLE>
</DATA>
```

For this example, let's say that identifiers must be 9 characters long and that any identifier that starts with the letter `X` must be reported as special. Example 5.4 contains a Schematron schema that performs this validation.

Example 5.4 – A Schematron schema that checks the length of the `<ID>` elements (`schematron-book-code-2025/examples/basics/check-data-with-ids.sch`)

```
<schema xmlns="http://purl.oclc.org/dsdl/schematron" schematronEdition="2025"
  queryBinding="xslt3">
  <pattern>
    <rule context="ID">
      <assert test="string-length(.) eq 9">
        An ID must be 9 characters long!
      </assert>
      <report test="starts-with(., 'X')">
        Special identifier found!
      </report>
    </rule>
  </pattern>
</schema>
```

- Example 5.4 uses a pattern (`<pattern>` element). However, a group (`<group>` element) could just as well have been used here. Because Example 5.4 only contains a single rule (`<rule>` element), the effect remains the same.
- `<pattern>` and `<group>` usually have no attributes (see Chapter 6 for a few exceptions).

  Every pattern and group is applied to every node in the document being validated.
- A `<rule>` element must have a `context` attribute. The contents of this attribute is an "XSLT match pattern." The one in Example 5.4, `context="ID"`, fires on every `<ID>` element.

  When a rule fires, the node it triggered on becomes the context item, and the assertions and reports in that rule are processed.

  For patterns, for each separate node in the document, only the first rule triggered is executed. For groups, all rules triggered are executed.
- An `<assert>` or `<report>` element must have a `test` attribute. Its contents must be an XPath boolean expression. An assertion fails when the expression is `false`, a report succeeds when it's `true`.

  All assertions and reports in the rule that fires are processed.

  A failed assertion or successful report results in a validation message, which comes from the text of the contents of the `<assert>` or `<report>` element.
- If at least one assert fails or report succeeds, the document is considered Schematron invalid.

Given this, when you validate Example 5.3 against the schema in Example 5.4, there will be two validation messages:

1. On the `<ID>ABC12345</ID>` element: **`An ID must be 9 characters long!`**
2. On the `<ID>XYZ123456</ID>` element: **`Special identifier found!`**

The Schematron processing algorithm

This section provides an overview of the algorithm a Schematron processor uses to apply a Schematron schema to an XML instance. This explanation is based on the way current XSLT-based processors do this. Other processors, such as the XQuery based XQS, use a different approach, but the overall effect and outcome remain the same.

1. Read the XML document and represent it internally using a tree-shaped data structure in the Schematron processor's memory. All parts of the XML document (elements, attributes, text, etc.) are represented as nodes in that tree.
2. The Schematron processor starts "walking" the tree and, one by one, visits every node. This includes not only elements and attributes but also the document node, text, comments, and processing instructions.
3. For every node in the tree, the processor loops over every `<pattern>` and `<group>` element in the Schematron schema.
4. The patterns and groups are processed:
   a. **Patterns:** For each pattern, it finds the *first* rule (`<rule>` element) whose `context` attribute matches the node being visited (the context node). In this case, *first* means *top-most* (or, in official XML terminology, "first in document-order"). It's not an error if no rule matches.
   b. **Groups:** For each group, find *all* rules (`<rule>` elements) whose `context` attribute matches the node being visited (the context node). It's not an error if no rule matches.
5. For all matching rules, process all assertions and reports (`<assert>` and `<report>` elements) inside that rule. It's not an error if no assertion or report fires.

Example 5.5 shows the Schematron algorithm expressed in a pseudo programming language (the numbers refer to the corresponding numbers in the preceding list).

Example 5.5 – The Schematron algorithm in a pseudo programming language

```
1. Read the input document and represent it as a tree
2. For every node in the input document
   3. For every pattern and group in the schema
      4.1. For patterns: for every rule in the pattern
           *  If (the rule matches) Then
                5. For every assert and report in the rule
                   * Process asserts/reports
                * Stop checking the rules for this pattern
              Else
                *  Check next the rule in the pattern
      4.2. For groups: For every rule in the group
           *  If (the rule matches) Then
                5. For every assert and report in the rule
                   * Process asserts/reports
              Else
                *  Check next the rule in the group
```

The order of things

The Schematron specification states that the order in which nodes are visited in step 2 of Example 5.5 is implementation-defined. This means that a processor could jump at random through the nodes in the tree, as long as it visits them all. In practice, processors most likely walk through the tree in depth-first order.[3]

The specification also states that the order in which patterns, groups, rules in groups, and assertions/reports are handled (steps 3 and 5) is implementation-defined. Again, this will usually be predictable, most likely the order in which the patterns, groups, assertions, and reports appear in the schema.

The only exception is rules in a pattern. Because of the if-then-else nature of a pattern (see the section titled "Rule processing in patterns" (p. 58)), these rules are processed in document order.

The bottom line is that you should not rely on the order in which a Schematron processor reads a document, processes patterns and groups, rules in groups, or outputs messages. Another processor (or even the next version of the same processor) might do things differently.

---

[3] There are several algorithms for traversing a tree structure, the most common being depth-first and breadth-first. This Wikipedia article contains a good description of tree traversal: https://en.wikipedia.org/wiki/Tree_traversal.

Rule processing in patterns

Let's dwell a little longer on step 4.1 of the algorithm presented in Example 5.5: the processing of rules (`<rule>` elements) in a pattern (`<pattern>` element). This has an if-then-else kind of behavior which may take some getting used to but is useful in a number of situations.

Suppose you have a Schematron schema for an imaginary publisher's catalog. Inside is a pattern that looks like Example 5.6.

Example 5.6 – A pattern with three rules

```
<pattern>
  <rule context="book">
    … (asserts and reports for book elements)
  </rule>
  <rule context="magazine">
    … (asserts and reports for magazine elements)
  </rule>
  <rule context="*">
    … (asserts and reports for other elements)
  </rule>
</pattern>
```

Now, suppose the Schematron processor is checking a `<magazine>` element. This matches the second rule in the pattern (`context="magazine"`) and, therefore, causes all assertions and reports for magazines to be checked. However, contrary to what you might expect, it does *not* check the assertions and reports in the third rule (`context="*"`). This is because rules in a pattern act as an `if/then/else` statement (see Example 5.7).

Example 5.7 – The algorithm for processing rules in a pseudo programming language

```
* If (it's a book element) Then
    … (process the asserts and reports for book elements)
  Else If (it's a magazine element) Then
    … (process the asserts and reports for magazine elements)
  Else
    … (process the asserts and reports for other elements)
```

If you come from an XSLT background, you can represent this algorithm using an `<xsl:choose>` (see Example 5.8).

Example 5.8 – The algorithm for processing rules using an XSLT `<xsl:choose>` element

```
<xsl:choose>
  <xsl:when test="(it's a book element)">
    … (process the asserts and reports for book elements)
  </xsl:when>
  <xsl:when test="(it's a magazine element)">
    … (process the asserts and reports for magazine elements)
  </xsl:when>
  <xsl:otherwise>
    … (process the asserts and reports for other elements)
  </xsl:otherwise>
</xsl:choose>
```

Now what if you want `<book>` and `<magazine>` elements to be checked by both by the assertions and reports for those specific elements *and* the assertions and reports for any element (the third rule)? The solution is easy: use a group (`<group>` element) instead of a pattern (`<pattern>` element). In a group, all rules are processed. Example 5.9 shows what this looks like.

Example 5.9 – Using a group to process all rules

```
<group>
  <rule context="book">
    … (asserts and reports for book elements)
  </rule>
  <rule context="magazine">
    … (asserts and reports for magazine elements)
  </rule>
  <rule context="*">
    … (generic asserts and reports, for all elements)
  </rule>
</group>
```

Schematron 2020 note

Schematron 2020 has no groups, only patterns. In order to obtain the same effect as in Example 5.9, you have to move the third rule into its own pattern:

Example 5.10 – Using multiple patterns to process all rules

```
<pattern>
  <rule context="book">
    … (asserts and reports for book elements)
  </rule>
  <rule context="magazine">
    … (asserts and reports for magazine elements)
  </rule>
</pattern>
<pattern>
  <rule context="*">
    … (generic asserts and reports, for all elements)
  </rule>
</pattern>
```

Since all patterns are processed for all nodes in the document being validated, this ensures that the generic rules are also processed.

Assert and Report processing

The previous sections mention "assertions and reports being processed." What does that mean?

Assertions and reports are tests performed on the contents of the XML document being validated:

- An assertion (`<assert test="…">` element) checks whether the condition in the `test` attribute is `false`. If so it reports a validation error.

  An assertion flags something that is invalid.

- A report (`<report test="…">` element) does the reverse: it generates a message when the condition in the `test` attribute is `true`.

  A report flags specific situations that require attention (or are interesting, peculiar, wonderful, celebration-worthy, or whatever).

report = not assert?

Programmers may be frowning now: so a report is equivalent to the boolean *not* of an assertion (or the other way around)? Yes, that's correct. For instance, take this report:

```
<report test="...">...</report>
```

The following will produce the same message:

```
<assert test="not(...)">...</assert>
```

Then why are there two elements which, from a programming point of view, have almost exactly the same functionality? The difference is of course in their meaning, their goal, not in the technical implementation.

You'll also find this difference reflected in the resulting SVRL: a triggered assertion results in a `<failed-assert>` element, a report in a `<successful-report>` element.

Schematron is a language with which you can assert whether a document is Schematron valid. It's therefore more natural to think in assertions when writing such a schema. As far as I've seen, most Schematron schemas use assertions only.

Because of this I focus on the `<assert>` element in the explanations and examples to come. However, be aware that everything said about the `<assert>` element also holds for the `<report>` element, with a negated test as the main difference.

Moreover, reports exhibit somewhat counterintuitive behavior: a *successful* report (a report that triggered) causes the document to become *invalid*. This makes the use of reports rather confusing. Nevertheless, in some cases, using reports can be useful.

Let's illustrate this with another example. Suppose you have a Schematron schema whose sole purpose is to check whether all `type` attributes, anywhere in the document, have a value of either `normal` or `special` and produce an understandable error message when this isn't the case. The simple Schematron schema in Example 5.11 does this.

Example 5.11 – A simple Schematron schema that checks the value of every `type` attribute (`schematron-book-code-2025/examples/basics/check-type-1.sch`)

```
<schema xmlns="http://purl.oclc.org/dsdl/schematron" schematronEdition="2025"
  queryBinding="xslt3">
  <pattern>
    <rule context="@type">
      <assert test="(. eq 'normal') or (. eq 'special')">
        The type must be normal or special
      </assert>
    </rule>
  </pattern>
</schema>
```

If you run this schema against the document in Example 5.12, the `type` attribute on the fourth `<thing>` element triggers this error message: **`The type must be normal or special`**

Example 5.12 – A document with an invalid `type` attribute according to the Schematron schema in Example 5.11. (`schematron-book-code-2025/data/things-with-types.xml`)

```
<things>
  <thing name="thing 1" type="normal"/>
  <thing name="thing 2" type="special"/>
  <thing name="thing 3" type="special"/>
  <thing name="thing 4" type="vintage"/>
</things>
```

The SVRL validation report looks like Example 5.13.

Example 5.13 – The SVRL generated when validating the document in Example 5.12 with the schema from Example 5.11.

```
<schematron-output xmlns="http://purl.oclc.org/dsdl/svrl"
                   schematronEdition="2025"
                   phase="#ALL">
   <active-pattern/>
   <fired-rule context="@type" document=".../things-with-types.xml"/>
   <fired-rule context="@type" document=".../things-with-types.xml"/>
   <fired-rule context="@type" document=".../things-with-types.xml"/>
   <fired-rule context="@type" document=".../things-with-types.xml"/>
   <failed-assert test="(. eq 'normal') or (. eq 'special')"
                  location="/Q{}things[1]/Q{}thing[4]/@type">
      <text>The type must be normal or special</text>
   </failed-assert>
</schematron-output>
```

Back to the schema in Example 5.11. Let's analyze in detail what's happening:

- The schema uses a pattern (`<pattern>` element). However, a group (`<group>` element) could have been used just as well. I used a pattern to keep the example compatible with Schematron 2020.
- The (only) rule in the (only) pattern has a `context="@type"` attribute. This means that this rule will trigger on every `type` attribute in the document.
- When this rule encounters a `type` attribute, it triggers the assertion and the `type` attribute becomes the context item. This means that you can reference it with a dot (`.`) in the test expression, as this example does.
- The `test` attribute on an `<assert>` or `<report>` element must contain a valid XPath boolean expression. This expression is evaluated and the result (`true` or `false`) is used by the Schematron processor:
  - An assertion will trigger when the value of the test is `false`.
  - A report will trigger when the test is `true`.
- The `test` attribute in the example contains the value:

  ```
  (. eq 'normal') or (. eq 'special')
  ```

  This checks whether the value of the context item is either `normal` or `special` and returns `true` if this is the case.
- Now look back to Example 5.12. The first three `<thing>` elements have a `type` attribute that conforms to the rules. So the expression in the `test` attribute will evaluate to `true` and no message will be produced.

  But the value of the `type` attribute on the fourth `<thing>` has an invalid type, `vintage`, which causes the test expression to evaluate to `false`. The Schematron processor uses the contents of the `<assert>` element as message text, resulting in the following error message:

  ```
  The type must be normal or special
  ```

Using reports instead of assertions

You can get the same result using reports instead of assertions. Example 5.14 shows how.

Example 5.14 – A variant of Example 5.11, but now using `report` instead of `assert`. (`schematron-book-code-2025/examples/basics/check-type-2.sch`)

```
<schema xmlns="http://purl.oclc.org/dsdl/schematron" schematronEdition="2025"
  queryBinding="xslt3">
  <pattern>
    <rule context="@type">
      <report test="not((. eq 'normal') or (. eq 'special'))">
        The type must be normal or special
      </report>
    </rule>
  </pattern>
</schema>
```

The expression in the `<assert>` element's test expression is almost identical to Example 5.11. The only difference is that the test is negated using the `not()` function.

The validation result is almost the same. The only difference in the SVRL report is that it will tell you a report was detected instead of an assert (see Example 5.15).

Example 5.15 – The SVRL generated when validating the document in Example 5.12 with the schema from Example 5.14.

```
<schematron-output xmlns="http://purl.oclc.org/dsdl/svrl"
                   schematronEdition="2025"
                   phase="#ALL">
  <active-pattern/>
  <fired-rule context="@type" document=".../things-with-types.xml"/>
  <fired-rule context="@type" document=".../things-with-types.xml"/>
  <fired-rule context="@type" document=".../things-with-types.xml"/>
  <fired-rule context="@type" document=".../things-with-types.xml"/>
  <successful-report test="not((. eq 'normal') or (. eq 'special'))"
                     location="/Q{}things[1]/Q{}thing[4]/@type">
    <text>The type must be normal or special</text>
  </successful-report>
</schematron-output>
```

This might seem to be almost the same, but the meaning is different. In most situations assertions are used to catch errors, and reports are used to flag situations that need disclosure. And remember, a successful report also causes the document to become invalid.

The message texts

The texts produced by the assertions and reports are completely up to you. Of course, it helps a lot if you try to write them from the user's perspective. Don't leave your users staring puzzled at messages they don't understand. Make messages clear and helpful.

The Schematron standard contains two, in my opinion, rather peculiar statements about this:

- For assertions (standard section 5.4.3): "The natural-language assertion shall be a positive statement of a constraint."
- For reports (standard section 5.4.14): "The natural-language assertion shall be a positive statement of a found pattern or a negative statement of a constraint."

In other words: the Schematron standard prescribes how to formulate messages. A message like **`Invalid value`** is considered wrong and should be reformulated to something positive, for instance **`The value must be between x and y`**. The original designer of Schematron (Rick Jelliffe) says about this: "Schematron is a Schema language *because* it requires you to state positively what is supposed to be found in the document." It's all about what assertions and reports actually *are*, what they're intended to be.

Of course, in practice its entirely up to you how you formulate your messages. No Schematron processor will ever refuse a Schematron schema because the messages aren't stated in a positive way. Personally, I see this as a philosophical issue with limited practical value. Some examples in this book use positive message texts, some don't. Yes, messages should be clear and helpful, but how to formulate them is, in my opinion, not something a standard should be concerned with. You have to make up your own mind.

More meaningful messages: inserting values

So far, the messages in the examples have been rather simple, consisting of a fixed piece of text. However, it would be nice, and it is often required, to have more meaningful messages that, for example, detail exactly what's wrong and identify the location of the error.

This section describes the basic mechanism for this: the `<value-of>` element. There are other elements you can use to improve message quality, such as adding emphasis or defining the reading direction. I don't describe these other elements here, but you can find a description in the section titled "Messages with markup: `<emph>`, `<span>`, and `<dir>` " (p. 141).

You can improve messages by using information from the document. For instance, a message that reads **`The type must be normal or special, not vintage`** reports both the offending type value and the correct values. This allows you to search the document for the word "vintage" and repair the incorrect instances.

Schematron uses the `<value-of>` element to do this. This element inserts the result of an XPath expression in a message. The expression is in the (mandatory) `select` attribute:

```
<value-of select="..."/>
```

The result of the expression in the `select` attribute, converted to a string, is inserted into your message. Example 5.16 puts the `<value-of>` element to work.

Example 5.16 – Using a `<value-of>` element to enhance a message. (`schematron-book-code-2025/examples/basics/check-type-3.sch`)

```
<schema xmlns="http://purl.oclc.org/dsdl/schematron" schematronEdition="2025"
  queryBinding="xslt3">
  <pattern>
    <rule context="@type">
      <assert test="(. eq 'normal') or (. eq 'special')">
        The type must be normal or special, not <value-of select="."/>
      </assert>
    </rule>
  </pattern>
</schema>
```

The `select` attribute of the `<value-of>` element in Example 5.16 references the context item, just like the `test` attribute of the `<assert>` element. This context item, set by the encompassing `<rule>` element and referenced with the dot (`.`) operator, is the same in both cases.

When run against the document in Example 5.12, the error message becomes **`The type must be normal or special, not vintage`**. The generated SVRL is shown in Example 5.17.

Example 5.17 – The SVRL generated when validating the document in Example 5.12 with the schema from Example 5.16.

```
<schematron-output xmlns="http://purl.oclc.org/dsdl/svrl"
                   schematronEdition="2025"
                   phase="#ALL">
   <active-pattern/>
   <fired-rule context="@type" document=".../things-with-types.xml"/>
   <fired-rule context="@type" document=".../things-with-types.xml"/>
   <fired-rule context="@type" document=".../things-with-types.xml"/>
   <fired-rule context="@type" document=".../things-with-types.xml"/>
   <failed-assert test="(. eq 'normal') or (. eq 'special')"
                  location="/Q{}things[1]/Q{}thing[4]/@type">
      <text>The type must be normal or special, not vintage</text>
   </failed-assert>
</schematron-output>
```

Let's make this message even more specific: The input document from Example 5.12 also has a `name` attribute on every `<thing>` element:

```
<thing name="thing 4" type="vintage"/>
```

You can do this by including the value of the `name` attribute in the error message, for instance:

`The type of thing 4 must be normal or special, not vintage.`

However, the context item is the `type` element, and you need to reach the `name` attribute. To reach that attribute you need to work with the XML document tree:

- Climb up in the tree to the `type` attribute's parent, the `<thing>` element, using the parent double-dot operator (`..`).
- Descend from the `<thing>` parent element to its child `name` attribute: `@name`.
- Concatenate these two parts using the slash (/) operator: `../@code`

Example 5.18 shows the result when you add this to the schema.

Example 5.18 – Adding the value of the `name` attribute to the message using `<value-of>` elements (`schematron-book-code-2025/examples/basics/check-type-4.sch`)

```
<schema xmlns="http://purl.oclc.org/dsdl/schematron" schematronEdition="2025"
  queryBinding="xslt3">
  <pattern>
    <rule context="@type">
      <assert test="(. eq 'normal') or (. eq 'special')">
        The type of <value-of select="../@name"/> must be normal or special,
        not <value-of select="."/>
      </assert>
    </rule>
  </pattern>
</schema>
```

Where has the context item gone?

Looking at resulting the XPath expression `../@name`, you might wonder where the context item has gone. Shouldn't the expression be `./../@name` instead?

Actually, both expressions, `../@name` and `./../@name`, are correct. Starting at the context item is implicit for XPath expressions that do not start with a slash. So you can write `./../@name`, but the starting `./` is superfluous.

The code in Example 5.18 is fine but a bit clumsy with all this climbing up and down in the tree. Another way of doing this is to make the rule fire on the parent `<thing>` element and from there test and, if necessary, report the values of the attributes. Example 5.19 does this, and both it and Example 5.18 result in the same message.

Example 5.19 – Using the `<thing>` element as target for the rule. (`schematron-book-code-2025/examples/basics/check-type-5.sch`)

```
<schema xmlns="http://purl.oclc.org/dsdl/schematron" schematronEdition="2025"
  queryBinding="xslt3">
  <pattern>
    <rule context="thing">
      <assert test="(@type eq 'normal') or (@type eq 'special')">
        The type of <value-of select="@name"/> must be normal or special,
        not <value-of select="@type"/>
      </assert>
    </rule>
  </pattern>
</schema>
```

Using Text-Value-Templates instead of `<value-of>`

If you're using the `xslt3` query language binding (see Chapter 7), there is another mechanism you can use as an alternative to `<value-of>` elements: Text-Value-Templates (TVTs). A TVT is an XPath expression inside curly braces, like this: `{…}`. The result of the expression, converted to a string, is inserted into your message. This works just like the `select` attribute of a `<value-of>` element. Example 5.20 uses TVTs and is equivalent to Example 5.16.

Example 5.20 – Using a TVT to enhance a message.
(`schematron-book-code-2025/examples/basics/check-type-3-tvt.sch`)

```
<schema xmlns="http://purl.oclc.org/dsdl/schematron" schematronEdition="2025"
  queryBinding="xslt3">
  <pattern>
    <rule context="@type">
      <assert test="(. eq 'normal') or (. eq 'special')">
        The type must be normal or special, not {.}
      </assert>
    </rule>
  </pattern>
</schema>
```

TVTs are a useful, easy, and concise mechanism to insert values into messages. When you come from an XQuery or XSLT (version 3.0 or higher) background, you're probably used to them. However, there are some potential problem areas to address:

- It (officially) works only with the `xslt3` query language binding. This may make your schemas too specific.
- What do you do if you need a curly brace in your message? The Schematron specification does not address this and leaves it to the processor to implement a solution. Consult your Schematron processor documentation (or experiment a bit) to determine how to do this.

  In XSLT, doubling the curly braces stops them from being interpreted as the beginning/end of a TVT. This may also work for your Schematron processor. Another way is to write an XPath expression that results in a curly brace or outputs whatever you need inside curly braces, for example: `The code is {'{' || @code || '}'}`
- Porting Schematron 2020 schemas to the 2025 edition using an `xslt3` query language binding may cause problems if the messages in the original schemas contain curly braces. It can be costly to go through and fix every instance of curly brackets. The Schematron specification describes no general mechanism to control TVT expansion.

If you run into these kinds of problems, check whether you can enable or disable TVT expansion in the processor. For example, the SchXslt2 processor (see the section titled "The SchXslt2 Schematron processor" (p. 46)) has an option to turn TVT expansion on or off.

Declaring and using variables: `<let>`

Adding a variable to your Schematron schema allows you to store some value and re-use it in rules, assertions, reports, and messages. This value can be anything you can access using an XPath expression: a constant, something from the document that is validated, a computed result, etc.

For a first example, let's revisit Example 5.19. Here the schema determines the value of the `type` attribute twice: Once on the `<assert>` element and once when creating the message (the second `<value-of>` element).

For a simple schema this kind of duplication of effort isn't a big deal, but it does violate the software engineering's DNRY (Do Not Repeat Yourself) principle. It would be better to retrieve the value only once. This will become more important when schemas and XPath expressions get bigger, more complicated, and harder to maintain.

Example 5.21 shows an enhanced version of Example 5.19, using a variable as intermediate storage for the value of the `type` attribute.

Example 5.21 – Using a variable for a thing's type
(`schematron-book-code-2025/examples/basics/check-type-6.sch`)

```
<schema xmlns="http://purl.oclc.org/dsdl/schematron" schematronEdition="2025"
  queryBinding="xslt3">
  <pattern>
    <rule context="thing">
      <let name="thing-type" value="@type"/>
      <assert test="($thing-type eq 'normal') or ($thing-type eq 'special')">
        The type of <value-of select="@name"/> must be normal or special,
        not <value-of select="$thing-type"/>
      </assert>
    </rule>
  </pattern>
</schema>
```

The <let> element creates a variable called `thing-type` and fills this with the `type` attribute. In both the <assert> and the second <value-of> element we refer to this variable with `$thing-type`.

Ground rules for variables

Declaring and using variables is, in most cases, simple and intuitive. You normally don't have to be aware of the exact rules. If you think you can do without them, feel free to skip this section and look at the example in the section titled "Variable usage example" (p. 75) for inspiration. But if you get stuck, or are an inquisitive XPath connoisseur, read on. The following assumes we're using an XSLT, XQuery or XPath type query language binding.

- You declare a variable using the <let> element: `<let name="…" value="…"/>`. It has an optional `as` attribute to specify the variable data type, which will be explained further on.
- You can declare variables as children of the <schema>, <library>, <phase>, <pattern>, and <rule> elements.
- You reference a variable using the prefix `$` (as in XSLT):

Example 5.22 – Declaring and using a variable

```
<let name="thing-type" value="@type"/>
<assert test="…">… <value-of select="$thing-type"/> …</assert>
```

- The (required) `name` attribute of the <let> element holds the name of the variable. It must follow the rules of an XML element/attribute name (the technical term is a *qualified name*). For example: `name-of-thing`, `totalWeight`, `delivery_date`, `top3-listings`, etc.

Variables in a namespace

Being a qualified name also means you can use (declared) namespace prefixes for your variables, like `local:first-date`, `ns1:value`, etc. However, this capability is rarely used and of interest only when your schema becomes really complicated. There are no examples of variables-in-a-namespace in this book.

The namespace for a variable is no different from any other namespace, which means it must be declared before it can be used. See the section titled "Declaring namespaces" (p. 78) for information about declaring namespaces.

- The `value` attribute of the `<let>` element holds the XPath expression that results in the value for the variable. For instance:

Example 5.23 – Some examples XPath expressions in the `<let>` element's `value` attribute

```
<let name="max-weight" value="50"/>
<let name="nr-of-things" value="count(/*/thing)"/>
<let name="name-of-thing" value="../@name"/>
```

Omitting the `value` attribute

The `value` attribute is optional, but the rules for what happens if you omit it are a bit weird. The Schematron standard says: "If no `value` attribute is specified, the value of the attribute is the element content of the `<let>` element."

That sounds reasonable until you find out that the only things allowed inside a `<let>` element are elements that are not in the Schematron namespace.

So this is not allowed:

```
<let name="max-weight">50</let>
```

But this is:

```
<let name="max-weight"><weight
xmlns="http://some/name/space">50</weight></let>
```

It is also unclear what the data type of such a variable should be. Maybe `document-node()` (an XML document of its own), or `element()` (the `<weight>` element in its namespace), or maybe `node()*` (meaning anything)? For example, SchXslt2 makes it `node()*`, but other processors can make different choices here.

Using the `<let>` element without a `value` attribute is not useful for most schemas. I strongly advise against using it, unless you really know what you're doing.

- The context item used when evaluating the XPath expression can be one of two things:
  - Outside of `<rule>` elements, it is the document node of the document being validated.
  - Inside `<rule>` elements, it is the node matched by the rule's `context` attribute. This is the same context item used for assertions, reports, and messages. You can see an example in Example 5.21.
- A variable must be declared before you use it.
- The usual scope of a variable is the element (and its children) it's declared in.

  The exception to this rule are phases (see the section titled "Selecting what checks are active: `<phase>` " (p. 89)): variables declared as a child of a `phase` element are in-scope when this phase is active. See also the section titled "Phase variables" (p. 98).
- You cannot re-declare a variable within the same element. The re-declaration of `count` in Example 5.24 is illegal.

Example 5.24 – Example of invalid variable re-declaration

```
<rule context="thing">
  <let name="count" select="6"/>
  <let name="count" select="7"/>
  ...
</rule>
```

- However, you can re-declare a variable in a child element (see Example 5.25).

Example 5.25 – Example of validly re-declaring a variable in a child element

```
<pattern>
  <let name="count" select="6"/>
  <rule context="thing">
    <let name="count" select="7"/>
    ...
  </rule>
</pattern>
```

Shadowing

Re-declaring is also known as *shadowing*. You don't change a variable's value, you only shadow its previous occurrence with a new one. The new value is in effect only inside the element it's declared in and not outside that element's scope.

I do not recommend shadowing variables. It obfuscates code, making it harder to follow logic and determine where a value comes from. If you want to create maintainable code, invent a new descriptive name for each variable.

- You can provide a data type for a variable using an additional `as` attribute on the `let` element:

```
<let name="…" as="…" value="…"/>
```

The data type names (the values for the `as` attribute) are determined by XPath and therefore the same as used in XSLT or XQuery: `xs:string`, `xs:integer`, `element(code)`, `document-node()`, etc. More on this in the section titled "XPath data types" (p. 212).

The `xs` namespace prefix

An XPath data type often uses the namespace prefix `xs`, which must be bound to the `http://www.w3.org/2001/XMLSchema` namespace. Your Schematron processor may or may not pre-define this namespace prefix. If it doesn't, you'll get an error message about a missing namespace declaration when using type names like `xs:string` or `xs:boolean`.

To avoid this, declare the `xs` namespace prefix:

```
<ns prefix="xs" uri="http://www.w3.org/2001/XMLSchema"/>
```

More on namespaces in the section titled "Declaring namespaces" (p. 78).

If you don't specify an `as` attribute, the data type is determined by the result of the expression in the `select` attribute.

Schematron 2020 note

The Schematron 2020 does not allow `as` attributes on `<let>` elements. It has no mechanism to explicitly specify the data type for a variable.

Variable usage example

Schematron 2020 note

The example presented in this section uses the Schematron 2025 feature to provide a data type for a variable. It is therefore incompatible with the 2020 edition.

Let's return to the parcels document (Example 4.2) to illustrate variable usage. The following example works with dates and durations.

The first attempt to formulate a Schematron schema for this was in Example 4.1. Example 5.26 enhances this example using variables.

Example 5.26 – Example of using variables in a Schematron schema (`schematron-book-code-2025/examples/basics/check-parcels.sch`)

```
<schema xmlns="http://purl.oclc.org/dsdl/schematron" schematronEdition="2025"
  queryBinding="xslt3">

  <!-- 1 - Define the xs namespace prefix so we can provide data types
    for variables. -->
  <ns prefix="xs" uri="http://www.w3.org/2001/XMLSchema"/>

  <!-- 2 - Define the number of days a parcel's date must be before the
    delivery date and turn this into a duration: -->
  <let name="delivery-day-limit" as="xs:integer" value="10"/>
  <let name="delivery-day-limit-as-duration" as="xs:dayTimeDuration"
    value="xs:dayTimeDuration('P' || $delivery-day-limit || 'D')"/>

  <!-- 3 - Grab important values from the root element: -->
  <let name="max-weight" as="xs:double" value="xs:double(/*/@max-weight)"/>
  <let name="delivery-date"  as="xs:date" value="xs:date(/*/@delivery-date)"/>

  <group>

    <rule context="/*">
      <!-- 4 - Compute the total parcels weight, store this in a variable
        and use this in the assert's test and in the message: -->
      <let name="total-parcels-weight" as="xs:double"
        value="sum(parcel/@weight)"/>
      <assert test="$total-parcels-weight le $max-weight">
        The total weight <value-of select="$total-parcels-weight"/> is
        more than the allowed maximum <value-of select="$max-weight"/>
      </assert>
    </rule>
```

```
    <rule context="parcel">
      <!-- 5 - Get the parcel's date and make sure it has the right
        data type: -->
      <let name="parcel-date" as="xs:date" value="xs:date(@date)"/>
      <assert
        test="($delivery-date - $parcel-date) gt
                $delivery-day-limit-as-duration">
          The parcel's date <value-of select="$parcel-date"/> must be
        more than <value-of select="$delivery-day-limit"/> days
        before the delivery date <value-of select="$delivery-date"/>
      </assert>
    </rule>

  </group>

</schema>
```

Let's look at the numbered sections in Example 5.26 in more detail:

1. This example uses data types for its variables. For this, we need to declare the namespace prefix `xs` for the namespace URI `http://www.w3.org/2001/XMLSchema`.
2. One of the rules we set for our parcels document was that a parcel's date must be at least 10 days before the delivery date.

Variables for magic values

From a maintenance point of view it's not a good idea to use hard-coded "magic" values (like `10`) in your code.[4] This is especially true when the value is used multiple times. When the value changes, and it will, it's easy to forget to change the value everywhere it's used. Even if you use such a value only once, it's still better to define it as a variable in some central location (like here, at the top of the document) with a name that tells you what the value represents, which makes it self-documenting. You can also easily find and update the value when it changes.

Example 5.26 defines an integer variable `delivery-day-limit` with value `10` and a second variable `delivery-day-limit-as-duration` of type `xs:dayTimeDuration` The value of this second variable is constructed by first converting the value of `delivery-day-limit` into a valid duration string (`P10D`) and then converting it into a duration using the type name `xs:dayTimeDuration()` as a function.

[4] A magic value is a hard-coded value (like `10` in Example 5.26) that gives you no information about what it represents.

3. The input document's root element holds two important values in attributes. We need these values in our assertions later on. It's therefore a good idea to grab these values only once and put them in variables at a global level.
4. The first rule checks the total maximum weight. It computes this, stores it in a variable (`total-parcels-weight`), and then uses it in the following assertion. Notice that the message includes the values of some of our variables to make it more clear and informative.
5. The second rule reads the date value from the context `<parcel>` element into a variable (`parcel-date`) and uses this in its assertion. Again we use variables to make the message clearer.

Using variables in this example is not only better from a software engineering point of view, but probably also for efficiency. In particular, the computations required to calculate the global variables defined in 2 and 3, are done just once. For this simple example it doesn't matter much, but with large documents or complex schemas, it could make a difference.

Let's see how this works. The document in Example 5.27 is deliberately invalid.

Example 5.27 – Invalid parcels document to illustrate the workings of the schema in Example 5.26 (`schematron-book-code-2025/data/parcels-invalid.xml`)

```
<parcels max-weight="100" delivery-date="2021-10-10">
  <parcel weight="50" date="2021-09-29">
    <contents>A large quantity of mouth masks</contents>
  </parcel>
  <parcel weight="55" date="2021-10-05">
    <contents>Toys for children</contents>
  </parcel>
</parcels>
```

If you validate Example 5.27 using the schema in Example 5.26, you get the following errors:

```
The total weight (105) is more than the allowed maximum (100)
The parcel's date (2021-10-05) must be more than 10 days before the delivery
date (2021-10-10)
```

Declaring namespaces

There is a good chance that you will encounter namespaces during your Schematron adventures. For instance, you will see them when you need to validate documents that use an international standard like XHTML (web pages), DocBook (text), QTI (questions and tests), or HL7 (healthcare messages). Also, company- and product-specific XML documents often use namespaces.

This is a topic that often causes confusion. If you don't feel comfortable with this subject, please read Appendix B first.

In a Schematron schema, namespaces and their prefixes must be declared before you use them. You declare a namespace using the `<ns uri="..." prefix="..."/>` element. All namespace declarations must be direct children of the root `<schema>` element. For instance, Example 5.28 declares the XHTML namespace and assigns it the prefix `xh`.

Example 5.28 – Declaring the XHTML namespace and assigning it the prefix `xh`

```
<ns uri="http://www.w3.org/1999/xhtml" prefix="xh"/>
```

After this you can refer to the XHTML namespace with the prefix `xh` (see Example 5.29)

Example 5.29 – Declaring the XHTML namespace with prefix `xh` and using it in a rule

```
<schema xmlns="http://purl.oclc.org/dsdl/schematron" schematronEdition="2025"
  queryBinding="xslt3">

  <ns uri="http://www.w3.org/1999/xhtml" prefix="xh"/>

  <pattern>
    <rule context="xh:title">
      <assert test="string-length(.) le 35">Title too long!</assert>
    </rule>
  </pattern>

</schema>
```

Not `xmlns`

If you've used namespaces before, you're probably used to declaring them with `xmlns` "attributes" (strictly speaking they're not attributes, but let's not worry about that now). So you would expect Schematron to define the XHTML namespace like this:

```
<schema xmlns="http://purl.oclc.org/dsdl/schematron"
  schematronEdition="2025"
  queryBinding="xslt3"
  xmlns:xh="http://www.w3.org/1999/xhtml">
  …
</schema>
```

Although it's perfectly all right and valid to write this, you will not be able to use the `xh` prefix in Schematron's XPath expressions as you would like to. The Schematron processor will report that you haven't declared the `xh` prefix, a rather frustrating situation because in the "normal" XML sense, that's exactly what you did!

As a final note: having to declare a namespace (prefix) using the `<ns>` element has the consequence that Schematron has no notion of a default namespace. This means that when you write an XPath expression in Schematron that uses an element or attribute that is in a namespace, you must use the namespace prefix. An example of how to work around this can be found in the section titled "Handling a default namespace" (p. 164).

CHAPTER 6
Advanced Schematron

Chapter 5 dealt with the basics of Schematron: what you must know to start writing Schematron schemas. This chapter goes a step further and dives into some of the more advanced features of Schematron.

You can live without these features, but as your schemas get more complicated, it's good to know they're here. So even if you're just starting to use Schematron, I would advise you to browse this chapter. When the need arises, you'll know where to look.

Providing multiple messages: <diagnostics>

The section titled "Assert and Report processing" (p. 60) describes how to define a message in an `<assert>` or `<report>` element. For instance:

```
<assert test="…">Some message…</assert>
```

Besides defining messages directly in `<assert>` and `<report>` elements, Schematron also provides the ability to centralize message definitions. This is done using the `<diagnostics>` element, which allows you to define reusable diagnostic messages. This capability is also helpful in other use cases, which I'll describe later.

To get a taste, Example 6.1 is a simple example that rewrites Example 5.19.

Example 6.1 – Using the `<diagnostics>` element to define a message. (`schematron-book-code-2025/examples/advanced/diagnostics-1.sch`)

```
<schema xmlns="http://purl.oclc.org/dsdl/schematron" schematronEdition="2025"
  queryBinding="xslt3">

  <group>
    <rule context="thing">
      <!-- 1 - Refer to a message in a <diagnostics> section with the
        diagnostics attribute. -->
      <assert test="(@type eq 'normal') or (@type eq 'special')"
        diagnostics="message-1"/>
    </rule>
  </group>

  <!-- 2 - A <diagnostics> section contains centralized definitions
    of messages.-->
  <diagnostics>
    <!-- 3 - A <diagnostic> element contains a single message. It is
      referenced by id. -->
    <diagnostic id="message-1">
      Invalid type on <value-of select="@name"/>: <value-of select="@type"/>.
    </diagnostic>
  </diagnostics>

</schema>
```

1. The `<assert>` element no longer contains a message. Instead it references a diagnostic message using the identifier of the message (`message-1`) in the `diagnostics` attribute.
2. The `<diagnostics>` element is a container for diagnostic messages.
3. A `<diagnostic>` element defines a diagnostic message. It has a mandatory `id` attribute, containing an identifier for the message.

The use of diagnostics shows up in your SVRL as shown in Example 6.2. The SVRL element `<failed-assert>` now has a child `<diagnostic-reference>` that shows the message.

Example 6.2 – The SVRL generated when validating the document in Example 5.12 with the schema from Example 6.1.

```
<schematron-output xmlns="http://purl.oclc.org/dsdl/svrl"
                   schematronEdition="2025"
                   phase="#ALL">
   <active-group/>
   <fired-rule context="thing" document=".../things-with-types.xml"/>
   <fired-rule context="thing" document=".../things-with-types.xml"/>
   <fired-rule context="thing" document=".../things-with-types.xml"/>
   <fired-rule context="thing" document=".../things-with-types.xml"/>
   <failed-assert test="(@type eq 'normal') or (@type eq 'special')"
                  location="/Q{}things[1]/Q{}thing[4]">
      <diagnostic-reference diagnostic="message-1">
         <text>Invalid type on thing 4: vintage.</text>
      </diagnostic-reference>
   </failed-assert>
</schematron-output>
```

For this simple example, this capability doesn't add much value, but what if you want to issue the same message for other elements as well? For example, suppose the XML contains information not only about things, but also about alien artifacts. You can now use the already defined diagnostic to issue the same message when an artifact's type is wrong, as shown in Example 6.3.

Example 6.3 – Referencing the same diagnostic message twice.

```
<group>
  <rule context="thing">
    <assert test="(@type eq 'normal') or (@type eq 'special')"
      diagnostics="message-1"/>
  </rule>
  <rule context="artifact">
    <assert test="(@type eq 'zork') or (@type eq 'martian')"
      diagnostics="message-1"/>
  </rule>
</group>
```

Reusing messages makes your schemas more maintainable. I discuss three use cases in this chapter:

- **Reusable messages:** Grammar corrections or reformulations need to be done only once. The same is true for expressions in `<value-of>` elements, which can become complicated.
- **Multiple messages:** You can define more than one message for an assertion or report.
- **Localized messages:** You can more easily provide messages in different languages.

Multiple messages

There are cases where you may need to attach more than one message to a Schematron assertion or report. For example, you might have a generic error message (**`The type is wrong`**) and a specialized explanation (**`Types for … must be …`**).

Example 6.4 enhances Example 6.1 to do this.

Example 6.4 – Defining multiple messages for an assertion or report. (schematron-book-code-2025/examples/advanced/diagnostics-2.sch)

```
<schema xmlns="http://purl.oclc.org/dsdl/schematron" schematronEdition="2025"
  queryBinding="xslt3">

  <group>
    <rule context="thing">
      <assert test="(@type eq 'normal') or (@type eq 'special')"
        diagnostics="message-1 thing-explanation"/>
    </rule>
    <rule context="artifact">
      <assert test="(@type eq 'zork') or (@type eq 'martian')"
        diagnostics="message-1 artifact-explanation"/>
    </rule>
  </group>

  <diagnostics>
    <diagnostic id="message-1">
      Invalid type on <value-of select="@name"/>: <value-of select="@type"/>.
    </diagnostic>
    <diagnostic id="thing-explanation">
      Allowed types for a thing: normal, special.
    </diagnostic>
    <diagnostic id="artifact-explanation">
      Allowed types for an artifact: zork, martian.
    </diagnostic>
  </diagnostics>

</schema>
```

The `diagnostics` attribute of each of the `<assert>` elements now contains two whitespace-separated identifiers. Both messages will be reported when the assertion fires.

How this shows up in your environment is implementation-defined. For instance, when you use Example 6.4 to validate Example 5.12, oXygen concatenates the messages and comes up with:

```
Invalid type on thing 4: vintage. Allowed types for a thing: normal, special.
```

The SVRL validation report is shown in Example 6.5. The `<failed-assert>` element now has multiple `<diagnostic-reference>` children.

Example 6.5 – The SVRL generated when validating the document in Example 5.12 with the schema from Example 6.4.

```
<schematron-output xmlns="http://purl.oclc.org/dsdl/svrl"
                   schematronEdition="2025"
                   phase="#ALL">
   <active-group/>
   <fired-rule context="thing" document="…/things-with-types.xml"/>
   <fired-rule context="thing" document="…/things-with-types.xml"/>
   <fired-rule context="thing" document="…/things-with-types.xml"/>
   <fired-rule context="thing" document="…/things-with-types.xml"/>
   <failed-assert test="(@type eq 'normal') or (@type eq 'special')"
                  location="/Q{}things[1]/Q{}thing[4]">
      <diagnostic-reference diagnostic="message-1">
         <text>Invalid type on thing 4: vintage.</text>
      </diagnostic-reference>
      <diagnostic-reference diagnostic="thing-explanation">
         <text>Allowed types for a thing: normal, special.</text>
      </diagnostic-reference>
   </failed-assert>
</schematron-output>
```

Repeating yourself

Readers with a software engineering background might shudder looking at Example 6.4. The horror! The list of possible types, for both the things and artifacts, is defined twice: once in the XPath expression of the assertions and once as text, in the explanatory messages. I did this to avoid over complicating the example. However, you can use XPath sequences to improve the code. Example 6.6 does this, but I'll leave it to you as an exercise to work out the details.

Example 6.6 – An improved version of Example 6.4.
(schematron-book-code-2025/examples/advanced/diagnostics-2-improved.sch)

```
<schema xmlns="http://purl.oclc.org/dsdl/schematron"
  schematronEdition="2025" queryBinding="xslt3">

  <let name="thing-types" value="('normal', 'special')"/>
  <let name="artifact-types" value="('zork', 'martian')"/>

  <group>
    <rule context="thing">
      <assert test="@type = $thing-types"
        diagnostics="message-1 thing-explanation"/>
    </rule>
    <rule context="artifact">
      <assert test="@type = $artifact-types"
        diagnostics="message-1 artifact-explanation"/>
    </rule>
  </group>

  <diagnostics>
    <diagnostic id="message-1">
      Invalid type on <value-of select="@name"/>:
      <value-of select="@type"/>.
    </diagnostic>
    <diagnostic id="thing-explanation">
      Allowed types for a thing:
      <value-of select="string-join($thing-types, ', ')"/>.
    </diagnostic>
    <diagnostic id="artifact-explanation">
      Allowed types for an artifact:
      <value-of select="string-join($artifact-types, ', ')"/>.
    </diagnostic>
  </diagnostics>

</schema>
```

Besides using multiple references to diagnostic messages, as we've done so far, it's also possible to define multiple messages by combining a direct message in the assertion/report with one or more references to diagnostic messages (see Example 6.7).

Example 6.7 – Defining multiple messages for an assertion or report.
(schematron-book-code-2025/examples/advanced/diagnostics-2b.sch)

```
<schema xmlns="http://purl.oclc.org/dsdl/schematron" schematronEdition="2025"
  queryBinding="xslt3">

  <group>
    <rule context="thing">
      <assert test="(@type eq 'normal') or (@type eq 'special')"
        diagnostics="thing-explanation">
        Invalid type on <value-of select="@name"/>: <value-of select="@type"/>
      </assert>
    </rule>
  </group>

  <diagnostics>
    <diagnostic id="thing-explanation">
      Allowed types for a thing: normal, special.
    </diagnostic>
  </diagnostics>

</schema>
```

As with the previous example, how this is visually represented in an IDE is implementation-defined. The SVRL validation report is shown in Example 6.8. The <failed-assert> element now has both a <diagnostic-reference> and a <text> child element.

Example 6.8 – The SVRL generated when validating the document in Example 5.12 with the schema from Example 6.7.

```
<schematron-output xmlns="http://purl.oclc.org/dsdl/svrl"
                   schematronEdition="2025"
                   phase="#ALL">
   <active-group/>
   <fired-rule context="thing" document="…/things-with-types.xml"/>
   <fired-rule context="thing" document="…/things-with-types.xml"/>
   <fired-rule context="thing" document="…/things-with-types.xml"/>
   <fired-rule context="thing" document="…/things-with-types.xml"/>
   <failed-assert test="(@type eq 'normal') or (@type eq 'special')"
                  location="/Q{}things[1]/Q{}thing[4]">
      <diagnostic-reference diagnostic="thing-explanation">
         <text>Allowed types for a thing: normal, special.</text>
      </diagnostic-reference>
      <text>Invalid type on thing 4: vintage</text>
   </failed-assert>
</schematron-output>
```

Localization of messages

Diagnostics are also a useful tool for localization; they allow you to provide messages in different languages. Example 6.9 enhances Example 6.1 so it can report problems in Dutch and English.

Example 6.9 – A Schematron schema with localized messages.
(`schematron-book-code-2025/examples/advanced/diagnostics-3.sch`)

```
<schema xmlns="http://purl.oclc.org/dsdl/schematron" schematronEdition="2025"
  queryBinding="xslt3">

  <group>
    <rule context="thing">
      <!-- 1 - Refer to the diagnostics in all languages: -->
      <assert test="(@type eq 'normal') or (@type eq 'special')"
        diagnostics="type-message-en type-message-nl"/>
    </rule>
  </group>

  <diagnostics>
    <!-- 2 - Provide the diagnostics in all languages and set the language
      using the xml:lang attribute: -->
    <diagnostic id="type-message-en" xml:lang="en">
      Invalid type on <value-of select="@name"/>: <value-of select="@type"/>.
    </diagnostic>
    <diagnostic id="type-message-nl" xml:lang="nl">
      Ongeldig type voor <value-of select="@name"/>: <value-of select="@type"/>.
    </diagnostic>
  </diagnostics>

</schema>
```

1. The `<assert>` element, in its `diagnostics` attribute, references the diagnostic messages for both languages (using a whitespace separated list of diagnostic message identifiers).
2. The diagnostic messages are defined for both languages. Each has a unique identifier and defines its language using the `xml:lang` attribute.

The result of this shows up in the SVRL, as shown in Example 6.10.

Example 6.10 – The SVRL generated when validating the document in Example 5.12 with the schema from Example 6.9.

```
<schematron-output xmlns="http://purl.oclc.org/dsdl/svrl"
                   schematronEdition="2025"
                   phase="#ALL">
   <active-group/>
   <fired-rule context="thing" document="…/things-with-types.xml"/>
   <fired-rule context="thing" document="…/things-with-types.xml"/>
   <fired-rule context="thing" document="…/things-with-types.xml"/>
   <fired-rule context="thing" document="…/things-with-types.xml"/>
   <failed-assert test="(@type eq 'normal') or (@type eq 'special')"
                  location="/Q{}things[1]/Q{}thing[4]">
      <diagnostic-reference diagnostic="type-message-en">
         <text lang="en">Invalid type on thing 4: vintage.</text>
      </diagnostic-reference>
      <diagnostic-reference diagnostic="type-message-nl">
         <text lang="nl">Ongeldig type voor thing 4: vintage.</text>
      </diagnostic-reference>
   </failed-assert>
</schematron-output>
```

There are now multiple `<diagnostic-reference>` child elements for the `<failed-assert>` element, each with an `xml:lang` attribute. By post-processing this SVRL with, for instance, a (simple) XSLT stylesheet, you can make the message come out as either **`Invalid type on …`** or **`Ongeldig type voor …`**.

oXygen, for Schematron 2020, natively supports multi-lingual schemas and can do the language filtering for you. It is likely that they will implement something similar for Schematron 2025.

Selecting what checks are active: `<phase>`

Schematron phases can be used to selectively enable/disable patterns and groups in a schema. Maybe some patterns/groups are CPU intensive, and you don't always want to apply them. Or maybe some of them are applicable only to final documents, but you need to keep them together with the patterns for documents that are works in progress.

Another typical use case is reference checking: if your document contains identifiers that reference something else, you might want to turn off checking references until everything is complete. To support these kinds of situation, Schematron has phases.

Here is an example. Suppose you are writing an article about Schematron in some fictitious markup language. Example 6.11 contains an example of a valid document in that language.

Example 6.11 – A valid example of a document about Schematron. (`schematron-book-code-2025/data/simple-document.xml`)

```
<document>

  <title>The wonderful world of Schematron</title>

  <para>Welcome to the wonderful world of Schematron
    <footnote-reference idref="more-schematron-info"/>. …</para>
  <para>It is a useful tool for …</para>
  <para>Here are some examples …</para>

  <!-- Footnotes: -->
  <footnotes>
    <footnote id="more-schematron-info">
      More information to be found at …
    </footnote>
  </footnotes>

</document>
```

Our fictitious XML markup language has the following rules:

- Titles must be no longer than 45 characters.
- There must be at least 3 paragraphs of text.
- Footnotes are referenced by identifiers.

Example 6.12 contains a Schematron schema to check these rules.

Example 6.12 – A Schematron schema for checking the validity of Example 6.11.
(schematron-book-code-2025/examples/advanced/phases-1a.sch)

```
<schema xmlns="http://purl.oclc.org/dsdl/schematron" schematronEdition="2025"
  queryBinding="xslt3">

  <group>
    <rule context="title">
      <assert test="string-length(.) le 45">The title is longer than 45
        characters</assert>
    </rule>
  </group>

  <group>
    <rule context="/*">
      <assert test="count(//para) ge 3">There must be at least 3
        paragraphs</assert>
    </rule>
  </group>

  <group>
    <rule context="footnote-reference">
      <let name="footnote-id" value="@idref"/>
      <assert test="exists(//footnote[@id eq $footnote-id])">
        Footnote id <value-of select="$footnote-id"/> not found</assert>
    </rule>
  </group>

</schema>
```

The document in Example 6.11 survives scrutiny by this schema with flying colors. But a full check is less useful if you write this document in phases. For example:

- First you create the document structure. Therefore, the only things you want to check are warnings for overly long titles.
- After that you write the text but not the footnotes, yet.
- Last, but not least, you add the footnotes.

Phases allow a Schematron schema to apply only the tests you need at each point in the process. Example 6.13 shows how.

Example 6.13 – A Schematron schema for checking the validity of Example 6.11 using phases. (schematron-book-code-2025/examples/advanced/phases-1b.sch)

```
<schema xmlns="http://purl.oclc.org/dsdl/schematron" schematronEdition="2025"
  queryBinding="xslt3">

  <!-- 1 - Define a phase that only checks the title length -->
  <phase id="titles-only">
    <active pattern="check-title-length"/>
  </phase>

  <!-- 2 - Define a phase that checks the title length and the number of
    paragraphs -->
  <phase id="titles-and-paragraphs">
    <active pattern="check-title-length"/>
    <active pattern="check-para-count"/>
  </phase>

  <!-- 3 - The actual groups: -->
  <group id="check-title-length">
    <rule context="title">
      <assert test="string-length(.) le 45">The title is longer than 45
        characters</assert>
    </rule>
  </group>

  <group id="check-para-count">
    <rule context="/*">
      <assert test="count(//para) ge 3">There must be at least 3
        paragraphs</assert>
    </rule>
  </group>

  <group id="check-footnote-references">
    <rule context="footnote-reference">
      <let name="footnote-id" value="@idref"/>
      <assert test="exists(//footnote[@id eq $footnote-id])">
        Footnote id <value-of select="$footnote-id"/> not found</assert>
    </rule>
  </group>

</schema>
```

Each <group> element in Example 6.13 has an id attribute.

1. The first <phase> element defines a phase with identifier titles-only. The child element <active> defines that only the group or pattern that checks the title length is active. The active group or pattern is referenced by its identifier, check-title-length.
2. The second <phase> element defines a phase with the identifier titles-and-paragraphs. It has two <active> children that reference the groups/patterns that must be active: the title length and the paragraph count checks.
3. There is no phase defined for all patterns in the schema. You could have done this but it's unnecessary. By default, a Schematron validation uses all available groups/patterns unless you override this by specifying a phase.

Groups or patterns?

It may seem confusing that even though Example 6.13 uses groups (<group> elements), the <active> elements have an attribute called pattern to refer to these groups.

The reason for this is historical. Schematron 2020 and earlier editions only had patterns (<pattern> elements), not groups (<group> elements). Therefore, they named the attribute, unsurprisingly, pattern. Schematron 2025 did not change this name, but it now also refers to groups.

Let's use this schema on a document in the making (see Example 6.14).

Example 6.14 – A document in the making about Schematron. (schematron-book-code-2025/data/simple-document-invalid.xml)

```
<document>

  <title>The wonderful world of Schematron and much more information that you
    want to know but were afraid to ask</title>

  <para>Welcome to the wonderful world of Schematron
    <footnote-reference idref="more-schematron-info"/>. …</para>
  …

  <!-- Footnotes: -->
  <footnotes>
    <!-- To be done -->
  </footnotes>

</document>
```

The title of Example 6.14 is too long, there's only one paragraph, and the footnote is missing. Let's validate this document using the phases introduced in Example 6.13.

- At first, we're only interested in overly long titles, so we run the schema activating the `title-only` phase. This message is issued:

  ```
  The title is longer than 45 characters
  ```

- We continue by activating the `titles-and-paragraphs` phase to check the number of paragraphs. The previous message is issued plus:

  ```
  There must be at least 3 paragraphs
  ```

- Finally, we want to do a full check and run the schema without activating a particular phase. The two previous messages are issued plus:

  ```
  Footnote id more-schematron-info not found
  ```

Of course, for only three messages this is not a big deal, but in a real-life situation, not having to wade through lots of not-yet-relevant messages can be a real time (and annoyance) saver.

Activating a phase

There are several ways to activate a phase:

- You can specify a default phase that must be activated if no other methods have been used. This is explained in the section titled "Specifying a default phase" (p. 95).
- All Schematron processing environments have implementation-defined ways to activate a phase manually at the start of the validation process. the section titled "Manual phase activation" (p. 96) shows some examples.
- Finally, Schematron 2025 introduced dynamic phase selection: activating a phase based on the contents of the document being validated. This is explained in the section titled "Dynamic phase selection" (p. 96).

Usually a phase is identified by its identifier (the value of the `id` attribute of the `<phase>` element). In addition, there are three special values you can use:

`#DEFAULT` Specifies that the default phase should be used: the value of the `defaultPhase` attribute of the `schema` root element. This is explained in the section titled "Specifying a default phase" (p. 95).

If no default phase is specified, all patterns/groups become active (like when using `#ALL`).

`#ALL` Act like there are no phases. All groups/patterns become active. This is also the default if no other activation mechanism is used.

`#ANY` Specifies dynamic phase selection. This is explained in the section titled "Dynamic phase selection" (p. 96).

Schematron 2020 note

Schematron 2020 does not have dynamic phase selection. Therefore the value `#ANY` is not supported.

Specifying a default phase

You can specify a default phase for Schematron validations by adding a `defaultPhase` attribute to the `<schema>` root element. The processor will use this phase if no other phase activation method is specified or if the phase activation value is `#DEFAULT`.

For example, to make the `titles-and-paragraphs` phase the default in Example 6.13, change the root element as shown in Example 6.15.

Example 6.15 – Specifying a default phase on the Schematron schema's root element

```
<schema xmlns="http://purl.oclc.org/dsdl/schematron" schematronEdition="2025"
  queryBinding="xslt3" defaultPhase="titles-and-paragraphs">
  …
</schema>
```

Manual phase activation

Schematron processors usually allow you to specify the phase before starting a validation. The method is implementation-defined, so consult your processor's documentation for details. Here are a few examples:

- oXygen, for Schematron 2020, gives you the option of choosing a phase directly or getting a prompt to choose one (see Figure 6.1).

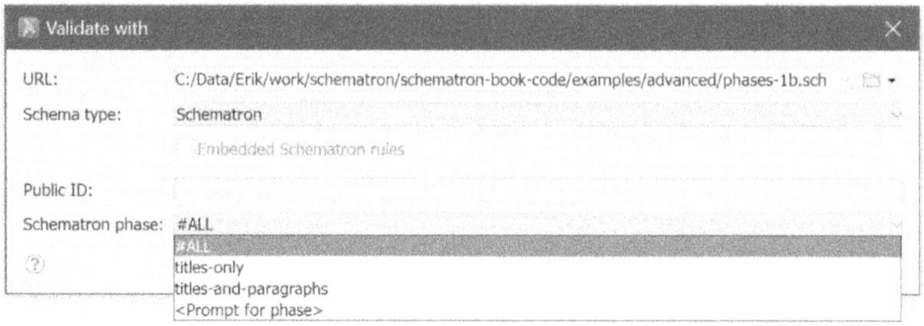

Figure 6.1 – Choosing a phase using oXygen

  They are likely to implement something similar for Schematron 2025.

- XMLBlueprint does not, as of the beginning of 2026, support Schematron phases.
- SchXslt2 has an option called `schxslt:phase` to specify the phase (the namespace prefix `schxslt` should be bound to the namespace `http://dmaus.name/ns/2023/schxslt`). This option must be specified when transpiling your schema. See the section titled "The SchXslt2 Schematron processor" (p. 46) for more information.
- XQS has a compiler option called `phase` to specify the phase. On the command line this must be specified as `-bphase=...`. See the section titled "The XQS Schematron processor" (p. 49) for more information.

Dynamic phase selection

> **Schematron 2020 note**
>
> Schematron 2020 has no dynamic phase selection, so this feature cannot be used in this (and older) editions.

Dynamic phase selection is a mechanism to select which phase becomes active, based on the contents of the document that is validated. For this to happen two things are needed:

- Phase activation must be triggered using the special value `#ANY`. How to pass such a value to the Schematron processor is implementation-defined.
- All phases eligible for dynamic phase selection must have a `when` attribute on the `<phase>` element. Its value must be an XPath expression that can be evaluated/cast to a Boolean.

When dynamic phase selection is active, the following happens:

- The Schematron processor looks for the first phase (`<phase>` element) with a `when` attribute, in document order.
- The expression in the `when` attribute is evaluated (with the document-node of the document being validated as context item).
  - If the expression evaluates to `true`, this phase becomes active.
  - If it evaluates to `false` the next phase, in document order, with a `when` attribute is checked.
- If no `when` attribute evaluates to `true`, all phases become active. This is the same as what happens when you pass the value `#ALL` instead of `#ANY`.

For example, assume you want to validate the following memo document:

Example 6.16 – Example document for demonstrating dynamic phase selection

```
<important-memo status="final">
  …
</important-memo>
```

The validation rules depend on the value of the `status` attribute on the root element. A final memo (`status="final"` in this example) must adhere to stricter rules than a memo that is not yet finished.

Using dynamic phase selection, you can express this as follows:

Example 6.17 – Example of using dynamic phase selection in a Schematron schema

```
<schema xmlns="http://purl.oclc.org/dsdl/schematron" schematronEdition="2025"
    queryBinding="xslt3">

  <phase id="validation-for-final-documents" when="/*/@status eq 'final'">
    <!-- Activate all patterns and groups for a final document: -->
    <active pattern="…"/>
    …
  </phase>

  <phase id="lax-validation" when="/*/@status ne 'final'">
    <!-- Activate all patterns and groups for a non-final document: -->
    <active pattern="…"/>
    …
  </phase>

  …

</schema>
```

SchXslt2 transpiler support

The SchXslt2 transpiler does not, as of the beginning of 2026, implement dynamic phase selection. See the section titled "The SchXslt2 transpiler" (p. 47) for more information.

Phase variables

Schematron 2020 note

Schematron 2020 also supports phase variables. However, Example 6.18 in this section uses features that are not supported in Schematron 2020: the `severity` attribute and dynamic evaluation of these kinds of attributes.

An interesting feature of phases is that you can declare variables specific to a phase. This means that you can, for instance, give some variable a different value depending on what phase is active. Example 6.18 gives an example of this.

Example 6.18 – Using phase variables to set the message severity.
(schematron-book-code-2025/examples/advanced/phase-variables.sch)

```
<schema xmlns="http://purl.oclc.org/dsdl/schematron" schematronEdition="2025"
  queryBinding="xslt3">
  <ns prefix="xs" uri="http://www.w3.org/2001/XMLSchema"/>

  <phase id="phase-preliminary">
    <let name="message-severity" as="xs:string" value="'warning'"/>
    <active pattern="preliminary-checks"/>
  </phase>

  <phase id="phase-final">
    <let name="message-severity" as="xs:string" value="'error'"/>
    <active pattern="preliminary-checks"/>
    <active pattern="final-checks"/>
  </phase>

  <group id="preliminary-checks">
    <rule context="…">
      <assert severity="$message-severity" test="…">…</assert>
      <assert severity="$message-severity" test="…">…</assert>
    </rule>
  </group>

  <group id="final-checks">
    <rule context="…">
      <assert severity="$message-severity" test="…">…</assert>
      <assert severity="$message-severity" test="…">…</assert>
    </rule>
  </group>

</schema>
```

- The schema in Example 6.18 has two phases: `phase-preliminary` and `phase-final`.
- Both phases set the variable `$message-severity`: `phase-preliminary` sets the value to `warning` and `phase-final` sets it to `error`.
- This variable specifies the severity of the assertions. The `<assert>` in this example sets the `severity="$message-severity"` attribute. See the section titled "Specifying a severity: the `severity` attribute" (p. 155) for more information on this.

Partial document validation using phases

Schematron 2020 note

Schematron 2020 has no partial document validation, so this feature cannot be used in this (and older) editions.

Another feature of phases is partial document validation. This means that, based on the active phase, validation is restricted to a subset of the document being validated. This can be helpful, for instance, when you're sure that all patterns/groups for a phase are relevant for certain parts of the document only. Partial document validation allows you to restrict the validation to these parts and ignore the rest.

To use partial document validation, add the `from` attribute to the `<phase>` element. Its value must be an XPath expression that selects the relevant part(s) of the document. This expression is evaluated when the phase becomes active, with the document-node of the document being validated as context item. It's not an error if nothing matches, but in that case, of course, nothing is processed.

For example, assume you want to validate the following document containing information on books and magazines:

Example 6.19 – Example document for demonstrating partial document validation

```
<publications>

  <book …>
    …
  </book>

  <magazine …>
    …
  </magazine>

  … (more book and magazine elements)

</publications>
```

For some reason, maybe validations are very time consuming, you sometimes want to validate the books and sometimes the magazines. Using partial document validation, you can express this as shown in Example 6.20.

Example 6.20 – Example of using partial document validation in a Schematron schema

```
<schema xmlns="http://purl.oclc.org/dsdl/schematron" schematronEdition="2025"
  queryBinding="xslt3">

  <phase id="book-validation-phase" from="/*/book">
    <!-- Activate all patterns and groups for books: -->
    <active pattern="…"/>
    …
  </phase>

  <phase id="magazine-validation-phase" when="/*/magazine">
    <!-- Activate all patterns and groups for a magazines: -->
    <active pattern="…"/>
    …
  </phase>

  …

</schema>
```

Reusing rules: abstract rules

"Do not repeat yourself" is a well-known adage from software engineering. We've already seen how Schematron diagnostics help you avoid repeating messages. Abstract rules are a mechanism to help you avoid repeating rules. A similar mechanism also exists for patterns (see the section titled "Reusing patterns and groups: Abstract patterns and groups" (p. 106)).

If you're just writing a single schema, you will rarely need abstract patterns. Of the three mechanisms for reuse (diagnostics, abstract rules, and abstract patterns), they are probably used the least. It's much more common to use alternative mechanisms (see the section titled "Alternative to abstract rules" (p. 105) for more).

However, the true power of abstract rules becomes apparent when you need to reuse patterns in multiple schemas: modularization. See the section titled "Schema modularization" (p. 117) for more information.

Let's start our look at the abstract rule mechanism with a fresh example. Suppose you have some kind of loading manifest, containing a list of crates:

Example 6.21 – A loading list with crates (schematron-book-code-2025/data/crates.xml)

```
<crate-contents>
  <crate width="0.5" height="0.5" length="0.6" material="wood">books</crate>
  <crate width="0.5" height="0.8" length="1.6" material="wood">fishing
    rods</crate>
  <crate width="1.5" height="0.8" length="1.3" material="metal">
    dumbbells</crate>
</crate-contents>
```

Length, width, and height information is expressed in meters; crates may not be larger than one cubic meter. In addition, wooden crates are only allowed to contain books.

The Schematron schema in Example 6.22 checks this.

Example 6.22 – A Schematron schema for checking the loading list regulations (schematron-book-code-2025/examples/advanced/abstract-rules-1.sch)

```
<schema xmlns="http://purl.oclc.org/dsdl/schematron" schematronEdition="2025"
  queryBinding="xslt3">

  <group>

    <rule context="crate[@material eq 'wood']">
      <assert test="(@length * @height * @width) le 1">
        The crate with <value-of select="."/> is too big
      </assert>
      <assert test=". eq 'books'">
        A wooden crate may only contain books. This one contains
        <value-of select="."/>
      </assert>
    </rule>

    <rule context="crate[@material eq 'metal']">
      <assert test="(@length * @height * @width) le 1">
        The crate with <value-of select="."/> is too big
      </assert>
    </rule>

  </group>

</schema>
```

Validating Example 6.21 against the schema in Example 6.22 results in the following two messages:

```
A wooden crate may only contain books. This one contains fishing rods
The crate with dumbbells is too big
```

The schema in Example 6.22 contains a repeated assertion for the volume check. The assertion that checks the maximum volume appears in two rules: once when the crate material is wood and again when the crate material is metal.

Example 6.23 gets rid of this duplication using abstract rules. Note that in this explanation, I use the term *concrete* rule for the kinds of rules used so far in this book.

Example 6.23 – A Schematron schema for checking the loading list regulations, using an abstract rule for the volume check
(`schematron-book-code-2025/examples/advanced/abstract-rules-2.sch`)

```
<schema xmlns="http://purl.oclc.org/dsdl/schematron" schematronEdition="2025"
  queryBinding="xslt3">

  <group>

    <!-- 1 - Define the volume check rule as abstract -->
    <rule abstract="true" id="volume-check">
      <assert test="(@length * @height * @width) le 1">
        The crate with <value-of select="."/> is too big
      </assert>
    </rule>

    <rule context="crate[@material eq 'wood']">
      <!-- 2 - Use the abstract rule for the volume check for wooden crates -->
      <extends rule="volume-check"/>
      <assert test=". eq 'books'">
        A wooden crate may only contain books. This one contains
        <value-of select="."/>
      </assert>
    </rule>

    <rule context="crate[@material eq 'metal']">
      <!-- 3 - Use the abstract rule for the volume check for metal crates -->
      <extends rule="volume-check"/>
    </rule>

  </group>

</schema>
```

1. The rule for the volume check is now defined as an abstract rule. The following applies:
   - An abstract rule must have an `abstract="true"` attribute.
   - An abstract rule must have an identifier using the `id` attribute so you can reference it.
   - An abstract rule must not have a `context` attribute. Its context is taken from the rule that uses it (extends it).
2. The concrete rule for wooden crates needs the volume check. Therefore, it references the abstract rule using `<extends rule="volume-check"/>`.
3. The same goes for the metal crates.

A concrete rule can extend multiple abstract rules (contain multiple `<extends>` child elements). An abstract rule can itself extend other abstract rules (contain `<extends>` child elements).

Despite the fancy object-oriented term "extends," there's nothing object oriented about this capability. Abstract rules are implemented as macros. The `<extends>` element is simply replaced by all the child elements of the abstract rule. So, a variable in an abstract rule will be evaluated in the context of the rule that references it. This can be convenient, for example, if you want to give a variable in an abstract rule a different value depending on where it is used. However, this can lead to naming conflicts if you are not careful.

Global abstract rules

The abstract rule in Example 6.23 can only be used in the group it was defined in. This is because it is a child of the `<group>` element. If you want to use the same abstract rule(s) in multiple groups (or patterns), put them in a special container element `<rules>`, as shown in Example 6.24.

Schematron 2020 note

Schematron 2020 has no `<rules>` element, so all abstract rules are local to the pattern they're defined in. The only way to get around this is to use external abstract patterns (see the section titled "Abstract rules in external documents" (p. 120)).

Example 6.24 – A Schematron schema for checking the loading list regulations, using global abstract rules
(`schematron-book-code-2025/examples/advanced/abstract-rules-2b.sch`)

```
<schema xmlns="http://purl.oclc.org/dsdl/schematron" schematronEdition="2025"
  queryBinding="xslt3">

  <rules>
    <rule abstract="true" id="volume-check">
      <assert test="(@length * @height * @width) le 1">
        The crate with <value-of select="."/> is too big
      </assert>
    </rule>
  </rules>

  <group>

    <rule context="crate[@material eq 'wood']">
      <extends rule="volume-check"/>
      <assert test=". eq 'books'">
        A wooden crate may only contain books. This one contains
        <value-of select="."/>
      </assert>
    </rule>

    <rule context="crate[@material eq 'metal']">
      <extends rule="volume-check"/>
    </rule>

  </group>

</schema>
```

Alternative to abstract rules

You may have noticed that there is already a perfect mechanism for solving the repeated rules problem: instead of abstract rules you can in most, if not all, cases reformulate your schema a bit to avoid rule repetition.

In Example 6.25, the first rule fires for every crate and tests for the maximum volume. The second rule fires only for wooden crates, testing for the contents. The result is the same, but the Schematron schema in Example 6.25 is shorter and, arguably, easier to understand. This may explain why the abstract rules feature is used less often that the other reuse features.

Example 6.25 – A Schematron schema for checking the loading list regulations, using reformulated rules to avoid rule repetition (schematron-book-code-2025/examples/advanced/abstract-rules-1b.sch)

```
<schema xmlns="http://purl.oclc.org/dsdl/schematron" schematronEdition="2025"
  queryBinding="xslt3">

  <group>

    <rule context="crate">
      <assert test="(@length * @height * @width) le 1">
        The crate with <value-of select="."/> is too big
      </assert>
    </rule>

    <rule context="crate[@material eq 'wood']">
      <assert test=". eq 'books'">
        A wooden crate may only contain books. This one contains
        <value-of select="."/>
      </assert>
    </rule>

  </group>

</schema>
```

Reusing patterns and groups: Abstract patterns and groups

Abstract patterns and groups are useful when your document contains structures that look alike and must abide by the same rules, but differ in element names or other details.

As an example (adapted from the one in the standard and shown in Example 6.26), let's take a document with two different, table-like, structures.

Example 6.26 – An XML document with two table-like structures (`schematron-book-code-2025/data/tables.xml`)

```
<tables>

  <!-- HTML table: -->
  <table>
    <tr>
      <td>Yes!</td>
      <td>No!</td>
    </tr>
  </table>

  <!-- Calendar table-like structure: -->
  <year>
    <week>
      <day>Monday</day>
      <day>Tuesday</day>
      <!-- Etc. -->
    </week>
  </year>

</tables>
```

- The first structure is a straight HTML table contained in a `<table>` element. A table must have rows (`<tr>`), and a row must have cells (`<td>`).
- The second one is a calendar structure, contained in a `<year>` element. A year must have weeks (`<week>` elements), and a week must have days (`<day>` elements).

We could, with what we know by now, easily create a Schematron schema that checks this. However, given the similarities between the table and calendar structures, it repeat several rules and assertions. Example 6.27 avoids the repetition using abstract patterns.

Example 6.27 – A Schematron schema that uses abstract patterns to test Example 6.26 (schematron-book-code-2025/examples/advanced/abstract-patterns-1a.sch)

```
<schema xmlns="http://purl.oclc.org/dsdl/schematron" schematronEdition="2025"
  queryBinding="xslt3">

  <!-- 1 - Define the abstract pattern -->
  <pattern abstract="true" id="table-pattern">

    <!-- 2 - Define the parameters for the abstract pattern -->
    <param name="table"/>
    <param name="row" />
    <param name="entry"/>

    <rule context="$table">
      <assert test="$row">
        The element <value-of select="local-name()"/> is a table structure.
        Tables must contain the correct row elements.
      </assert>
    </rule>

    <rule context="$table/$row">
      <assert test="$entry">
        The element <value-of select="local-name()"/> is a table row.
        Rows must contain the correct cell elements.
      </assert>
    </rule>

  </pattern>

  <!-- 2 - Pattern for HTML tables: -->
  <pattern is-a="table-pattern" >
    <param name="table" value="table"/>
    <param name="row" value="tr"/>
    <param name="entry" value="td"/>
  </pattern>

  <!-- 3 - Pattern for a calendar table-like structure: -->
  <pattern is-a="table-pattern" >
    <param name="table" value="year"/>
    <param name="row" value="week"/>
    <param name="entry" value="day"/>
  </pattern>

</schema>
```

1. First, define an abstract pattern. This looks like a normal pattern, but the `abstract="true"` attribute defines it as abstract. The `id` attribute assigns it an identifier.
2. Define the parameters for the abstract pattern. These values must be available when the pattern is instantiated. You can use a `<param>` element with a `value` attribute in the instantiation (see 3 and 4). As an alternative, you can supply a default value, using a `value` attribute on the `<param>` element.

> **Schematron 2020 note**
>
> Schematron 2020 does not allow you to declare the abstract pattern parameters at the start of an abstract pattern.

3. To instantiate an abstract pattern, set the value of the `is-a` attribute on the `<pattern>` element to the identifier of the abstract pattern. Instead of `<rule>` elements, use `<param>` elements to define the values of the pattern-parameters you declared in the abstract pattern. Here, the parameters are the names of the table, row, and entry elements.
4. You can instantiate the abstract pattern as often as needed, using different element names.

What happens under the hood is that every abstract pattern (and group) is turned into a concrete pattern (or group), substituting the parameters. So Example 6.27 becomes Example 6.28.

Example 6.28 – Example 6.27 with all abstract patterns expanded (`schematron-book-code-2025/examples/advanced/abstract-patterns-1b.sch`)

```
<schema xmlns="http://purl.oclc.org/dsdl/schematron" schematronEdition="2025"
  queryBinding="xslt3">

  <pattern>
    <rule context="table">
      <assert test="tr">
        The element <value-of select="local-name()"/> is a table structure.
        Tables must contain the correct row elements.
      </assert>
    </rule>
    <rule context="table/tr">
      <assert test="td">
        The element <value-of select="local-name()"/> is a table row.
        Rows must contain the correct cell elements.
      </assert>
    </rule>
  </pattern>
```

```
  <pattern>
    <rule context="year">
      <assert test="week">
        The element <value-of select="local-name()"/> is a table structure.
        Tables must contain the correct row elements.
      </assert>
    </rule>
    <rule context="year/week">
      <assert test="day">
        The element <value-of select="local-name()"/> is a table row.
        Rows must contain the correct cell elements.
      </assert>
    </rule>
  </pattern>

</schema>
```

Abstract patterns/groups are a useful construct to avoid repeated code. A few detailed notes:

- Both patterns (`<pattern>` elements) and groups (`<group>` elements) can be abstract.
- Although Example 6.27 defines the abstract pattern before it is instantiated, you can place the abstract pattern/group definitions and instantiations in any order.
- Parameters for an abstract pattern/group must be defined using `<param>` elements as (first) children of the `<pattern>` or `<group>` element. The required `name` attribute holds the name of the parameter, the optional `value` attribute its default value (the value to be used when, on instantiation, no value was provided for this parameter).
- As with abstract rules, abstract patterns/groups are macros. Each parameter reference is simply replaced with the value of the `value` attribute on the corresponding `<param>` element.
- Related to that, a `<param>` element's `value` attribute is not an XPath expression. It's just a piece of text, used in place of the parameter.
- Abstract pattern/group parameters and variable references share the same syntax: a name preceded by `$` (for example, `$name`). Using the same name for both a parameter and a variable can lead to confusing and subtle bugs. For complex schemas I recommend that you use a unique naming convention for pattern-parameters (for example, you could start all parameter names with `p-`) to keep them distinct from variables.

Global schema parameters: <param>

Schematron 2020 note

Schematron 2020 has no global parameters, so this feature cannot be used in this (and older) editions.

Sometimes it is useful to be able to adjust certain values in your schema without having to change the schema itself. For example, consider Example 6.29, which contains information about parcels.

Example 6.29 – A document containing information about parcels with their dimensions. (schematron-book-code-2025/data/parcels-with-dimensions.xml)

```
<parcels>
  <parcel id="P1345" width="50" height="100" depth="45"/>
  <parcel id="P9998760" width="35" height="15" depth="105"/>
  <parcel id="P6660" width="120" height="120" depth="75"/>
  …
</parcels>
```

We would like to find out, using Schematron, whether some parcels are too wide, high, or deep. But since our delivery vehicles have different dimensions, the actual limits cannot be fixed in the schema, they must be flexible. The schema in Example 6.30 achieves this using global parameters:

Example 6.30 – A document containing information about parcels with their dimensions. (schematron-book-code-2025/examples/advanced/global-parameters-1.sch)

```
<schema xmlns="http://purl.oclc.org/dsdl/schematron" schematronEdition="2025">
  <ns prefix="xs" uri="http://www.w3.org/2001/XMLSchema"/>

  <param name="max-width" value="100"/>
  <param name="max-height" value="100"/>
  <param name="max-depth" value="100"/>

  <group>
    <rule context="parcel">
      <assert test="xs:integer(@width) le $max-width">
        Parcel <value-of select="@id"/> is too wide
      </assert>
      <assert test="xs:integer(@height) le $max-height">
        Parcel <value-of select="@id"/> is too high
      </assert>
```

```
      <assert test="xs:integer(@depth) le $max-depth">
        Parcel <value-of select="@id"/> is too deep
      </assert>
    </rule>
  </group>

</schema>
```

The global parameters `max-width`, `max-height`, and `max-depth` are defined at the top of the schema using `<param>` elements. The `value` attribute holds the default value for the parameter: the value to be used when no value for this parameter was provided.

So when we validate Example 6.29 against the schema in Example 6.30 without explicitly providing values, all parameters are set to the value `100`. This results in the following messages:

```
Parcel P9998760 is too deep
Parcel P6660 is too wide
Parcel P6660 is too high
```

Some details:

- Global parameters are defined using `<param>` elements as direct children of the root `<schema>` element.
- The required `name` attribute contains the name of the parameter. The same rules apply as for the names of variables (see the section titled "Declaring and using variables: `<let>`" (p. 70)).
- The `value` attribute, which is required for global parameters, contains the default value for the parameter. Its content must be an XPath expression.
- Unfortunately, the `<param>` element has no `as` attribute to specify its data type. If this is important to you, make sure the expression in the `value` attribute returns the right data type. For example:
  - A string parameter: `<param name="s" value="'abcd'"/>`
  - A decimal parameter: `<param name="d" value="xs:decimal(100.5)"/>`
  - A duration parameter: `<param name="t" value="xs:duration('PT10S')"/>` (this value defaults to 10 seconds)

What remains is how to specify an actual value for a parameter when the validation starts. This is, as expected, implementation-defined.

Detailing rules: `visit-each`

Schematron 2020 note

Schematron 2020 has no `visit-each` attribute for `<rule>` elements, so this feature cannot be used in this (and older) editions.

Sometimes it is necessary to validate at a more detailed level than usual. An example is validating a piece of text for things that occur on the word level. Assume we have some document containing descriptions that contain codes, in text. These codes start with (upper-case) CD, followed by some integer number. Here is a very simple example:

Example 6.31 – A document containing descriptions with codes. (`schematron-book-code-2025/data/description-with-codes.xml`)

```
<descriptions>
  <description>The part CD2345 consists of CD456, CDwrong and CD234a.</description>
</descriptions>
```

Validating Example 6.31 using "classic" Schematron could be done using Example 6.32.

Example 6.32 – A schema for validating Example 6.31 (`schematron-book-code-2025/examples/advanced/visit-each-1.sch`)

```
<schema xmlns="http://purl.oclc.org/dsdl/schematron" schematronEdition="2025"
  queryBinding="xslt3">
  <ns prefix="xs" uri="http://www.w3.org/2001/XMLSchema"/>

  <group>
    <rule context="description" >
      <assert test="every $w in tokenize(., '[\s,.]+')[starts-with(., 'CD')]
          satisfies (substring($w, 3) castable as xs:integer)">
        Invalid codes found!
      </assert>
    </rule>
  </group>

</schema>
```

The expression in the `test` attribute of the `<assert>` element is rather complicated and might need some explanation:

- At its heart is the following XPath instruction:

  ```
  every (variable) in (sequence-expression) satisfies (condition)
  ```

  A `(variable)` iterates over every member of `(sequence-expression)`. If for all its values `(condition)` returns `true`, the full expression returns `true`. If not it returns `false`.[1]

- The first part of the sequence-expression `tokenize(., '[\s,.]+')` splits (tokenizes, turns into separate tokens) the text of the description (the context item `.`) into separate words.

  The separator for the `tokenize()` function, what we consider word boundaries here, is the regular expression `[\s,.]+`. This means: a string of one or more (the `[...]` with the `+` at the end) combinations of any whitespace (the `\s` part), commas (`,`) or dots (`.`).

  The result of the `tokenize(...)` part of the expression is a sequence of all the words in the `<description>` element: `The`, `part`, `CD2345`, etc.

- We're interested in codes only, so we add a predicate to the result of the `tokenize()` function that filters out all words that start with (upper-case) `CD`: `[starts-with(., 'CD')]`.

  The result is a sequence of all the codes in the text: `CD2345`, `CD456`, `CDwrong` and `CD234a`.

- In the condition to satisfy, we check whether the part of the code after the initial `CD` characters `substring($w, 3)` can be cast to (converted to) an integer. If so, the code is OK; if not, it contains an error.

  The codes `CDwrong` and `CD234a` do not pass this test. Therefore, the result of the full `every ... in ... satisfies ...` test is `false`. The `<assert>` fails, invalidating the document.

Example 6.33 shows the SVRL output from validating Example 6.31 using the schema shown in Example 6.32.

[1] XPath also has a `some (variable) in (sequence-expression) satisfies (condition)` expression.

Example 6.33 – The SVRL result of validating Example 6.31 using the schema in Example 6.32

```
<schematron-output xmlns="http://purl.oclc.org/dsdl/svrl"
                   schematronEdition="2025"
                   phase="#ALL">
   <ns-prefix-in-attribute-values prefix="xs"
uri="http://www.w3.org/2001/XMLSchema"/>
   <active-group/>
   <fired-rule context="description" document=".../description-with-codes.xml"/>
   <failed-assert test="every $w in tokenize(., '[\s,.]+')[starts-with(., 'CD')]
satisfies (substring($w, 3) castable as xs:integer)"
                  location="/Q{}descriptions[1]/Q{}description[1]">
      <text>Invalid codes found!</text>
   </failed-assert>
</schematron-output>
```

This works as expected: we get the validation message `Invalid codes found!` and the validation fails. However, this doesn't tell us *which* codes are invalid. The SVRL in Example 6.33 flags the full `<description>` element as invalid. An IDE will probably put a red squiggly line underneath it. Unfortunately, this leaves it as an exercise for us to find out exactly which codes were meant.

The `visit-each` attribute for `<rule>` elements is meant to alleviate this problem. It contains an XPath expression that, based on what made the rule fire, selects a sequence of items for further evaluation. Example 6.34 shows a schema that uses this for validating Example 6.31.

Example 6.34 – A schema for validating Example 6.31 using `visit-each` (`schematron-book-code-2025/examples/advanced/visit-each-2.sch`)

```
<schema xmlns="http://purl.oclc.org/dsdl/schematron" schematronEdition="2025"
  queryBinding="xslt3">
  <ns prefix="xs" uri="http://www.w3.org/2001/XMLSchema"/>

  <group>
    <rule context="description"
      visit-each="tokenize(., '[\s,.]')[starts-with(., 'CD')]">
      <assert test="substring(., 3) castable as xs:integer">
        Invalid code: <value-of select="."/>
      </assert>
    </rule>
  </group>

</schema>
```

The expression in the `visit-each` attribute takes the context of the rule and divides this further into words containing codes (how this expression works is explained above). The assert is evaluated for every member of the result of the `visit-each` expression. Its test expression can now simply check whether a code is correct and report it if it doesn't.

Example 6.35 shows the SVRL output from validating Example 6.31 using the schema shown in Example 6.34.

Example 6.35 – The SVRL result of validating Example 6.31 using the schema in Example 6.34

```
<schematron-output xmlns="http://purl.oclc.org/dsdl/svrl"
                   schematronEdition="2025"
                   phase="#ALL">
   <ns-prefix-in-attribute-values prefix="xs"
uri="http://www.w3.org/2001/XMLSchema"/>
   <active-group/>
   <fired-rule visit-each="tokenize(., '[\s,.]')[starts-with(., 'CD')]"
               context="description"
               document="…/description-with-codes.xml"/>
   <failed-assert test="substring(., 3) castable as xs:integer"
                  location="/Q{}descriptions[1]/Q{}description[1]">
      <text>Invalid code: CDwrong</text>
   </failed-assert>
   <failed-assert test="substring(., 3) castable as xs:integer"
                  location="/Q{}descriptions[1]/Q{}description[1]">
      <text>Invalid code: CD234a</text>
   </failed-assert>
</schematron-output>
```

As you can see, every invalid code now results in a separate `<failed-assert>` element. This makes it much easier to find the offending codes and fix them. An IDE could use this information to put a red squiggly line underneath only the invalid codes and not the whole text. Whether this actually happens is, of course, implementation-defined.

`visit-each` and the context item

Be aware that `visit-each` usually changes the context item inside the rule to something not rooted in the document. In Example 6.34, for instance, the context item inside the rule is a string that is not part of, not linked to, the document (tree) being validated.

In most cases this won't cause a problem, but it may affect advanced applications, for example:

- Expressions that rely on the context item being a node in the tree become impossible. For instance, the assert might need to access an attribute on the element that contains the context item string. The usual `../@some-attribute` no longer works and there is no easy way around this.
- XPath functions like `base-uri()` and `resolve-uri()` no longer work because they have no access to the surrounding node's base URI. This can be a problem if you want to resolve a relative URI into an absolute one.
- The XPath `key()` function also needs the context item to be a node in the document tree. However, there is an easy way around this:
  - Add a global variable that references the document:

    ```
    <let name="doc" as="document-node()" value="."/>
    ```

  - Use this variable as third argument in the `key()` function:

    ```
    key(…, …, $doc)
    ```

To alleviate these problems, SchXslt2 makes the variable `$schxslt:rule-context` available inside a rule. However, be aware that using this feature makes your schema processor-dependent.

Schema modularization

Schematron schemas can become complicated. In addition, they are sometimes part of a family of schemas, where parts (for instance rules and patterns) are reused in different schemas. This calls for modularization: the approach of breaking down a schema into smaller, self-contained units or modules. This allows re-use and can improve code readability and maintainability.

Schematron has a number of features that support modularization:

- You can directly include a schema fragment from an external document into your schema (the section titled “Including documents: `<include>` ” (p. 118)).
- You can use abstract rules (see the section titled “Reusing rules: abstract rules” (p. 101)) stored in external documents (the section titled “Abstract rules in external documents” (p. 120)).
- With the introduction of Schematron 2025, you can create and use complete libraries with schema parts (the section titled “Using libraries: `<library>` and `<extends>` ” (p. 122)).

Including documents: `<include>`

Like most programming and validation languages, Schematron schemas can include external documents, whole or in parts. This is useful when you want to share definitions, such as patterns or rules, between different schemas. This capability is similar to `<xsl:include>` in XSLT or `<xs:include>` in W3C XML Schema, with a restriction that I discuss at the end of this section.

Let's return to Example 6.9, which defines multilingual diagnostic messages inside a `<diagnostics>` element. Suppose you want to put this `<diagnostics>` element in a separate document to make it easier for a translator to work on it. To do this, you need to rewrite the schema as shown in Example 6.36.

Example 6.36 – A Schematron schema that includes an external document
(`schematron-book-code-2025/examples/advanced/diagnostics-included.sch`)

```
<schema xmlns="http://purl.oclc.org/dsdl/schematron" schematronEdition="2025"
  queryBinding="xslt3">

  <pattern>
    <rule context="thing">
      <assert test="@type = ('normal', 'special', 'deprecated')"
        diagnostics="type-message-en type-message-nl"/>
    </rule>
  </pattern>

  <include href="separate-diagnostics.sch"/>

</schema>
```

The included file looks like this:

Example 6.37 – The document included by Example 6.36
(`schematron-book-code-2025/examples/advanced/separate-diagnostics.sch`)

```
<diagnostics xmlns="http://purl.oclc.org/dsdl/schematron">
  <diagnostic id="type-message-en" xml:lang="en">
    Invalid type on <value-of select="@name"/>: <value-of select="@type"/>.
  </diagnostic>
  <diagnostic id="type-message-nl" xml:lang="nl">
    Ongeldig type voor <value-of select="@name"/>: <value-of select="@type"/>.
  </diagnostic>
</diagnostics>
```

And that's all you need to do, no bells or whistles. The `<include>` element inserts the contents of the referenced document. It works just like a simple external entity or XInclude.

It sounds simple (and it is), but in practice this simplicity has a limitation: you cannot include schema parts if they don't share a common root element. For instance, patterns often belong together. Reviewing Example 6.25, we see that both patterns are necessary. If you wanted to include them (maybe because you also needed them in some other schema), it would take two `<include>` elements. This might be manageable for just two, but what if you have a lot…

In other words, the Schematron `<include>` element has no Schematron-specific semantics. If you need a more advanced include capability, see the section titled "Using libraries: `<library>` and `<extends>` " (p. 122).

Including fragments of documents

The include mechanism does not limit you to including full documents; you can also include fragments. For this, the fragment must have an `xml:id` attribute as its identifier. A document containing fragments does not have to be a valid schema, as long as the result, once all inclusions are done, is a valid schema. Example 6.38 shows what a fragment document might look like.

Example 6.38 – A document containing schema fragments, as used by Example 6.39 (`schematron-book-code-2025/examples/advanced/separate-diagnostics-2.sch`)

```
<my-diagnostics xmlns="http://purl.oclc.org/dsdl/schematron">

  <diagnostics  xml:id="type-diagnostics">
    <diagnostic id="type-message-en" xml:lang="en">
      Invalid type on <value-of select="@name"/>: <value-of select="@type"/>.
    </diagnostic>
    <diagnostic id="type-message-nl" xml:lang="nl">
      Ongeldig type voor <value-of select="@name"/>: <value-of select="@type"/>.
    </diagnostic>
  </diagnostics>

  <diagnostics xml:id="other-diagnostics">
    …
  </diagnostics>

  <diagnostics xml:id="even-more-diagnostics">
    …
  </diagnostics>

</my-diagnostics>
```

- The document in Example 6.38 has a made-up root element `<my-diagnostics>` (it could be anything). You can of course also make it a valid Schematron schema.
- The included fragments must be in the correct Schematron namespace. In Example 6.38, the root element includes `xmlns="http://purl.oclc.org/dsdl/schematron"` to define the namespace.
- The fragments to include must have an `xml:id` attribute with a unique identifier value to be able to identify them.

To reference such a fragment, add a fragment identifier (`#...`) to the value of the `href` attribute, as shown in Example 6.38.

Example 6.39 – A schema including a fragment from the external document shown in Example 6.38
(schematron-book-code-2025/examples/advanced/diagnostics-included-2.sch)

```
<schema xmlns="http://purl.oclc.org/dsdl/schematron" schematronEdition="2025"
  queryBinding="xslt3">

  <pattern>
    <rule context="thing">
      <assert test="@type = ('normal', 'special', 'deprecated')"
        diagnostics="type-message-en type-message-nl"/>
    </rule>
  </pattern>

  <include href="separate-diagnostics-2.sch#type-diagnostics"/>

</schema>
```

Abstract rules in external documents

The section titled "Reusing rules: abstract rules" (p. 101) explains abstract rules: the Schematron feature to re-use rules within patterns and groups. To allow modularization, abstract rules can also be included from external documents.

Abstract rules within the same schema are referenced using an `<extends>` element with a `rule` attribute containing the identifier of the abstract rule (see for instance Example 6.23). To use external abstract rules, replace the `rule` attribute on the `<extends>` element with an `href` attribute that points to the file that contains the abstract rule (see Example 6.40). The `<extends>` element has either a `rule` or an `href` attribute but not both.

Example 6.40 – A Schematron schema for checking the loading list rules, using a separate rule document to avoid rule repetition
(schematron-book-code-2025/examples/advanced/abstract-rules-3.sch)

```
<schema xmlns="http://purl.oclc.org/dsdl/schematron" schematronEdition="2025"
  queryBinding="xslt3">

  <pattern>

    <rule context="crate[@material eq 'wood']">
      <extends href="volume-check.sch"/>
      <assert test=". eq 'books'">
        A wooden crate may only contain books. This one contains
        <value-of select="."/>
      </assert>
    </rule>

    <rule context="crate[@material eq 'metal']">
      <extends href="volume-check.sch"/>
    </rule>

  </pattern>

</schema>
```

The referenced `volume-check.sch` document looks like Example 6.41.

Example 6.41 – The volume check rule document, as referenced by Example 6.40
(schematron-book-code-2025/examples/advanced/volume-check.sch)

```
<rule xmlns="http://purl.oclc.org/dsdl/schematron">
  <assert test="(@length * @height * @width) le 1">
    The crate with <value-of select="."/> is too big
  </assert>
</rule>
```

Rules in an external document referenced by an `<extends href="...">` element do not need to be defined as abstract.

The same fragment mechanism used to include documents (see the section titled "Including fragments of documents" (p. 119)) can also be applied to external abstract rules. You can put your abstract rules together in an external document, add `xml:id` attributes to them, and reference them using a fragment identifier (#...) in the `href` attribute.

Using libraries: `<library>` and `<extends>`

Schematron 2020 note

> Schematron 2020 and older editions do not support the `library`.

Schematron 2025 introduces a more advanced way to modularize schemas: libraries. A library is a document with a `<library>` root element. Its content is like a full Schematron schema, with the exception of phases, `<phase>` elements. To use a library, add an `<extends href=..."/>` element as a direct child of a `<schema>` element.

For example, assume we need to make our complete abstract pattern schema from Example 6.27 reusable because we need it in different schemas. Using the include mechanism, as described in the section titled "Including documents: `<include>` " (p. 118), would be cumbersome: it takes several `<include>` elements to get all the definitions on board. A better solution is to turn this code into a library, as shown in Example 6.42.

Example 6.42 – The schema from Example 6.27 turned into a library (`schematron-book-code-2025/examples/advanced/library.sch`)

```
<library xmlns="http://purl.oclc.org/dsdl/schematron">

  <pattern abstract="true" id="table-pattern">

    <param name="table"/>
    <param name="row" />
    <param name="entry"/>

    <rule context="$table">
      <assert test="$row">
        The element <value-of select="local-name()"/> is a table structure.
        Tables must contain the correct row elements.
      </assert>
    </rule>

    <rule context="$table/$row">
      <assert test="$entry">
        The element <value-of select="local-name()"/> is a table row.
        Rows must contain the correct cell elements.
      </assert>
    </rule>

  </pattern>
```

```
  <pattern is-a="table-pattern" >
    <param name="table" value="table"/>
    <param name="row" value="tr"/>
    <param name="entry" value="td"/>
  </pattern>

  <pattern is-a="table-pattern" >
    <param name="table" value="year"/>
    <param name="row" value="week"/>
    <param name="entry" value="day"/>
  </pattern>

</library>
```

To use this library, add an `<extends>` element that includes it, as shown in Example 6.43.

Example 6.43 – A schema that uses the library from Example 6.42 (`schematron-book-code-2025/examples/advanced/library-usage.sch`)

```
<schema xmlns="http://purl.oclc.org/dsdl/schematron" schematronEdition="2025"
  queryBinding="xslt3">

  <extends href="library.sch"/>

  (more Schematron code)

</schema>
```

If your schemas get really complicated, libraries can also include other libraries. This allows for intricate structures if you need them.

CHAPTER 7

Query language binding and using other languages

Schematron supports query language binding (sometimes abbreviated to QLB). Query language binding allows you to specify the underlying programming language for, among other things, expressions in `<let>` and `<value-of>` elements. Some bindings, most notably XSLT and XQuery, allow you to add code in an additional programming language, thereby greatly expanding the scope of what you can do.

Theoretically, query language binding lets you choose an underlying language. In practice however, this is not the case. As far as I know, all publicly available Schematron processors support XSLT/XQuery/XPath bindings only. The Schematron specification mentions a few others, but these are generally not supported.

Having said that, it is, of course, possible that you're working in an environment that uses a Schematron processor that supports other query language bindings. If that's the case, you'll have to find out what works and what doesn't yourself.

Being able to use only XSLT/XQuery/XPath type bindings is not as limiting as it sounds. Often, Schematron is used in environments that also use XSLT or XQuery, so developers are already used to these languages. XSLT and XQuery are powerful languages for handling XML documents. Being able to use them opens up a world of possibilities. Most additional language processors have very interesting extensions that support capabilities such as manipulating the file system or querying SQL databases.

So let's not mourn the limitations of the Schematron query language binding but, instead, rejoice at the possibilities of using XSLT or XQuery. This chapter starts with an introduction to query language binding in general. However, if you're mostly interested in using XSLT feel free to skip ahead to the section titled "Using XSLT in Schematron" (p. 130). XQuery enthusiasts can skip to the section titled "Using XQuery in Schematron" (p. 137).

Introduction to query language binding

The Schematron specification defines query language binding as: "named set, specified in a document, of the languages and conventions used for assertion tests, rule-context expressions and so on, by a particular Schematron implementation".

You need two things for a Schematron query language binding:

- A name (probably "identifier" would be a better term) that uniquely identifies the binding. This name is used as the value of the `queryBinding` attribute on the schema's root element. A query language binding name is case-insensitive (so `xslt`, `XSLT`, and `XsLt` all mean the same thing).
- A query language binding document that defines what this binding actually means. The Schematron specification (section 6.5) describes what such a document should contain.

Your own query language binding

In theory you could define your own query language binding for some language of your choice and build a Schematron processor that supports it. To stay within the Schematron specifications, just pick a non-reserved query binding name, write a (usually short) document containing the necessary details and implement the language.

In practice, I expect this to be so rarely done that I don't cover the details about how to do that in this book. If you're that far into Schematron, you should have enough knowledge to take the information in the official standard and implement a new query language binding yourself.

The Schematron standard reserves a number of query binding names but does not provide definitions for all of them. Table 7.1 contains an overview of the reserved names and their status.

- The "Defined?" column indicates whether this binding is defined in the Schematron standard. If the binding is undefined, I provide a "most obvious meaning," based on its name. Be aware that this is just me (the author of this book) speaking. Since the binding is undefined you can make it mean anything you like, but be aware that at some point it may be defined differently from what you might like.
- The "Supported?" column indicates whether one of the publicly available Schematron processors, as of early 2026, support this binding (see the section titled "Schematron validation processors" (p. 45) for information about available processors).

Table 7.1 – Schematron reserved query language bindings

Name	Defined?	Supported?	Description
`exslt`	No	No	The most obvious meaning is how it was defined in Schematron 2020: this binding augments the default `xslt` binding with EXSLT functions. EXSLT is an initiative to provide standardized extensions for XSLT. You can find it at https://exslt.github.io/. EXSLT can be considered outdated (the last change is from 2003), but most of its proposed extensions have found their way into recent XPath versions.
`stx`	No	No	The most obvious meaning is how it was defined in Schematron 2020 edition: STX (Streaming Transformations for XML)[1] is an XML-based language for transforming XML documents without building a tree in memory, an approach known as *streaming*. The STX initiative never went beyond the working draft stage. Its last update was in April 2007. Its ideas found their way into XSLT 3.0.
`xpath`	No	No	Most obvious meaning: XPath 1.0 expressions can be used. If so, it's almost the same as the `xslt` binding, but without the ability to use `<xsl:key>` and `<xsl:copy-of>` instructions.
`xpath2`	Yes	No	The `xpath2` binding allows the use of XPath 2.0 expressions for matching nodes and computing values. An important restriction of this binding is that the use of variables is not allowed.

1 https://stx.sourceforge.net/documents/spec-stx-20070427.html

Name	Defined?	Supported?	Description
`xpath3`	Yes	No	The `xpath3` binding allows the use of XPath 3.0 expressions for matching nodes and computing values. As with `xpath2`, the use of variables is not allowed.
`xpath31`	Yes	No	The `xpath31` binding allows the use of XPath 3.1 expressions for matching nodes and computing values. An important restriction of this binding is that the use of variables is not allowed.
`xpath4`	No	No	Most obvious meaning: allow the use of XPath 4 expressions for matching nodes and computing values. XPath 4 is, at the time of this writing (early 2026), still in development.
`xquery`	No	Yes	Most obvious meaning: allow XPath 1.0 expressions and define additional declarations and functions using XQuery 1.0.
`xquery3`	Yes	Yes	The `xquery3` binding allows the use of XPath 3.0 expressions for matching nodes and computing values. It may also support anything that is allowed in an XQuery 3.0 prolog. You could for instance define an XQuery function and use this function in your expressions. An example can be found in the section titled "Using XQuery in Schematron" (p. 137).
`xquery31`	Yes	Yes	The `xquery31` binding is an extension of the `xquery3` binding. It allows the use of XQuery 3.1 and XPath 3.1.
`xquery4`	No	No	Most obvious meaning: an extension of the `xquery31` binding, allowing the use of XQuery 4 and XPath 4. Both XQuery 4 and XPath 4 are, at the time of this writing (early 2026), still in development.

Name	Defined?	Supported?	Description
`xslt`	Yes	Yes	The `xslt` binding is the default binding if you don't set the `queryBinding` attribute. Expressions for matching nodes and computing values must follow the XSLT 1.0 standard. This implies the use of XPath 1.0. It also supports the <xsl:key> element, which can make lookups (for example, for identifiers) much faster. This binding also supports the <xsl:copy-of> element inside <property> elements (see the section titled "Properties" (p. 144)).
`xslt2`	Yes	Yes	This language binding is an extension of the `xslt` binding. It allows you to use XSLT 2.0 expressions, implying XPath 2.0. This gives you more options for expressions and also more standard functions. Results of expressions are no longer limited to strings but can be any data type. An important additional feature is that it allows you to define XSLT functions in your schema and use these functions in expressions.
`xslt3`	Yes	Yes	This language binding is an extension of the `xslt2` binding. It allows you to use XSLT 3.0 expressions, implying XPath 3.1. Most examples in this book use the `xslt3` binding.
`xslt4`	No	No	Most obvious meaning: an extension of the `xslt3` binding, allowing the use of XSLT 4 and implying XPath 4. Both XSLT 4 and XPath 4 are, at the time of this writing (early 2026), still in development.

Using XSLT in Schematron

Historically, Schematron has usually been implemented using XSLT. Therefore, `xslt` type bindings are supported by most of the current, publicly available Schematron processors, allowing you to use features such as keys and user-defined functions in your schemas. This section concentrates on the most recent XSLT type binding (in 2026): `xslt3`.

For those interested in using XQuery instead of XSLT, please skip ahead to the section titled "Using XQuery in Schematron" (p. 137).

Using XSLT keys

Referencing in XML documents is often done using identifiers. For instance, Example 7.1 contains orders that reference items by identifier.

Example 7.1 – Example of an XML document that contains references using identifiers. (`schematron-book-code-2025/data/orders-with-ids.xml`)

```
<orders>
  <item id="bolts" price="5.49">A box with 20 bolts</item>
  <item id="nuts" price="3.78">A box with 20 nuts</item>
  <!-- … many, many more items… -->
  <order>
    <ordered-item id-ref="bolts" quantity="5"/>
    <ordered-item id-ref="nuts" quantity="10"/>
  </order>
  <!-- … many, many more orders… -->
</orders>
```

The value of each `id-ref` attribute on an `<ordered-item>` element must contain the identifier of an `<item>` element in the same document.

Example 7.2 checks this. The `<let>` element stores the identifier to check in the variable `$item-id`. The `<assert>` uses it to check whether an `<item>` element with the same identifier exists. Straightforward and correct.

Example 7.2 – Schematron schema that checks the identifier references for Example 7.1. (schematron-book-code-2025/examples/query-binding/check-orders-1.sch)

```
<schema xmlns="http://purl.oclc.org/dsdl/schematron" schematronEdition="2025"
  queryBinding="xslt3">
  <ns prefix="xs" uri="http://www.w3.org/2001/XMLSchema"/>

  <group>
    <rule context="ordered-item">
      <let name="item-id" as="xs:string" value="@id-ref"/>
      <assert test="exists(/*/item[@id eq $item-id])">
        The referenced item <value-of select="$item-id"/> does not exist
      </assert>
    </rule>
  </group>

</schema>
```

But what if the document contains thousands of `<item>` elements? Every `<ordered-item>` element causes the schema processor to search every `<item>` element, again and again. That's inefficient and time consuming. A solution is to create a key. This is an in-memory data structure that allows fast lookup of elements using a key index value. XSLT has an instruction for this, `<xsl:key>`, which you can use with an `xslt` binding. Example 7.3 is equivalent to Example 7.2, but much more efficient.

Example 7.3 – Schematron schema that checks the identifier references for Example 7.1 using a key (schematron-book-code-2025/examples/query-binding/check-orders-2.sch)

```
<!-- 1 - Define the XSLT namespace: -->
<schema xmlns="http://purl.oclc.org/dsdl/schematron" schematronEdition="2025"
  queryBinding="xslt3" xmlns:xsl="http://www.w3.org/1999/XSL/Transform">

  <!-- 2 - Define a key using the XSLT key instruction: -->
  <xsl:key name="item-ids" match="/*/item" use="@id"/>

  <group>
    <rule context="ordered-item">
      <!-- 3 - Reference the key using the key() function: -->
      <assert test="exists(key('item-ids', @id-ref))">
        The referenced item <value-of select="@id-ref"/> does not exist
      </assert>
    </rule>
  </group>

</schema>
```

1. To use instructions from XSLT, you need to declare the XSLT namespace. Hence the `xmlns:xsl="http://www.w3.org/1999/XSL/Transform"` namespace declaration on the root element. Every element that starts with `xsl:` is now considered an XSLT instruction.
2. The XSLT `<xsl:key>` instruction defines a key. It has three components:
   - The name of the key, in this case `item-ids`.
   - The nodes the key is about, in this case the `/*/item` elements.
   - The value of the key, in this case the identifier of the item, contained in its `id` attribute.

   What happens under the hood is that the Schematron processor creates a data structure that allows fast lookup of `<item>` elements using the value of their `id` attribute.
3. The `match` attribute of the `<assert>` element uses the XSLT `key()` function to look up values in the data structure. This function takes two or three parameters:
   - The key name, in this case `item-ids`, written as a quoted string (`'item-ids'`).
   - The value to look up, in this case the `id-ref` attribute of the `<ordered-item>` element.
   - The third (optional and unused here) parameter allows you to limit the returned nodes to a specific part of the document (a *subtree*). You do this by specifying the root node of the part you're interested in. Default value is the document node `/`.

   The `key()` function performs a fast and efficient lookup and returns the `<item>` element(s) associated with the given identifier. If the identifier is not found the `key()` function returns an empty sequence.

For documents like Example 7.1, keys can speed things up considerably. There are many more nifty things you can do with keys. If you're curious, read the sections about `<xsl:key>` and the `key()` function in the XSLT books listed in the section titled "XSLT" (p. 297).

A warning before we end this topic: keys don't come for free. Building a key takes time, and you have to weigh this against the time raw lookups take (as done in Example 7.2). In general, don't use keys on small documents. The tipping point is fuzzy. If this is important to you, experiment and measure!

Another example of using XSLT keys in Schematron can be found in the section titled "Checking multiple identifier references" (p. 172).

Using W3C XML Schema to check identifier references

In W3C XML Schema it's possible to check for correct identifier references as well. An example of a schema that does this for Example 7.1 can be found in `schematron-book-code/examples/query-binding/orders.xsd`.

There are however a few noticeable differences:

- You have no control over the error message when using a schema. On my system the error message looks like this:

  ```
  Key 'key-id-ref' with value '…' not found for identity constraint
  of element 'orders'.
  ```

  Not terribly puzzling for the initiated, but it takes some background knowledge (what's an "identity constraint"?) to fully understand it. Schematron, on the other hand, gives you full control over the message.

- As tests get more complicated, XML Schema may no longer be able to handle them. For instance, sometimes identifier references are not singular but a whitespace separated list of values, like `id-refs="nuts bolts"`.

  When you have only one type of identifier, you can handle this case using the `xs:ID` data type for identifiers and `xs:IDREFS` for references. However, if you have multiple types of identifiers (that is, identifiers that refer to different kinds of things in the XML document), this no longer works.

Using XSLT functions

Modularizing code using functions is a very common thing to do when programming. However, Schematron itself lacks the ability to define functions. For this, it relies on its query language binding feature.

For example, suppose you have a reference document that tells you the expected price for items of different types. In Example 7.4, there is a `<data>` element for each type that includes the name of the type (`type` attribute) and the expected price (`price` attribute).

There is also a default price, defined in the `default-price` attribute on the root element. The default is used when you encounter a thing that has a type that is not in the reference document.

Example 7.4 – A list with type codes and prices
(`schematron-book-code-2025/examples/query-binding/type-codes-and-prices.xml`)

```
<type-codes-and-prices default-price="10.0">
  <data type="A125" price="17.25"/>
  <data type="X96" price="89.34"/>
</type-codes-and-prices>
```

You can use this reference document to check whether things listed in documents like Example 7.5 contain the expected price for their type.

Example 7.5 – Data containing type codes and prices
(`schematron-book-code-2025/data/things-with-type-codes-and-prices.xml`)

```
<things>
  <thing name="thing 1" type="A125" price="17.25"/>
  <thing name="thing 2" type="A125" price="17.26"/>
  <thing name="thing 3" type="X96" price="89.34"/>
  <thing name="thing 4" type="Y78" price="10.01"/>
</things>
```

To check the price of a thing in Example 7.5, you need to compare it with the expected price for a thing of that type in Example 7.4. If the type is not listed in the reference document, compare the price with the default price.

You could express this directly in Schematron as a complicated and rather long XPath expression, but it's much nicer and more maintainable to define a function for this using XSLT, which is what Example 7.6 does.

Example 7.6 – Schematron schema that checks the prices in Example 7.5 against Example 7.4 (schematron-book-code-2025/examples/query-binding/check-type-codes-and-prices.sch)

```
<!-- 1 - Define the XSLT namespace on the root element: -->
<schema xmlns="http://purl.oclc.org/dsdl/schematron" schematronEdition="2025"
  queryBinding="xslt3" xmlns:xsl="http://www.w3.org/1999/XSL/Transform">
  <ns prefix="xs" uri="http://www.w3.org/2001/XMLSchema"/>

  <!-- 2 - Define a namespace for the functions as an <ns> element: -->
  <ns uri="#functions" prefix="f"/>

  <!-- 3 - Define your function using XSLT: -->
  <xsl:function name="f:get-price" as="xs:double">
    <xsl:param name="type" as="xs:string"/>
    <xsl:variable name="prices-document" as="document-node()"
      select="doc('type-codes-and-prices.xml')"/>
    <xsl:variable name="data-element-for-type" as="element(data)?"
      select="$prices-document//data[@type eq $type]"/>
    <xsl:choose>
      <xsl:when test="exists($data-element-for-type)">
        <xsl:sequence select="xs:double($data-element-for-type/@price)"/>
      </xsl:when>
      <xsl:otherwise>
        <xsl:sequence select="
            xs:double($prices-document/type-codes-and-prices/@default-price)
          "/>
      </xsl:otherwise>
    </xsl:choose>
  </xsl:function>

  <group>
    <rule context="thing">
      <!-- 4 - Use the defined function to get the price: -->
      <let name="expected-price" as="xs:double" value="f:get-price(@type)"/>
      <assert test="$expected-price eq xs:double(@price)">
        The price for <value-of select="@name"/> should be
        <value-of select="$expected-price"/>
      </assert>
    </rule>
  </group>

</schema>
```

1. This example embeds XSLT code in the schema. So, you have to define the XSLT namespace on the root element: `xmlns:xsl="http://www.w3.org/1999/XSL/Transform"`
2. XPath function names must also be in a namespace. This example defines the namespace `#functions` with the prefix `f`. You use the prefix when defining and using the `f:get-price` function. The namespace and prefix values were chosen at random; you can use anything you like (for more on namespaces, see the section titled "Declaring namespaces" (p. 78)).
3. Define your function(s) using the XSLT programming language. In this example, the function is called `f:get-price`, and it takes the value of the `type` attribute as input and if it locates a `<data>` element that has that type, it returns the value of the `price` attribute. If no `<data>` element matches the input type, it returns the default (`default-price`).

   Since this is not a book about XSLT, I'm not going to explain the function itself. As with all programming languages, Example 7.5 is not the only way to express the same functionality.
4. This rule uses the `f:get-price()` function to get the expected price from Example 7.4 and then uses it in the `<assert>` element's test expression.

Using other XSLT features

Schematron 2020 note

The Schematron 2020 XSLT bindings only support the use of the `<xsl:copy-of>` instruction in Schematron properties (last bullet). All other additional features are unsupported.

In addition to using keys and embedding XSLT functions in Schematron, you can use several other XSLT features:

- Attribute value templates (AVTs) are allowed in `flag`, `role`, and `severity` attributes (see Chapter 8 for an explanation of these attributes). An AVT is an XPath expressions between curly braces (`{…}`) in your attribute value.

  For example, assume we have some error severity level in a variable called `$errlvl` and we want to use this in the value of the `role` attribute. This could be done as follows:

  ```
  role="error-level-{$errlvl}"
  ```

  To stop a curly brace from being part of an AVT, double it.

- Text value templates (TVTs) are allowed in constructing messages in Schematron `<assert>` and `<report>` elements (see the section titled "Patterns, groups, rules, assertions, and reports" (p. 53)). A TVT is an XPath expressions between curly braces (`{…}`) in your text. It is an alternative to using the Schematron `<value-of>` element (see the section titled "More meaningful messages: inserting values" (p. 65)).

  For example, assume we have some computed value in variable called `$value` and we want to use this in the text of an assertion. This could be done as follows:

  ```
  <assert test="…">The value must be {$value}</assert>
  ```

  To stop a curly brace from being part of a TVT, double it.
- Use the `<xsl:import>`, `<xsl:include>`, or `<xsl:use-package>` instructions to reference external XSLT code.
- Import a schema using `<xsl:import-schema>`.
- Define an accumulator using `<xsl:accumulator>`.
- You can use the `<xsl:copy-of>` instruction inside a Schematron `<property>` element. For more information see the section titled "Properties" (p. 144).

Using XQuery in Schematron

> **Schematron 2020 note**
>
> As far as I'm aware, there is no Schematron 2020 processor that supports XQuery type bindings.

An XQuery type query language binding allows you to use XQuery within Schematron. Annexes M and N in the standard, which describe these bindings, say that anything allowed in an XQuery prolog *may* be used: declaring functions, importing modules, etc. However, the way to do this is left open. This means that what is actually possible here, and how, is implementation-defined.

One of the problems XQuery binding implementers face is that XQuery is text, not XML, and Schematron does not allow you to simply add pieces of text to your schema. It is however allowed to add XML in a non-Schematron namespace. Therefore there must always be some, binding implementation-defined, wrapper element around XQuery code.

XQuery binding compatibility

The need to have some wrapper element highlights an important difference between XSLT and XQuery bindings. XSLT is expressed in XML in its own namespace and can therefore simply be inserted into a schema. XQuery is text and needs some, binding implementation-defined, wrapper element.

This means there is a very good chance that Schematron schemas using XSLT will be compatible between Schematron processors. This is not the case for XQuery, since different processors might use different approaches in wrapping the XQuery code.

However, that being said, in practice there isn't much choice in processors. So the extent to which this is or becomes a problem remains to be seen.

Let's have a look at how the XQS Schematron processor (see the section titled "The XQS Schematron processor" (p. 49)) implements this. XQS defines two wrapper elements, both in the XQuery namespace `http://www.w3.org/2012/xquery`. We'll assign this namespace the prefix `xqs` (`xmlns:xqs="http://www.w3.org/2012/xquery"`).

- Use the `<xqs:function>` element to wrap an XQuery function. For example:

```
<xqs:function>
  declare function local:square($n as xs:double) as xs:double { $n * $n };
</xqs:function>
```

- Use the `<xqs:prolog>` element to wrap other prolog statements, like importing a module. For example:

```
<xqs:prolog>
  import module namespace fun='#my-functions' at 'my-functions.xqm';
</xqs:prolog>
```

The section titled "Using XSLT functions" (p. 133) shows the use of an XSLT function in a Schematron schema. Let's implement Example 7.6 again, now using XQuery. The result is in Example 7.7.

Example 7.7 – Schematron schema that implements Example 7.6 using XQuery
(schematron-book-code-2025/examples/query-binding/check-type-codes-and-prices-xquery.sch)

```
<schema xmlns="http://purl.oclc.org/dsdl/schematron" schematronEdition="2025"
  queryBinding="xquery31" xmlns:xqs="http://www.w3.org/2012/xquery">
  <ns prefix="xs" uri="http://www.w3.org/2001/XMLSchema"/>

  <xqs:function xml:space="preserve">
    declare function local:get-price($type as xs:string) as xs:double {
      let $prices-document as document-node() := doc('type-codes-and-prices.xml')
      let $data-element-for-type as element(data)? :=
        $prices-document//data[@type eq $type]
      return
        if (exists($data-element-for-type))
        then
          xs:double($data-element-for-type/@price)
        else
          xs:double($prices-document/type-codes-and-prices/@default-price)
    };
  </xqs:function>

  <group>
    <rule context="//thing">
      <let name="expected-price" as="xs:double" value="local:get-price(@type)"/>
      <assert test="$expected-price eq xs:double(@price)">
        The price for <value-of select="@name"/> should be
        <value-of select="$expected-price"/>
      </assert>
    </rule>
  </group>

</schema>
```

Some additional remarks:

- Maybe you've noticed: the context attribute for the (only) rule in this schema reads `context="//thing"` and not `context="thing"`, as you might expect. This is because, unlike XSLT bound schemas, XQS always evaluates context expressions using the document-node as context item. The expression `context="thing"` would only have matched if `<thing>` was the root element, which it isn't.

  Other ways we could have expressed the same are `context="/*/thing"` or `context="/things/thing"`.

- In XSLT we had to define a special namespace for our function. XQuery predefines the namespace prefix `local` for this, attached to the namespace `http://www.w3.org/2005/xquery-local-functions`. Therefore we can use this prefix to define and use our function without having to bother declaring it.
- Notice there is an `xml:space="preserve"` attribute on the `<xqs:function>` element. This keeps pretty-printers from screwing up your carefully formatted XQuery code.
- XQS has an implementation-defined special instruction as the equivalent of `<xsl:copy-of>` for use in Schematron properties (see the section titled "Properties" (p. 144)): `<xqs:copy-of>`.

CHAPTER 8

Additional features

Whatever system you devise for categorizing things, there are always left-over bits and pieces (one of the reasons you always end up with a junk drawer). Schematron is no exception. After describing the core of Schematron in Chapter 5 through Chapter 7, there are still some additional features. While these are less often used, they are nonetheless there for a reason.

Messages with markup: `<emph>`, `<span>`, and `<dir>`

Schematron allows limited markup in the messages defined in `<assert>`, `<report>`, and `<diagnostic>` elements. Example 8.1 contains an example.

Example 8.1 – Example of using markup in an assert message

```
<assert test="...">
  Do <emph>not</emph> use the <value-of select="local-name()"/> element here!
</assert>
```

Three markup elements are allowed:

- The `<emph>` element specifies that the enclosed text should be rendered with emphasis. It has no attributes.
- The `<span>` element is a general-purpose, text-spanning element (like in HTML). It has a `class` attribute to signify what should happen with its contents.

  The standard does not specify what a `<span>` element or its `class` signify. CSS styling is an obvious possibility, but other ways to control appearance are also possible.
- The `<dir>` element specifies the writing direction of the text. By default this is left-to-right, but if there's a piece of text in a language that reads from right-to-left (for example Arabic), you can surround it with `<dir value="rtl">`.

Using markup in messages is not common, and how markup is handled is implementation defined. SchXslt2 and XQS copy the markup elements through to the SVRL. Therefore, markup can be use by an application that processes SVRL, letting you render the result as a custom report.

There are several other places where markup is allowed (for example in properties, see the section titled "Properties" (p. 144)). See the Schematron reference in Appendix C for details.

Flags

The `<rule>`, `<assert>`, and `<report>` elements have an optional `flag` attribute. The value of this attribute is the name of a boolean variable. The value of this variable is initially `false`. When a rule, assertion, or report on which this flag is defined fires, the value becomes `true`.

Example 8.2 shows how you could use this mechanism to identify some assertions as more serious than others.

Example 8.2 – Example of using flags to identify important assertions

```
<?xml version="1.0" encoding="UTF-8"?>
<schema xmlns="http://purl.oclc.org/dsdl/schematron" schematronEdition="2025"
  queryBinding="xslt3">
  <group>
    <rule context="…">
      <assert test="…" flag="serious-error">This is bad</assert>
      <assert test="…">This is not so bad</assert>
    </rule>
    <rule context="…">
      <assert test="…" flag="serious-error">This is also bad</assert>
    </rule>
  </group>
</schema>
```

In the validation result you can check whether the `serious-error` flag was set to `true` and, if so, trigger an appropriate follow-up (display a big red error message, sound a horn, sue the person who produced the document, etc.).

How to detect that a flag-variable is set to `true` is implementation defined. Flags do show up in the SVRL, so they're probably most useful in a scenario where you post-process the SVRL after the validation has taken place. For example, when the first assertion of Example 8.2 fires, the following shows up in the SVRL (see Example 8.3).

Example 8.3 – SVRL fragment when an assertion with a flag fires

```
<failed-assert location="…" test="…" flag="serious-error">
  <text>This is bad</text>
</failed-assert>
```

Dynamic flags

If the value of the `flag` attribute is a variable reference, for instance `flag="$flag-1"`, its value is dynamically evaluated. This allows you to vary the value of a flag based on the value of a variable or parameter.

For example, suppose you have a toolchain that uses Schematron validation. The value of a Schematron validation flag is important in processing the resulting SVRL, but its actual value is determined elsewhere. Using Schematron global parameters (see the section titled "Global schema parameters: `<param>`" (p. 111)) you could now pass this value to the schema. Example 8.4 shows how to do this.

Example 8.4 – Example of determining a flag value using schema parameters

```
<?xml version="1.0" encoding="UTF-8"?>
<schema xmlns="http://purl.oclc.org/dsdl/schematron" schematronEdition="2025"
  queryBinding="xslt3">

  <param name="bad-case-flag-value" value="'bad'"/>

  <group>
    <rule context="…">
      <assert test="…" flag="$bad-case-flag-value">This is bad</assert>
    </rule>
  </group>
</schema>
```

Another important use-case is setting a flag value based on the Schematron phases using phase variables (see the section titled "Phase variables" (p. 98)). Depending on the active phase, the variable `flag-value` is set to a different value. This value is then used to set the value of the `flag` attribute. Example 8.5 shows how to do this.

Example 8.5 – Example of determining a flag value using phase variables

```
<?xml version="1.0" encoding="UTF-8"?>
<schema xmlns="http://purl.oclc.org/dsdl/schematron" schematronEdition="2025"
  queryBinding="xslt3">
  <ns prefix="xs" uri="http://www.w3.org/2001/XMLSchema"/>

  <phase id="preliminary-check">
    <let name="flag-value" as="xs:string" value="'warning-flag'"/>
    <active pattern="some-generic-checks"/>
    …
  </phase>

  <phase id="final-check">
    <let name="flag-value" as="xs:string" value="'error-flag'"/>
    <active pattern="some-generic-checks"/>
    …
  </phase>

  <group id="some-generic-checks">
    <rule context="…">
      <assert test="…" flag="$flag-value">This is bad</assert>
    </rule>
  </group>

  …

</schema>
```

You can also use dynamic evaluation with the `role` (see the section titled "Specifying a role: the `role` attribute" (p. 154)) and `severity` (see the section titled "Specifying a severity: the `severity` attribute" (p. 155)) attributes.

Properties

Schematron properties allow you to add additional arbitrary information to assertions and reports. As with markup, what happens with this information is implementation defined and probably useful only in a scenario where the SVRL validation results are post-processed.

Example 8.6 shows a simple (invalid) example. It is a document with invoice information (derived from our first example, Example 1.1).

Example 8.6 – Invalid example XML document with invoice information
(schematron-book-code-2025/data/invoices-2.xml)

```
<invoices date="2020-11-11" total="10117.82">
  <invoice date="2020-10-04" total="10000.50" id="12345"/>
  <invoice date="2020-10-16" total="100.83" id="56789"/>
  <invoice date="2020-10-18" total="16.5" id="56789"/>
</invoices>
```

This example is invalid because the `total` attribute on the root element is incorrect (off by one cent, which is probably a rounding error) and the identifier `56789` is used twice. The schema in Example 8.7 dutifully reports these problems.

Example 8.7 – Schematron schema to validate Example 8.6
(schematron-book-code-2025/examples/additional-features/properties-1.sch)

```
<schema xmlns="http://purl.oclc.org/dsdl/schematron" schematronEdition="2025"
  queryBinding="xslt3">
  <ns uri="http://www.w3.org/2001/XMLSchema" prefix="xs"/>

  <group>
    <rule context="/invoices">
      <assert test="xs:double(@total) eq sum(invoice/@total)">
        Total <value-of select="@total"/> not correct
      </assert>
    </rule>
    <rule context="invoice">
      <let name="id" value="@id"></let>
      <assert test="count(../invoice[@id eq $id]) eq 1">
        Id <value-of select="@id"/> not unique
      </assert>
    </rule>
  </group>

</schema>
```

Now suppose you want to post-process the SVRL validation result to produce a report with hints for the developers of your invoicing XML application, but you don't want these hints to be visible to the normal users.

Therefore, you shouldn't put them into the assertion text. Instead, one way to do this is to add the developer information in Schematron properties. This will place that information into the SVRL output.

Example 8.8 adds developer information using Schematron properties.

Example 8.8 – Example 8.7 with developer hints added in properties (schematron-book-code-2025/examples/additional-features/properties-2.sch)

```
<schema xmlns="http://purl.oclc.org/dsdl/schematron" schematronEdition="2025"
  queryBinding="xslt3">

  <ns uri="http://www.w3.org/2001/XMLSchema" prefix="xs"/>

  <properties>
    <property id="programmer-alert">Programmers, watch out!</property>
    <property id="check-rounding-error">
      Please check for rounding errors!
    </property>
    <property id="check-subsystem">Did subsystem XYZ fail again?</property>
  </properties>

  <group>
    <rule context="/invoices">
      <assert test="xs:double(@total) eq sum(invoice/@total)"
          properties="programmer-alert check-rounding-error">
        Total <value-of select="@total"/> not correct
      </assert>
    </rule>
    <rule context="invoice">
      <let name="id" value="@id"></let>
      <assert test="count(../invoice[@id eq $id]) eq 1"
          properties="programmer-alert check-subsystem">
        Id <value-of select="@id"/> not unique
      </assert>
    </rule>
  </group>

</schema>
```

Both `<assert>` elements in Example 8.8 have a `properties` attribute that references multiple `<property>` elements by identifier. This attribute allows you to specify multiple identifiers as a whitespace-separated list.

The direct validation outcomes of Example 8.8 are still the same as those of Example 8.7. However, the properties are visible in the resulting SVRL, shown in Example 8.9.

Example 8.9 – The SVRL generated when validating the document in Example 8.6 with the schema from Example 8.8.

```
<schematron-output xmlns="http://purl.oclc.org/dsdl/svrl"
                   schematronEdition="2025"
                   phase="#ALL">
   <ns-prefix-in-attribute-values prefix="xs"
uri="http://www.w3.org/2001/XMLSchema"/>
   <active-group/>
   <fired-rule context="/invoices" document=".../invoices-2.xml"/>
   <failed-assert test="xs:double(@total) eq sum(invoice/@total)"
                  location="/Q{}invoices[1]">
      <property-reference property="programmer-alert">
         <text>Programmers, watch out!</text>
      </property-reference>
      <property-reference property="check-rounding-error">
         <text>Please check for rounding errors!</text>
      </property-reference>
      <text>Total 10117.82 not correct</text>
   </failed-assert>
   <fired-rule context="invoice" document=".../invoices-2.xml"/>
   <fired-rule context="invoice" document=".../invoices-2.xml"/>
   <failed-assert test="count(../invoice[@id eq $id]) eq 1"
                  location="/Q{}invoices[1]/Q{}invoice[2]">
      <property-reference property="programmer-alert">
         <text>Programmers, watch out!</text>
      </property-reference>
      <property-reference property="check-subsystem">
         <text>Did subsystem XYZ fail again?</text>
      </property-reference>
      <text>Id 56789 not unique</text>
   </failed-assert>
   <fired-rule context="invoice" document=".../invoices-2.xml"/>
   <failed-assert test="count(../invoice[@id eq $id]) eq 1"
                  location="/Q{}invoices[1]/Q{}invoice[3]">
      <property-reference property="programmer-alert">
         <text>Programmers, watch out!</text>
      </property-reference>
      <property-reference property="check-subsystem">
         <text>Did subsystem XYZ fail again?</text>
      </property-reference>
      <text>Id 56789 not unique</text>
   </failed-assert>
</schematron-output>
```

Properties can go further than this:

- <property> elements have an optional scheme attribute that, according to the specification, "should be an IRI or other public identifier which specifies the notation used for the metadata value." For instance, if your property contains an ISO 3166-1 country code like NL, UK, or DE, you can add this information to your property as follows:

  ```
  <property id="country" scheme="ISO 3166-1">NL</property>
  ```

- Properties also have an optional role attribute which can contain even more information about the property. Its value is neither defined nor restricted, so you can come up with anything you like. For instance, the standard contains the following example:

  ```
  <property id="australianDollar" scheme="ISO 4217" role="currency">AUD</property>
  ```

- The <property> element can contain additional attributes (in a different namespace). Properties can contain arbitrary XML (in any namespace). This example property contains a W3C XML Schema fragment:

  ```
  <property id="non-negative-decimal"
  xmlns:xsd="http://www.w3.org/2001/XMLSchema">
    <xsd:simpleType type="xs:decimal">
      <xsd:maxInclusive value="0" />
      <xsd:fractionDigits value='2'/>
    </xsd:simpleType>
  </property>
  ```

- With an XSLT query binding, you can use the <xsl:copy-of> element to add information to the property. For instance, this example copies the full context node (the node that triggered the Schematron rule) to the property:

  ```
  <property id="context" xmlns:xsl="http://www.w3.org/1999/XSL/Transform">
    <xsl:copy-of select="."/>
  </property>
  ```

  For XQuery, the XQS processor defines an, implementation defined, additional element: <xqs:copy-of> (the xqs namespace prefix here is bound to the namespace http://www.w3.org/2012/xquery).

The official Schematron schema (the one that comes with the standard) only allows for a single <properties> element to appear in your Schematron schema. However, in most cases, multiple <properties> elements are accepted by Schematron processors.

Adding structured comments: <title> and <p>

You usually document a schema using XML comments (<!-- ... -->). Adding well-worded comments in strategic places makes code more comprehensible for somebody else (or yourself in a few month times). The following example documents Example 8.7:

Example 8.10 – The schema from Example 8.7 with documentation in XML comments added (schematron-book-code-2025/examples/additional-features/properties-1b.sch)

```
<schema xmlns="http://purl.oclc.org/dsdl/schematron" schematronEdition="2025"
  queryBinding="xslt3">
  <ns uri="http://www.w3.org/2001/XMLSchema" prefix="xs"/>
  <!-- This schema validates an invoice list. -->

  <group>
    <!-- Checking whether the total attribute is ok: -->
    <rule context="/invoices">
      <assert test="xs:double(@total) eq sum(invoice/@total)">
        Total <value-of select="@total"/> not correct
      </assert>
    </rule>
  </group>

  <group>
    <!-- Checking whether invoice ids are unique: -->
    <rule context="invoice">
      <let name="id" value="@id"></let>
      <assert test="count(../invoice[@id eq $id]) eq 1">
        Id <value-of select="@id"/> not unique
      </assert>
    </rule>
  </group>

</schema>
```

Schematron also has native means for documenting schemas: it allows <title> and <p> elements in places where you might want to add documentation. For example, you can add these elements as direct children of the root <schema> element or inside a <pattern> or <group> element. Example 8.11 rewrites Example 8.10 using this feature.

Example 8.11 – The schema from Example 8.7 with documentation using Schematron's `<title>` and `<p>` element (schematron-book-code-2025/examples/additional-features/properties-1c.sch)

```
<schema xmlns="http://purl.oclc.org/dsdl/schematron" schematronEdition="2025"
  queryBinding="xslt3">
  <ns uri="http://www.w3.org/2001/XMLSchema" prefix="xs"/>
  <title>Invoice list validation</title>
  <p>This schema validates an invoice list.</p>

  <group>
    <title>Total attribute</title>
    <p>This group checks whether the total attribute is correct.</p>
    <rule context="/invoices">
      <assert test="xs:double(@total) eq sum(invoice/@total)">
        Total <value-of select="@total"/> not correct
      </assert>
    </rule>
  </group>

  <group>
    <title>Identifier uniqueness</title>
    <p>This group checks whether invoice identifiers are unique.</p>
    <rule context="invoice">
      <let name="id" value="@id"></let>
      <assert test="count(../invoice[@id eq $id]) eq 1">
        Id <value-of select="@id"/> not unique
      </assert>
    </rule>
  </group>

</schema>
```

Why and when would you want to use `<title>` and `<p>` instead of the more usual XML comments? Both methods enable you to explain your code. However, an advantage of using these elements, and the reason Schematron's designers added them, is that it becomes much easier to extract documentation from the schema.

Schemas are code. There are situations, especially when the code size increases, where you may want to extract information from your code into a separate documentation structure. Maybe you want to produce a PDF that lists everything your schema checks. Or you have a support website with information about the schemas. Having the base information in structured markup instead of XML comments makes it much easier to create either of these outputs and more.

Having said that, I'm not claiming that it is easy to create documentation this way. You have to write code that extracts the information, build the result page(s), add structure, and more. As far as I know there is currently nothing available that does this. However, if you ever decide to do this, parsing `<title>` and `<p>` elements will be much easier than parsing XML comments.

Here are some details about using structured comments:

- The `<title>` element is allowed only as (single) child of the `<schema>`, `<pattern>`, and `<group>` elements.
- The `<p>` element is allowed as (multiple) children of the following elements:
  - `<schema>` (after an optional `<title>` element)
  - `<pattern>` and `<group>` (after an optional `<title>` element)
  - `<phase>`
  - `<rule>`
- There are limited ways to markup the contents of the `<title>` and `<p>` elements (see also the section titled "Messages with markup: `<emph>`, `<span>`, and `<dir>` " (p. 141)):
  - The `<title>` element allows in its contents the `<dir>` element (writing direction) only.
  - The `<p>` element allows all Schematron's markup elements.
- `<title>` and `<p>` elements in the schema are not copied to the resulting SVRL.

Validating documents referenced by XInclude

XML documents frequently include other documents. We have already see this with the Schematron `<include>` element. Including external documents is so common that there's a standard for it, called XInclude. Schematron can access documents that are referenced by XInclude as it processes the including document. Example 8.12 uses XInclude to include two sub-documents:

Example 8.12 – Master document that includes two other documents using XInclude (`schematron-book-code-2025/data/subdocuments-master.xml`)

```
<document xmlns:xi="http://www.w3.org/2001/XInclude">
  <xi:include href="subdocuments-1.xml"/>
  <xi:include href="subdocuments-2.xml"/>
</document>
```

The included documents are shown in Example 8.13 and Example 8.14.

Example 8.13 – The first included document by Example 8.12 (schematron-book-code-2025/data/subdocuments-1.xml)

```
<document>
  <p class="emphasize">This is the first included sub-document.</p>
</document>
```

Example 8.14 – The second included document by Example 8.12 (schematron-book-code-2025/data/subdocuments-2.xml)

```
<document>
  <p class="brightred">This is the second included sub-document.</p>
</document>
```

Suppose you want to check whether `<p>` elements in the included documents use the `brightred` class and issue a message if one does. The schema in Example 8.15 does this.

Example 8.15 – Schematron schema to validate the included documents of Example 8.12 (schematron-book-code-2025/examples/additional-features/subdocuments-1.sch)

```
<schema xmlns="http://purl.oclc.org/dsdl/schematron" schematronEdition="2025"
  queryBinding="xslt3">

  <ns prefix="xi" uri="http://www.w3.org/2001/XInclude"/>

  <pattern documents="/*/xi:include/@href">
    <rule context="p">
      <assert test="@class ne 'brightred'">
        The class <value-of select="@class"/> is forbidden
        (<value-of select="base-uri(.)"/>)!
      </assert>
    </rule>
  </pattern>

</schema>
```

- The `<ns>` element defines the XInclude namespace using the usual `xi` prefix.
- The Schematron processor encounters the `<pattern>` element with the `documents` attribute on it. It evaluates the attribute's contents, `/*/xi:include/@href`, as an XPath expression.

  Notice that this is an XPath expression that accesses the reference to the external file in the document you are processing. If you want to specify a file system path directly, you need to put it between quotes, for instance `documents="'subdocument.xml'"`.
- This results in a sequence of two values: `subdocuments-1.xml` and `subdocuments-2.xml`. Both values are interpreted as a reference to another document.
- The rules in the pattern are resolved against both of the referenced documents but not against the original master document.
- The line `<value-of select="base-uri(.)"/>` in the message displays the URI of the document. Displaying the URI is optional, but if you don't it can be difficult to determine which document the message refers to.

Some details:

- A document referenced in a `documents` attribute is evaluated only for rules found inside the pattern that references it. Rules in other patterns are not applied to the referenced document.
- Evaluation of a document referenced using a `documents` attribute is done in the context of that document's root node. Therefore, it is safest to use absolute XPath expressions, as in Example 8.15.
- When a pattern's `documents` attribute results in relative references (as in Example 8.15), these are resolved against the document that is validated.
- The resulting value of the `documents` attribute must be a URI. This means that if it resolves to an absolute path (and not a relative path as in Example 8.15), it must begin with `file:/`, for instance `file:/C:/docs/subdoc.xml`.

Finally, while useful, this mechanism has one, rather limiting, drawback: it cannot handle nested includes. For instance, if `subdocument-2.xml` (Example 8.14) included some other document, that sub-document would not be validated. Since nesting of includes is common in many XML applications, this limitation can be significant.

Specifying a role: the `role` attribute

Schematron 2020 note

> In Schematron 2020, the `role` attribute is most commonly used to signify the severity of assertions and reports. However, for Schematron 2025, this function has been taken over by the `severity` attribute (see the section titled "Specifying a severity: the `severity` attribute" (p. 155)).
>
> For Schematron 2020, oXygen uses the `role` attribute to change the representation of the messages. The values it acts on are: `info`, `warning`, `error`, and `fatal`. It is likely that something similar will be implemented for Schematron 2025.

The `role` attribute on an assertion, report, or property allows you to say something about its role. But what is a role? The Schematron standard defines it as "a name describing the function of the assertion or context node in the pattern" and provides neither (preferred) values nor examples. Therefore, what a role is, its values, what it's used for, and how it is used, is up to you.

Some details:

- The `role` attribute can appear on `<assert>` and `<report>` elements.
- It can also appear on the parent `<rule>` element, specifying the default role for all the assertions and reports in this rule. Usually a `role` attribute on a child `<assert>` or `<report>` element overrides this default, but this is not defined in the standard as such. Whether it works that way, however logical it may seem, is implementation defined.
- The `role` attribute can also appear on `<property>` elements (see the section titled "Properties" (p. 144)).
- The `role` attribute is present in the resulting SVRL, allowing you to act on it when post-processing validation results.
- Like the `flag` attribute, the `role` attribute can be dynamically evaluated. See the section titled "Dynamic flags" (p. 143) for details.

Specifying a severity: the `severity` attribute

Schematron 2020 note

Schematron 2020 has no `severity` attribute, so this feature cannot be used in this (and older) editions.

The `severity` attribute on assertions and reports allows you to say something about the severity of the message. The standard reserves the following values without further definition: `fatal`, `error`, `warning`, and `info`. The meaning of these values is implementation defined. The attribute shows up in the resulting SVRL, so it can be used when post-processing the results.

Like the `flag` attribute, the `severity` attribute can be dynamically evaluated. See the section titled "Dynamic flags" (p. 143) for details.

Specify a different location: the `subject` attribute

As we've learned, the Schematron `<rule>` element specifies the context: the location of the content we're validating. Child assertions and reports normally apply to this location. However, sometimes the context specified in the `<rule>` element is not the location you want to apply the rule to. This can happen if you try to choose a context that is efficient to locate.

For example, consider Example 8.16, which is a simple table.

Example 8.16 – Simple table document
(`schematron-book-code-2025/data/simple-table.xml`)

```
<table>
  <row>
    <entry>First cell</entry>
    <entry>Second cell</entry>
    <entry>Third cell</entry>
    <entry>Fourth cell</entry>
  </row>
</table>
```

Assume that tables are not allowed to have more than two columns. It is easy to check this with the schema in Example 8.17.

Example 8.17 – Schematron schema to check the number of columns for Example 8.16. (schematron-book-code-2025/examples/additional-features/subject-1a.sch)

```
<schema xmlns="http://purl.oclc.org/dsdl/schematron" schematronEdition="2025"
  queryBinding="xslt3">

  <group>
    <rule context="row">
      <assert test="count(entry) le 2">Row with superfluous column(s)</assert>
    </rule>
  </group>

</schema>
```

If you run this, the validation error identifies the `<row>` element, as specified by the `<rule>` element's `context` attribute. The oXygen IDE, for instance, shows this with a red squiggly line on this element.

But what if you want to specify the error on the first superfluous column (`<entry>` element)? This might be useful when the table gets more complex, or maybe users find it easier to fix this error when you specify the exact column. Example 8.18 takes care of this and correctly identifies the third and fourth `<entry>` elements of Example 8.16 as the error locations.

Example 8.18 – Schematron schema to check the number of columns for Example 8.16 (schematron-book-code-2025/examples/additional-features/subject-1b.sch)

```
<schema xmlns="http://purl.oclc.org/dsdl/schematron" schematronEdition="2025"
  queryBinding="xslt3">

  <pattern>
    <rule context="entry">
      <assert test="count(preceding-sibling::entry) lt 2">
        Superfluous column
      </assert>
    </rule>
  </pattern>

</schema>
```

`preceding-sibling::?`

If you're new to XPath, the `preceding-sibling::` construct is probably unfamiliar to you. It's an example of what is called an XPath *axis*. An XPath axis tells the XPath processor where to look to match the XPath expression that follows the axis.

For example, the XPath expression `preceding-sibling::entry` in Example 8.18 returns all `<entry>` elements that precede the context item and have the same parent. Since the assertion that contains this XPath expression is inside a rule that matches every `<entry>` element in the document, the context item is an `<entry>` element, and the XPath expression returns every `<entry>` element that comes before the context item and has the same parent element (in this case, `<row>`). It then counts the number of elements returned and issues a message if there are two or more.

XPath defines several axes. See https://www.w3schools.com/xml/xpath_axes.asp for more information. Another example of using axis can be found in the section titled "Validating doubled elements in mixed content" (p. 182).

Although XPath axes are useful and often the best way to accomplish a particular goal, in this set of examples, Example 8.18 is less clear and efficient than Example 8.17:

- There usually will be far fewer `<row>` than `<entry>` elements in a document, so using the `<row>` element as context is better for performance reasons.
- Example 8.18 is more complex and, therefore, less easy to interpret than Example 8.17. Simply counting the number of child `<entry>` elements is easy to grasp, while mucking about with preceding siblings adds complexity and might need a comment to explain it.

For situations like this the `subject` attribute comes to the rescue. Its content is an XPath expression that, evaluated against the context of the rule, leads to the subject of the error. Example 8.19 rewrites Example 8.18 using this feature.

Example 8.19 – Schematron schema to check the number of columns for Example 8.16, using the `subject` attribute to shift the error location to the first superfluous column. (`schematron-book-code-2025/examples/additional-features/subject-1c.sch`)

```
<schema xmlns="http://purl.oclc.org/dsdl/schematron" schematronEdition="2025"
  queryBinding="xslt3">

  <group>
    <rule context="row" >
      <assert test="count(entry) le 2" subject="entry[3]">
        Start of superfluous column(s)
      </assert>
    </rule>
  </group>

</schema>
```

The XPath expression in the `subject` attribute (`entry[3]`) is evaluated using the context of the rule (the `<row>` element). This flags the third `<entry>` element as the error location.

Some details:

- The `subject` attribute can appear on `<assert>` and `<report>` elements.
- It can also appear on the parent `<rule>` element, specifying the default subject for all assertions and reports of this rule. Usually a `subject` attribute on a child `<assert>` or `<report>` element overrides this default, but this is not defined in the standard. Whether it works that way, however logical it may seem, is implementation defined.
- In the resulting SVRL, the location of an assertion or report shows up in the `<failed-assert>` or `<successful-report>` element's `location` attribute. This allows you to identify the intended subject location when post-processing the SVRL.

The `<name>` element

The `<name/>` element inserts the name of the context item (usually the name of an element or attribute) into a message. It can be used in locations where `<value-of/>` is allowed.

When using XPath-enabled query bindings (the only ones currently available), the element is superfluous. You can use `<value-of select="name()"/>` instead. However, in the rare case that you are using a non-XPath-enabled query binding, `<name/>` can be useful.

The `icon`, `see`, and `fpi` attributes

Last in this chapter about additional features are three attributes: `icon`, `see`, and `fpi`. These attributes can be used in several places, including the root `<schema>` element and the `<pattern>`, `<rule>`, `<assert>`, and `<report>` elements. Usually, if you use one of these attributes on an element, its value overrides any value set for that attribute on an ancestor element.[1]

The meaning of these attributes is defined in the standard, but usage is implementation defined. They show up in the resulting SVRL, so they can be used when post-processing the results.

`icon`
: The `icon` attribute contains a link to a graphic file associated with an assertion or report, which, for example, you could display for a failed assertion.

`see`
: The `see` attribute contains a link to additional information about assertions or reports. For example, you could point to a web page with additional information about an error.[2]

`fpi`
: The `fpi` attribute is defined as "a formal public identifier for the schema, phase, or other element." This attribute and its rather cryptic definition are holdovers from the SGML days and unlikely to be relevant.

---

1 As logical as that may seem, this behavior is implementation defined.

2 The oXygen IDE uses the value of the `see` attribute in the Results window to provide a link to additional information.

CHAPTER 9

Schematron examples and recipes

This chapter contains some more advanced examples and recipes for applying Schematron. All code and data is in the book's example code GitHub repository. See the section titled "Finding and using the code examples" (p. 6) for information on finding and downloading examples.

> **Introducing advanced XPath techniques and operators**
>
> Because of the more advanced nature of this chapter, I use several XPath techniques and operators that are not covered in the technology primer in Appendix A. I explain anything not covered there in a note like this.

Validating a Schematron schema

Schematron schemas are XML documents and, as such, can be validated themselves. Doing this adds value, especially when you're writing a schema using a schema-aware editor. A schema-aware editor can flag mistakes and help you by showing what elements and attributes are valid at the current cursor position.

The official schemas for validating Schematron are part of the Schematron standard and listed in its PDF. To get them in machine-usable format, you have to copy the code from the PDF (page by page) and paste it into an appropriate document—a cumbersome procedure. To save everyone work and money (the PDF of the standard is not free), you can obtain these schemas (for Schematron and the reporting language SVRL) in two ways:

- Clone or download the GitHub repository https://github.com/Schematron/schema.
- Download them from the example code GitHub repository for this book, subdirectory `schematron-book-code-2025/schemas-2025`.

Whichever source you choose, you will get the following files:

- `schematron.rnc` and `svrl.rnc` are the RELAX NG compact schemas from the standard. These are straight copies, except the versions included in the GitHub repository for this book include a provenance comment added at the beginning of each file.
- `schematron.sch` and `svrl.sch` are the original Schematron schemas from in the standard. Again, these are straight copies, except the versions included in the GitHub repository for this book include a provenance comment added at the beginning of each file.

The Schematron schemas provide an additional layer of validation, on top of the RELAX NG schemas. It may sound like hocus pocus to use Schematron schemas to validate Schematron schemas, like Baron Munchhausen rescuing himself from the swamp by pulling his own hair. But there's no magic involved: nothing prevents you from using a Schematron schema to validate another Schematron schema.

- The GitHub repository for this book also includes the files `schematron-converted.xsd` and `svrl-converted.xsd`, which are the W3C XML Schemas, converted (by me, using the oXygen schema converter) from their RELAX NG Compact versions. These conversions are approximations (RELAX NG has some different features than W3C XML Schema) and needed a little patching to make them valid. Nonetheless, I am providing them because W3C XML Schema is more widely supported than RELAX NG.

> There are some subtle differences between the RELAX NG and the W3C XML Schemas, but, unless you need to be really strict, there is nothing to be concerned about. For instance, the RELAX NG schema requires at least a single `<pattern>` element, but the W3C variant allows zero-or-more. Be aware that there might be other differences that I didn't spot.

How to make these validations happen?

- Most XML-aware IDEs and editors automatically detect that you're editing a Schematron schema and provide validation without further ado. You don't even need the schemas provided in the example code of this book.
- The XML community has developed common ways to include a reference to a schema in an XML document. If your environment supports this functionality, it should trigger validation when you work with a file that contains such references. Here are some examples:
  - Referencing a RELAX NG compact schema:

Example 9.1 – A reference to the RELAX NG compact schema for Schematron (`schematron-book-code-2025/templates/empty-schema-relaxng-compact-validation.sch`)

```
<?xml-model
  type="application/relax-ng-compact-syntax"
  href="../schemas-2025/schematron.rnc"
?>
<schema xmlns="http://purl.oclc.org/dsdl/schematron" schematronEdition="2025"
  queryBinding="xslt3">
  <pattern/>
</schema>
```

- Referencing a W3C XML Schema:

  Example 9.2 – A reference to the W3C XML Schema for Schematron
  (schematron-book-code-2025/templates/empty-schema-w3c-schema-validation.sch)

```
<schema xmlns="http://purl.oclc.org/dsdl/schematron" schematronEdition="2025"
  queryBinding="xslt3"
  xmlns:xsi="http://www.w3.org/2001/XMLSchema-instance"
  xsi:schemaLocation="http://purl.oclc.org/dsdl/schematron
    ../schemas-2025/schematron-converted.xsd">
  <pattern/>
</schema>
```

- Referencing a Schematron schema:

  Example 9.3 – A reference to the Schematron schema for Schematron
  (schematron-book-code-2025/templates/empty-schema-schematron-validation.sch)

```
<?xml-model
  type="application/xml"
  schematypens="http://purl.oclc.org/dsdl/schematron"
  href="../schemas-2025/schematron.sch"
?>
<schema xmlns="http://purl.oclc.org/dsdl/schematron" schematronEdition="2025"
  queryBinding="xslt3">
  <pattern/>
</schema>
```

Test to find out what works in your environment. You will need to change the path to the schemas, `../schemas-2025/`... in the examples, to the real (relative or absolute) path in your environment.

In some environments you can have multiple schema references. If supported, you can have references to RELAX NG plus Schematron or W3C XML Schema plus Schematron, which gives you the benefit of checking the validity of your document against both the XML schema and the Schematron rules.

- Other environments may need a specific configuration to set up validation. You're on your own here, but it can be worth the effort to figure out what works in your environment.

Handling a default namespace

Even among XML specialists it's not unusual to run into a frustrating situation where you have written your code (in Schematron or another XML language) to the best of your abilities, checked it multiple times, and it still doesn't do anything. Nothing. Zilch. When this happens, the odds are that somewhere a namespace plays a role (if you don't know what I'm talking about, the XML namespace mechanism is explained in Appendix B).

Namespaces can be tricky, and their declarations are hard to spot. Because of the default namespace mechanism (`xmlns="..."`), elements that are in a namespace don't always need a prefix. And when this default namespace is declared somewhere way up in a long and complicated document, it's easy to miss. So when your code seems perfect but your XPath expressions refuse to work, look again and check the data for namespace usage.

Schematron, because of the way namespaces must be defined, doesn't have the concept of a default namespace (see the section titled "Declaring namespaces" (p. 78)). However, documents, the data to be checked, can use a default namespace. If you're new to namespaces it can be rather mysterious how to handle this. Fortunately, the solution is simple.

Suppose you're writing a Schematron schema that checks a piece of text written in DocBook. DocBook is a standard for texts like books, articles, and manuals (this book, for instance, is written entirely in DocBook). Example 9.4 contains a short piece of text expressed in DocBook.

Example 9.4 – Some text expressed in DocBook
(`schematron-book-code-2025/data/docbook-text.xml`)

```
<article xmlns="http://docbook.org/ns/docbook" version="5.0">
  <title>An example document</title>

  <sect1>
    <title>The first section</title>

    <para>A paragraph of text.</para>
    <para>A <emphasis>second</emphasis> paragraph of text!</para>
  </sect1>

</article>
```

One thing you might want to validate for this example is that sections on the first level (`<sect1>` elements) must have at least three paragraphs of text (`<para>` elements). This makes Example 9.4 invalid. A first attempt at writing a Schematron schema for this might look like Example 9.5.

Example 9.5 – A first, non-working, attempt at a Schematron schema validating Example 9.4 (`schematron-book-code-2025/examples/examples-recipes/check-docbook-1.sch`)

```
<schema xmlns="http://purl.oclc.org/dsdl/schematron" schematronEdition="2025"
  queryBinding="xslt3">
  <pattern>
    <rule context="sect1">
      <assert test="count(para) ge 3">
        This section must contain at least three paragraphs of text
      </assert>
    </rule>
  </pattern>
</schema>
```

When you run this schema against the data in Example 9.4, nothing will happen. Your computer will proclaim the data as valid, which it clearly isn't. Something is wrong, and, yes, it has to do with namespaces:

- Because of the default namespace declaration `xmlns="http://docbook.org/ns/docbook"` on the root element of Example 9.4, all of its elements are in the DocBook namespace.
- However, the two XPath expressions in Example 9.5, `sect1` and `count(para) ge 3`, do not reference a namespace: they expect the elements to be in the null namespace.
- To an XML processor, a `<sect1>` or `<para>` element in the null namespace is considered different from elements with the same names in the DocBook namespace.
- Therefore, although the element names are the same, nothing happens. The namespaces in the document and the XPath expressions in the Schematron schema differ.

This situation is confusing because the element names in Example 9.4 are written exactly the same as the names used in the Schematron schema of Example 9.5. It's the default namespace declaration on the root element of Example 9.4 that causes the problem.

How can we solve this? Schematron has no default namespace mechanism forXPath expressions, so the only remaining option is to use Schematron's namespace mechanism, the `<ns>` element:

- Define the DocBook namespace using the `<ns>` element and assign some prefix to it:

  ```
  <ns prefix="db" uri="http://docbook.org/ns/docbook"/>
  ```

  You are free to choose the value of the prefix attribute, but the value of the `uri` attribute must match the DocBook namespace name (its URI).
- Use this prefix in the XPath expressions that refer to DocBook elements: `db:sect1` and `count(db:para) ge 3`.

Example 9.6 shows the resulting Schematron schema,

Example 9.6 – A working Schematron schema validating Example 9.4 (`schematron-book-code-2025/examples/examples-recipes/check-docbook-2.sch`)

```
<schema xmlns="http://purl.oclc.org/dsdl/schematron" schematronEdition="2025"
  queryBinding="xslt3">

  <ns prefix="db" uri="http://docbook.org/ns/docbook"/>

  <pattern>
    <rule context="db:sect1">
      <assert test="count(db:para) ge 3">
        This section must contain at least three paragraphs of text
      </assert>
    </rule>
  </pattern>
</schema>
```

The XPath expressions in Example 9.6 reference the DocBook namespace using the namespace prefix mechanism. Example 9.4 references the DocBook namespace using the default namespace mechanism. However, the mechanism for referencing a namespace doesn't matter: as long as the referenced namespace name is the same, the elements are considered the same.

Using Schematron for schema validation

When you validate using schema languages such as DTD, W3C XML Schema, or RELAX NG the messages do not always make sense to non-technical users. The message will say something is wrong, but it may not say exactly what is wrong, and it can be unclear what you need to do to fix the problem. One of Schematron's major strengths is that you control the messages. Because of this, some people use Schematron for validations that are usually done with other languages.

However, Schematron cannot easily check everything that other validation languages check. For instance, checking the order of elements (`<a>` elements must always come before `<b>` elements) is hard to implement efficiently. Other checks, like the presence of attributes/elements and checks on their data types, can be done but need a lot of repetitive and boring code.

The repetitive nature of this kind of code led to the idea of generating a Schematron schema from another schema language. For W3C XML Schema and RELAX NG, which are expressed in XML, you can use XSLT. It's not easy, because schemas can be complex, but it is possible.

Writing such a generator is beyond the scope of this book, but in this section, I provide you with some guidance on how to implement some of the more classic schema checks using Schematron.

Example 9.7 contains a sample XML instance to illustrate these checks.

Example 9.7 – The XML for validation using Schematron
(`schematron-book-code-2025/data/xml-for-validation.xml`)

```
<data timestamp="2026-03-01T12:12:23">
  <thing thingid="12345">Something</thing>
  <thing thingid="12346">Another thing</thing>
  <object>Object 1</object>
  <object remark="just an object">Object 2</object>
</data>
```

Here is a list of checks we will use to validate this example (the Schematron examples in this section refer to the numbers in this list, e.g., Validation 1, Validation 2, etc.):

1. The root element must be `<data>`.
2. The root has a required attribute called `timestamp`.
3. The value of the `timestamp` attribute must be a valid date/time.
4. There must be between one and three child `<thing>` elements.
5. A `<thing>` element has a required `thingid` attribute.
6. The value of the `thingid` attribute must be a valid integer.
7. Each `<thing>` element is followed by zero or more `<object>` elements.
8. The `<object>` element has an optional `remark` attribute.

Validation 1, Example 9.8, checks the root element.

Example 9.8 – Validating the root element
(schematron-book-code-2025/examples/examples-recipes/validation-1.sch)

```
<schema xmlns="http://purl.oclc.org/dsdl/schematron" schematronEdition="2025"
  queryBinding="xslt3">

  <!-- Validation check 1: -->
  <pattern>
    <rule context="/">
      <assert test="exists(data)">
        The root element must be data
      </assert>
    </rule>
  </pattern>

</schema>
```

Validations 2 and 3, Example 9.9, check the `timestamp` attribute.

Example 9.9 – Validating the attribute on the root element
(schematron-book-code-2025/examples/examples-recipes/validation-2-3.sch)

```
<schema xmlns="http://purl.oclc.org/dsdl/schematron" schematronEdition="2025"
  queryBinding="xslt3">
  <ns prefix="xs" uri="http://www.w3.org/2001/XMLSchema"/>

  <!-- Validation check 2 and 3: -->
  <pattern>
    <rule context="/data">
      <assert test="exists(@timestamp)">
        The root element must have a timestamp attribute
      </assert>
      <assert test="empty(@timestamp) or @timestamp castable as xs:dateTime">
        The timestamp attribute must hold a valid date/time
      </assert>
      <assert test="empty(@* except @timestamp)">
        Only the timestamp attribute is allowed on the root element
      </assert>
    </rule>
  </pattern>

</schema>
```

- The first `<assert>` in Example 9.9 checks whether an attribute called `timestamp` is present.
- The second `<assert>` checks whether the value of `timestamp` is a valid date/time.

> ### The XPath `castable as` operator
>
> The XPath `castable as` operator returns `true` when a piece of data can be cast to a certain type. If `@timestamp castable as xs:dateTime` in Example 9.9 returns `true`, this means that the value of the `timestamp` attribute is a valid date/time and can be transformed to the right data type without raising an error using `xs:dateTime(@timestamp)`.
>
> You can find more about working with dates and times in the section titled "Working with dates, times and durations" (p. 226).

  Why is `empty(@timestamp)` part of the second assertion? It is there to avoid a double error message if there is no `timestamp` attribute at all. So this test first makes sure the attribute exists and only then performs the check on its data type.

- The third `<assert>` in Example 9.9 checks whether there are any other attributes on the root element, which is not allowed.

> ### The XPath `except` operator
>
> The XPath `except` operator takes two sequences and returns all members of the first sequence that do not occur in the second sequence. So in this case it will return all attributes except the attribute that is allowed. If this result is empty, everything is fine, but if not, the assertion raises an error.
>
> What if there were more attributes allowed, for instance an `id` attribute? In that case you would write:
>
> ```
> empty(@* except (@timestamp, @id))
> ```

Validations 4 and 7, Example 9.10, check the <thing> and <object> elements.

Example 9.10 – Validating the root's child elements
(schematron-book-code-2025/examples/examples-recipes/validation-4-7.sch)

```
<schema xmlns="http://purl.oclc.org/dsdl/schematron" schematronEdition="2025"
  queryBinding="xslt3">

  <!-- Validation check 4 and 7: -->
  <pattern>
    <rule context="/data">
      <assert test="count(thing) ge 1 and count(thing) le 3">
        There must be between 1 and 3 thing elements
      </assert>
      <assert test="empty(* except (thing, object))">
       Only thing and object elements are allowed as children of the root element
      </assert>
    </rule>
  </pattern>

</schema>
```

- The first assertion in Example 9.10 counts the number of <thing> elements and makes sure the total is between 1 and 3.
- You don't need to check the <object> element, because it is optional and there is no upper limit on how many times it can appear.
- The second assertion checks whether there are any elements underneath the root other than the allowed <thing> and <object> elements. This assertion uses the same technique as was used in Example 9.9 to check for extra attributes on the root element.

Validations 5 and 6, Example 9.11, check the thingid attribute. This check is similar to the check for validations 2 and 3 in Example 9.9.

Example 9.11 – Validating the `thingid` attribute on the `<thing>` element (`schematron-book-code-2025/examples/examples-recipes/validation-5-6.sch`)

```
<schema xmlns="http://purl.oclc.org/dsdl/schematron" schematronEdition="2025"
  queryBinding="xslt3">
  <ns prefix="xs" uri="http://www.w3.org/2001/XMLSchema"/>

  <!-- Validation check 5 and 6: -->
  <pattern>
    <rule context="/data/thing">
      <assert test="exists(@thingid)">
        A thing must have a thingid attribute
      </assert>
      <assert test="empty(@thingid) or @thingid castable as xs:integer">
        A thingid must be a valid integer
      </assert>
      <assert test="empty(@* except @thingid)">
        Only the thingid attribute is allowed on the thing element
      </assert>
    </rule>
  </pattern>

</schema>
```

Finally, validation 8, Example 9.12, checks whether the `<object>` element has any attributes other than `remark`, which is optional.[1]

Example 9.12 – Validating the attributes on the `<object>` element (`schematron-book-code-2025/examples/examples-recipes/validation-8.sch`)

```
<schema xmlns="http://purl.oclc.org/dsdl/schematron" schematronEdition="2025"
  queryBinding="xslt3">

  <!-- Validation check 8: -->
  <pattern>
    <rule context="/data/object">
      <assert test="empty(@* except @remark)">
        Only the remark attribute is allowed on the object element
      </assert>
    </rule>
  </pattern>

</schema>
```

[1] `schematron-book-code/examples/examples-recipes/validation-combined.sch` contains a full Schematron schema that combines all eight of these checks.

I hope you agree with me that this is not the most exciting code. Writing all this by hand is boring and error-prone. Bottom line: you can partially implement classic schema checks in Schematron, but I would only do this when controlling the error messages is critically important.

Checking multiple identifier references

Referencing in XML documents is often done using identifiers. The section titled "Using XSLT keys" (p. 130) shows how to use XSLT indexes to check such references. Sometimes a single attribute can contain references to multiple identifiers. For instance, `idrefs="id1 id2 id3"` references three identifiers. Schematron can check whether all of these references exist.

This example works with an excerpt from Shakespeare's play *Macbeth*, adapted from the full text on http://gutenberg.org/ and turned into XML using a fictitious play markup language.[2] A role in the play (there are 39 of them…) is defined by a <Role> element. Each role gets an identifier using the `role-id` attribute. For instance, Example 9.13 defines the role of Macbeth.

Example 9.13 – Example of defining a role in the XML rendering of Macbeth.

```
<Role role-id="MACBETH">
  <Name>Macbeth</Name>
  <PreferredSex>male</PreferredSex>
  <Description>General in the King's army</Description>
</Role>
```

Clauses link to a role using the `role-ref` attribute (entrances and exits also use the `role-ref` attribute). Example 9.14 shows a clause that contains a piece of text spoken by Macbeth, who is identified by the `role-ref` attribute.

Example 9.14 – Example of referencing roles in the XML rendering of Macbeth.

```
<Clause role-ref="MACBETH">
  <Text>I go, and it is done; the bell invites me.<Br/>
    Hear it not, Duncan, for it is a knell<Br/>
    That summons thee to heaven or to hell.
  </Text>
</Clause>
<Exits>
  <Exit role-ref="MACBETH"/>
</Exits>
```

[2] The full text is in the GitHub repository for this book (`schematron-book-code/data/macbeth.xml`).

The task is to validate whether every `role-ref` attribute references a role in the play.

> ### Checking multiple identifier references using other schema languages
>
> A W3C XML or RELAX NG schema can handle a single identifier attribute (in this case `role-id`), as having type `xs:ID` and multiple attributes as having type `xs:IDREFS`. In this case, these schemas can flag any reference errors.
>
> However, the full Macbeth text contains two types of identifiers: roles (`role-id` attribute) and scenes (`scene-id` attribute). If both of these attributes are of type `xs:ID`, a W3C XML or RELAX NG processor can't tell if a document has a role in a place where it should have a scene or vice versa.
>
> Schematron can check this. Although the examples in this section do not use the scene identifiers, I think you can see that Example 9.15 will fail if a scene identifier is incorrectly used in a `role-id` attribute.

Example 9.15 is a Schematron schema that checks whether all the roles referenced in `role-ref` attributes actually exist. For this example, I'm using the XSLT key mechanism, which is explained in the section titled "Using XSLT keys" (p. 130)).

Example 9.15 – Checking the role references in Macbeth, assuming `role-ref` attributes contain a single identifier
(`schematron-book-code-2025/examples/examples-recipes/check-role-refs-1.sch`)

```
<schema xmlns="http://purl.oclc.org/dsdl/schematron" schematronEdition="2025"
  queryBinding="xslt3" xmlns:xsl="http://www.w3.org/1999/XSL/Transform">

  <xsl:key name="role-ids" match="/*/Roles/*" use="@role-id"/>

  <pattern>
    <rule context="@role-ref">
      <assert test="exists(key('role-ids', .))">
        The referenced role id <value-of select="."/> does not exist
      </assert>
    </rule>
  </pattern>
</schema>
```

When you validate the entire play against this schema it reports 72 validation problems. These problems can be divided into two types:

- Some `role-ref` attributes contain multiple references. For instance on line 320:

  ```
  <Entry role-ref="DUNCAN MALCOLM DONALBAIN LENNOX ATTENDANTS"/>
  ```

  Multiple players enter the stage at this point, which is expressed in a single `role-ref` attribute.
- Some `role-ref` attributes contain the special value `#all` (for instance on line 305), which signifies that this applies to all players who are on stage at that moment in the play.

Let's solve these problems one by one.

To handle a `role-ref` attribute with multiple values, we have to break it into its constituents and check each separately. Example 9.16 does this.

Example 9.16 – Checking the role references in Macbeth, handling multiple references in the `role-ref` attributes
(`schematron-book-code-2025/examples/examples-recipes/check-role-refs-2.sch`)

```
<schema xmlns="http://purl.oclc.org/dsdl/schematron" schematronEdition="2025"
  queryBinding="xslt3" xmlns:xsl="http://www.w3.org/1999/XSL/Transform">

  <xsl:key name="role-ids" match="/*/Roles/*" use="@role-id"/>

  <pattern>
    <rule context="@role-ref">
      <assert test="
        every $ref in tokenize(., '\s+')[.]
          satisfies exists(key('role-ids', $ref))
      ">
        Role reference(s) in "<value-of select="."/>" not found
      </assert>
    </rule>
  </pattern>
</schema>
```

The value of the `role-ref` attribute is turned into its members. Each member is checked (using the key lookup we've already seen in Example 9.15). When one of these lookups fails, the assertion fails and a message is issued. If you run Example 9.16 against the play, only the `role-ref="#all"` attributes are still reported as invalid.

The XPath `tokenize()` function

The expression `tokenize(., '\s+')[.]` in Example 9.16 separates the value of the `role-ref` attribute into its constituents:

- The `tokenize()` function takes a string as its first argument and splits it into a sequence of substrings.
- The second argument of `tokenize()` tells the function where to split the string. This argument must be a regular expression (or regexp).[3] The regexp `\s+` matches a string of one or more whitespace characters (spaces, tabs, newlines, etc.).
- The `[.]` after the `tokenize()` function is a predicate (like in the section titled "Predicates in tree navigation" (p. 205)). It examines the sequence of strings coming out of the `tokenize()` function for empty strings, which happens when the attribute value starts or ends with whitespace.

  The effective boolean value of an empty string is `false`, so the predicate `[.]` kicks them out of the sequence.

The result of all this is that the value of the `role-ref` attribute is turned into a sequence of substrings, each of which holds a separate identifier.

The XPath `every … satisfies …` expression

The expression `every $ref in … satisfies …` in Example 9.16 checks all members of a sequence against some boolean expression.

If the boolean expression returns `true` for every member of the sequence, the expression in its entirety returns `true`, otherwise it returns `false`.

[3] A regular expression is a sequence of characters that are used to search for patterns in text. A detailed discussion of regular expressions is beyond the scope of this book, but you can find a good, detailed introduction on Wikipedia at: https://en.wikipedia.org/wiki/Regular_expression.

The last thing we need to add to our Schematron schema is a check for the special value `#all`. Example 9.17 is what probably comes to mind first.

Example 9.17 – Checking the role references in Macbeth, handling multiple references and the special value `#all` in the `role-ref` attributes
(`schematron-book-code-2025/examples/examples-recipes/check-role-refs-3.sch`)

```
<schema xmlns="http://purl.oclc.org/dsdl/schematron" schematronEdition="2025"
  queryBinding="xslt3" xmlns:xsl="http://www.w3.org/1999/XSL/Transform">

  <xsl:key name="role-ids" match="/*/Roles/*" use="@role-id"/>

  <pattern>
    <rule context="@role-ref">
      <assert test="
        every $ref in tokenize(., '\s+')[.]
          satisfies exists(key('role-ids', $ref))
        or
          . eq '#all'
      ">
        Role reference(s) in "<value-of select="."/>" not found
      </assert>
    </rule>
  </pattern>
</schema>
```

This example works, but there is a different, possibly less obvious, way to solve this using a different technique: another `<rule>` element in the pattern.

Remember that for a pattern, only the first matching rule is executed for every node being checked. So if you catch instances of `role-ref="#all"` before checking for identifiers, the identifier check never happens. Example 9.18 uses this technique.

Example 9.18 – An alternative for Example 9.17: catch any `role-ref="#all"` attributes before checking the identifier references (`schematron-book-code-2025/examples/examples-recipes/check-role-refs-4.sch`)

```
<schema xmlns="http://purl.oclc.org/dsdl/schematron" schematronEdition="2025"
  queryBinding="xslt3" xmlns:xsl="http://www.w3.org/1999/XSL/Transform">

  <xsl:key name="role-ids" match="/*/Roles/*" use="@role-id"/>

  <pattern>
    <rule context="@role-ref[. eq '#all']">
      <assert test="true()"/>
    </rule>
    <rule context="@role-ref">
      <assert test="
        every $ref in tokenize(., '\s+')[.]
          satisfies exists(key('role-ids', $ref))
      ">
        Role reference(s) in "<value-of select="."/>" not found
      </assert>
    </rule>
  </pattern>
</schema>
```

The rule element `<rule context="@role-ref[. eq '#all']/>` catches `role-ref="#all"` attributes. When it fires, its only `<assert>` test gets executed. This assertion never fails, because its test expression is the constant `true()`. It may look like a trick to have a constant, never-failing assertion, but you must include it because `<rule>` elements cannot be empty. When this rule fires, the second rule is never checked. While this method may look more complex, it is actually a straightforward use of Schematron that may be a bit more efficient than the previous example.

Validating processing instructions and comments

Schema languages, like DTD, W3C XML Schema, and RELAX NG, are unable to check processing instructions (`<? ... ?>`) or XML comments (`<!-- ... -->`). They can check neither their presence nor their contents, but Schematron can.

The anatomy of a processing instruction

Consider Example 9.19, which is a fictitious processing instruction.

Example 9.19 – An example processing instruction

```
<?xmlvalidate type="something" check="full"?>
```

This processing instruction has two parts:

- **Name:** `xmlvalidate`
- **Value:** `type="something" check="full"`

The value of a processing instruction often leads to misunderstandings. In most cases, like Example 9.19, the value looks like one or more attributes. However, that is not the case. What comes after the processing instruction's name is just a string. XML parsers do not attempt to turn this into separate attributes.

If you do want to process the value as though it is a list of attributes, you have two choices:

- If you're using Saxon EE combined with an `xslt2` or `xslt3` query language binding, use the Saxon-specific function `saxon:get-pseudo-attribute()`.[4]
- You can write a parser yourself using regular expressions. This goes beyond the scope of this book.

To see how you can validate processing instructions and comments, suppose you have data coming from an external supplier that you need to validate. In addition to the normal element and attribute validations, you also want to validate the following things:

- The data must have the processing instruction `<?process type="full"?>` up front.
- The first child of the root element must be a comment that contains at least the name of the data supplier, `ACMEDATA`.

[4] See https://www.saxonica.com/documentation11/index.html#!functions/saxon/get-pseudo-attribute.

Example 9.20 is a valid example of such a document.

Example 9.20 – Some XML data with a processing instruction and comment (schematron-book-code-2025/data/data-with-pi.xml)

```
<?process type="full"?>
<external-data>
  <!-- Produced by ACMEDATA -->
  …
</external-data>
```

As Appendix A explains, XPath treats XML as a tree-shaped data structure. This data structure contains the elements, attributes, and text as well as any processing instructions and comments. When navigating XPath expressions, you can use `processing-instruction()` and `comment()` to match processing instructions and comments, respectively. You can match a processing instruction by name by adding the name between the parentheses. For example, you could match a processing instruction named “process” using `processing-instruction(process)`.

Why do you need parentheses at the end of `comment()` and `processing-instruction()`?

You might wonder why the terms `processing-instruction()` and `comment()` are suffixed by parentheses, almost as if they’re functions.

The reason for this is that if you omit these parentheses they’re indistinguishable from <processing-instruction> and <comment> elements. XPath wouldn’t know whether you wanted to address an element or a processing instruction/comment. The same reasoning applies to `text()`, which matches any text and `node()`, which matches any node.

Example 9.21 checks the validity of documents like Example 9.20.

Example 9.21 – A Schematron schema that checks the validity of data like Example 9.20 (schematron-book-code-2025/examples/examples-recipes/check-pi-comments-1.sch)

```
<schema xmlns="http://purl.oclc.org/dsdl/schematron" schematronEdition="2025"
  queryBinding="xslt3">

  <group>

    <!-- 1 - Test for a processing-instruction (pi) with the name 'process': -->
    <rule context="/">
      <assert test="processing-instruction(process)">
        There must be a leading process pi present
      </assert>
    </rule>

    <!-- 2 - Test the contents of this processing-instruction: -->
    <rule context="/processing-instruction(process)">
      <assert test="contains(., 'type=&quot;full&quot;')">
        The process pi must contain type="full"
      </assert>
    </rule>

    <!-- 3 - Check for a comment mentioning ACMEDATA: -->
    <rule context="/*">
      <assert test="comment()[contains(., 'ACMEDATA')]">
        There must be a comment mentioning ACMEDATA underneath the root
      </assert>
    </rule>

  </group>
</schema>
```

The schema contains a group with three rules:

1. The first rule checks for the presence of the processing instruction. It takes the document node as context (`context="/"`). Then it asserts whether this has a child processing instruction called `process` (`test="processing-instruction(process)"`).
2. The second rule checks for the contents of the processing instruction (`context="/processing-instruction(process)"`). If found, it becomes the context item, and the assertion checks whether its value matches the expected string.

Character entity usage

Notice the two instances of the string " in the test expression. This string is a character entity. Character entities are used to represent characters that, if inserted directly, would be interpreted as operators or delimiters. In this case, " represents a double quote (").

The character entity is necessary here because we want to check for a string that contains double quotes, but the test expression is inside an XML attribute delimited by double quotes. If the test was contains(., 'type="full"'), the XML interpreter would not be able to tell where the attribute value ended. Therefore, we have to write the quotes as character entities.

Here are some common character entities defined in XML:

- > for the greater-than character >
- < for the less-than character <
- & for the ampersand &
- ' for the single quote '

3. The third rule tests for a comment underneath the root element (/*) that contains the word ACMEDATA.

Example 9.21 can still be improved. For instance, when the processing instruction is moved to the end of the document (after the closing </external-data>), it's still considered valid. The same happens when the comment containing ACMEDATA is not the first child of the root element. Adjusting this requires some advanced XPath usage that would distract too much from the purpose of this book.[5]

[5] For the curious, see schematron-book-code-2025/examples/examples-recipes/check-pi-comments-2.sch, which is an improved and annotated example.

Validating doubled elements in mixed content

XML is often used for expressing textual data, like web pages, book contents, etc. This kind of data is called *mixed content*. For example:

```
<p>Hello <i>Schematron</i> lovers!</p>
```

The `<p>` element has children of type text and of type element (the `<i>` element).

One of the things that is very hard to express efficiently in validation languages like DTD, W3C XML Schema, or RELAX NG is *doubled markup*, that is, a situation where an element is nested inside an element of the same name. Here, the `<i>` element is doubled; one `<i>` is nested in another:

```
<p>Hello <i><i>Schematron</i></i> lovers!</p>
```

Here is an example of a doubled `<b>` element, hidden inside a child `<i>` element:

```
<p>Hello <b><i><b>Schematron</b></i></b> lovers!</p>
```

Expressing constraints like "a `<b>` element cannot be a child or a descendant of a `<b>` element" leads to a combinatorial explosion of schema rules in classic validation languages. This in turn leads to enormous and unmaintainable schemas, especially when the number of elements that can be used for marking up text goes up. As a result, doubled markup is usually not checked.

However, Schematron can handle this case using a simple assertion. Suppose you want to check Example 9.22 for doubled `<b>`, `<i>`, and `<u>` elements?

Example 9.22 – Data with a doubled `<b>` element
(`schematron-book-code-2025/data/doubled-elements.xml`)

```
<body>
  <p>Hello <i>you</i>, are you seeing <b><i><b>double</b></i></b>?</p>
</body>
```

The Schematron schema in Example 9.23 checks for these doubled elements.

Example 9.23 – A schema that checks Example 9.22 for doubled elements
(schematron-book-code-2025/examples/examples-recipes/check-doubled-elements-1.sch)

```
<schema xmlns="http://purl.oclc.org/dsdl/schematron" schematronEdition="2025"
  queryBinding="xslt3">

  <group>
    <rule context="i">
      <assert test="not(ancestor::i)">
        You cannot have doubled i elements
      </assert>
    </rule>
    <rule context="u">
      <assert test="not(ancestor::u)">
        You cannot have doubled u elements
      </assert>
    </rule>
    <rule context="b">
      <assert test="not(ancestor::b)">
        You cannot have doubled b elements
      </assert>
    </rule>
  </group>

</schema>
```

The three rules trigger on the elements we want to check. The assertions check whether an element (an ancestor) with the same name occurs between the element we triggered on and the root of the document.

Axis steps

Axis steps are expressions that, starting from a context node, select a related set of nodes. They are written as a name followed by a double colon (e.g., `ancestor::`). Here are some frequently used examples:[6]

- The `ancestor::` axis step selects all ancestors of the context node, up to the document node (its parent, grandparent, and so on).

[6] The XPath standard defines 13 axis steps. You can find an overview at https://www.w3.org/TR/xpath-31/#axes. See https://www.w3schools.com/xml/xpath_axes.asp for another useful list and explanation.

- The `preceding-sibling::` axis step selects all nodes that have the same parent but come before the context node in the document.
- The `following-sibling::` axis step does the same but for the nodes that come after the context node.

You can reduce Example 9.23 to a single rule using the XPath "or" operator (|).[7] XPath interprets `i|u|b` as `<i>` or `<u>` or `<b>`. This enables you to simplify Example 9.23 to Example 9.24:

Example 9.24 – A much shorter version of Example 9.23

(`schematron-book-code-2025/examples/examples-recipes/check-doubled-elements-2.sch`)

```
<schema xmlns="http://purl.oclc.org/dsdl/schematron" schematronEdition="2025"
  queryBinding="xslt3">

  <group>
    <!-- 1 - Trigger on all elements we want to check: -->
    <rule context="i|u|b">
      <!-- 2 - Store the name element that triggered this rule in a
        variable: -->
      <let name="current-element-name" value="local-name(.)"/>
      <!-- 3 - Use this variable to check whether there are any ancestors
        with the same name: -->
      <assert
        test="not(ancestor::*[local-name() eq $current-element-name])">
        You cannot have doubled <value-of select="$current-element-name"/>
        elements
      </assert>
    </rule>
  </group>

</schema>
```

1. Use the single pipe | operator to combine the elements to be checked. Note that this construct makes it easy to expand the list.
2. Store the name of the element that triggered the rule in the variable `current-element-name`.
3. Look for any ancestor element (`ancestor::*`) that has the same name.

---

[7] Officially, this is called the "union" operator, but for the purpose of this example it's easier to think of it as "or."

APPENDIX A

XPath technology primer

To apply Schematron, you need a basic knowledge of the underlying XPath technology. This appendix provides a basic XPath primer. It's mostly useful for beginners, but it can be of value for seasoned programmers in other languages who need to know their way around XPath.

XPath is a truly wonderful invention in the XML world. It's a standard for functions such as selecting data in XML documents or evaluating simple data expressions such as `1 + 2` or `"XP" || "ath"`. But these properties, as nifty as they are, don't make XPath wonderful. What makes XPath stand out is that it is used in every important XML-related language, including XSLT, XQuery, and Schematron. And this means that if you understand XPath, you're already halfway to understanding any XML language!

Schematron relies heavily on XPath, which means that if you want to write Schematron schemas, you will need to understand XPath. This appendix assumes only that you've seen XML and worked with it at least a little.

XPath is a huge subject and could easily fill a book. What I will try to do here is provide you with enough background information to understand the examples in this book. Even this takes a lot of pages! But if you master XPath to this level, writing simple to medium-complex Schematron schemas is definitely within reach. For those that want or need to know more, see the section titled "XPath" (p. 296).

Simplifications...

To prevent newcomers from dropping out, this appendix simplifies XPath quite a bit. I do not describe every nook, cranny, and detail. For instance, I cover only simple tree navigation, and I omit axis specifiers (`preceding-sibling::` etc.), maps, and arrays. I also make no distinction between XPath selection and (XSLT) match expression.

Yes, all of this omitted information is important if you want to master XPath. But to reach the level you need to use Schematron, you don't need to understand the full range of XPath capabilities.

XML as a tree

Trees as used here are concepts from computer science. To work with XML and XPath, you need to start thinking of an XML document as a tree of data.

For those that are new to this I can almost hear you think: "Tree? What tree? I just see text with a lot of angled brackets, not a tree...." Yes, superficially that seems to be the case. But all those angled brackets are just a way to describe a tree-shaped structure. How does this work and why is it important? Let's dive in.

Basic trees: documents, elements, and text

An XPath tree representation is an abstract way of thinking about how XML documents are structured. This abstraction is the basis for the XPath way of navigating XML documents. Let's start our orchard gardening with a very simple example document:

Example A.1 – A very simple XML document

```
<message>Hi there!</message>
```

An abstract tree representation for this document, in the XPath sense, looks like Figure A.1:

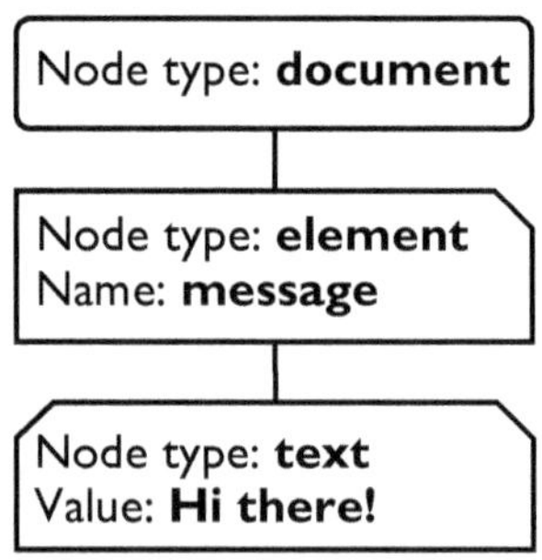

Figure A.1 – The XPath tree representation for Example A.1

Let's take a closer look at the tree in Figure A.1:

- XPath trees are made up of *nodes*: the various shaped boxes in Figure A.1. Our simple XML document in Example A.1 contains three nodes.
- Nodes always have a *type*. The tree in Figure A.1 contains nodes of three types: `document`, `element`, and `text`.
- A node can have other properties, depending on its type. For instance, the node of type `element` has a property called `name` with a value `message`.
- A tree for an XML document always starts with a node of type `document`.
- Every element in an XML document, like `<message>` in Example A.1, becomes a node of type `element`.

  An element always has a property called `name` that holds the name of the element, in this case: `message`.
- Text inside an element becomes a node of type `text`.

  Text nodes have a property called `value` that holds the actual literal text, in this case: `Hi there!`

Let's do this again for a somewhat less simple document:

Example A.2 – A less simple XML document

```
<messages>
  <dutch>
    <message>Hallo daar!</message>
  </dutch>
  <english>
    <message>Hi there!</message>
  </english>
</messages>
```

A tree for this document looks like Example A.2:

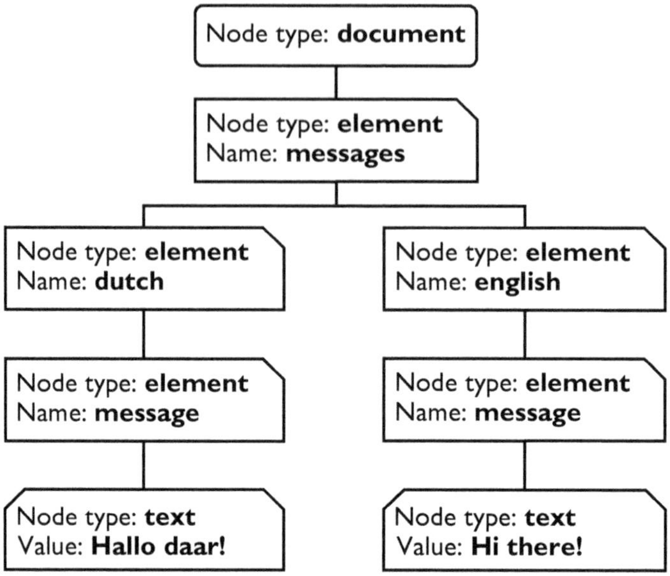

Figure A.2 – The XPath tree representation for Example A.2

- Again there is the starting node of type `document`.
- After that comes the element node for the `<messages>` root element.
- The root element has two element *children*: `<dutch>` and `<english>`. As you can see, the tree splits here and contains a node for each of them.
- The `<dutch>` and `<english>` elements each have a *child* `<message>` element.
- And each `<message>` element has a child node of type `text` that contains the contents.

As was done above, it's customary to talk about relations in such a tree in family terms:

- The `<messages>` element has two *child* nodes: the `<dutch>` and `<english>` elements.
- The *parent* of the `<english>` and `<dutch>` elements is the `<messages>` element.
- The `<dutch>` and `<english>` elements are *siblings*.

If you've never seen representations like this before, it often raises questions:

- **Why doesn't it look like a tree?** It's upside-down! Wouldn't "root system" be a better name?

  Regarding data structures, anything that branches like Figure A.1 and Figure A.2 is called a tree, regardless of how you draw it. Drawing the starting node at the top is just a convention.

- **Where are the closing tags?** For example, where in this tree is the closing `</message>` tag? Shouldn't there be an `element` node with name `/message` as child of the `text` node?

  The answer is no. The closing tag carries no information other than showing the end of an element in the text representation of XML. If you look at the tree representation of Figure A.2 or any XML document, you can see that the structure is clear; the end of the element is implicit in the tree structure. Adding a node for a closing tag would be confusing.

- **Why is there a `document` node?** Any well-formed piece of XML has a single root element only. So for the always-single root element, a parent seems unnecessary.

  Yes, there always is a single root element. But XML has two constructs that are allowed outside the root element: comments (`<!-- ... -->`) and processing instructions (`<?... ...?>`). It is valid to have these as siblings of the root element (before or after). Without a `document` node, you couldn't represent these "outliers" in the tree representation.

Representing comments and processing instructions in the tree

XML documents can also contain comments and processing instructions:

- Comments add information for humans, like `<!-- Start of chapter: -->` or `<!-- Incomplete! Fix this later! -->`
- Processing instructions add instructions for systems that process XML.

Comments and processing instructions are also represented in the tree, using nodes of type `comment` and `processing-instruction`. These node types rarely play a role in Schematron schemas. An example of how to work with them can be found in the section titled "Validating processing instructions and comments" (p. 177).

If you intend to do something with them, a warning: XML documents often start with the so-called *XML header*, for instance:

```
<?xml version="1.0" encoding="UTF-8"?>
```

Such a header is not considered a processing instruction (although it certainly mimics one). Therefore you will not find it in the tree representation of your document.

Attributes in the tree

Our examples so far haven't contained any attributes. How are these represented? The following element, appearing somewhere in a document, contains some:

Example A.3 – An element with some attributes (appearing somewhere in a document)

```
...
  <message class="special" color="red">Hi there!</message>
...
```

An abstract tree representation for this element looks like Figure A.3:

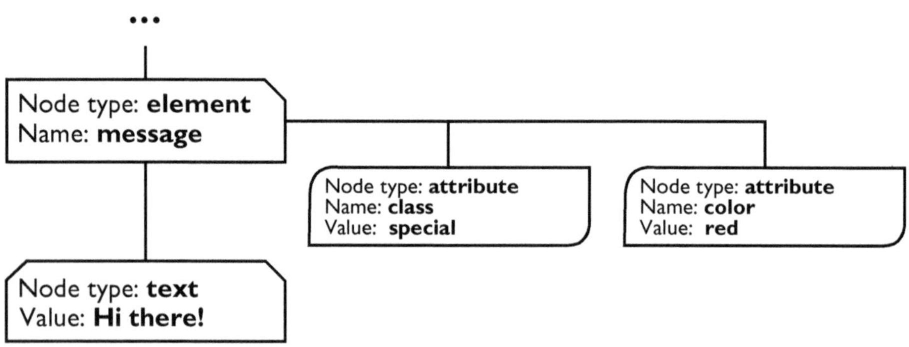

Figure A.3 – The XPath tree representation for Example A.3

Attributes are represented by nodes also. They appear as an offshoot of the element node that they belong to.

- Their node type is (unsurprisingly): `attribute`.
- They have a property `name` which holds the name of the attribute.
- They also have a property called `value` that holds the contents of the attribute.

Some questions that this might raise include:

- Why do attributes have a property that holds their value and not a node of type text, like elements have?

  Very good question, but maybe it should be stated the other way around: why have elements a separate node of type text, instead of a value property? That would make the model simpler, wouldn't it?

  The reason for text in elements being in separate nodes is that you can't represent mixed contents (like <p>hi <i>there</i>!</p>) without using separate nodes.[1] However, the value of an attribute is just a string, a piece of text. So for attribute values the model can be simple and a value property suffices.

- Does the order of the attributes matter?

  The simple answer here is: no. The XML specification says that the order of attributes is insignificant. So <p class="large" id="x123"/> is the same as, and must be processed the same as, <p id="x123" class="large"/>.

  Of course, attributes in a document, and therefore the nodes in the tree representation, are in an unavoidable sequence. But code, whether it is an XSLT stylesheet or a Schematron schema, should never rely on the order of attributes.

Representing mixed content

Mixed contents is XML where text and elements are mingled, for instance:

Example A.4 – An element containing mixed contents (appearing somewhere in a document)

```
...
  <para>This is <bold>OK</bold>!</para>
...
```

You most often encounter this in situations where human readable text needs to be represented in XML, for instance on an (X)HTML page or in book content.

[1] You can find descriptions and examples of mixed content in the section titled "Representing mixed content" (p. 191).

With the node types we've encountered so far it's not difficult to turn Example A.4 into a tree, as shown in Figure A.4.

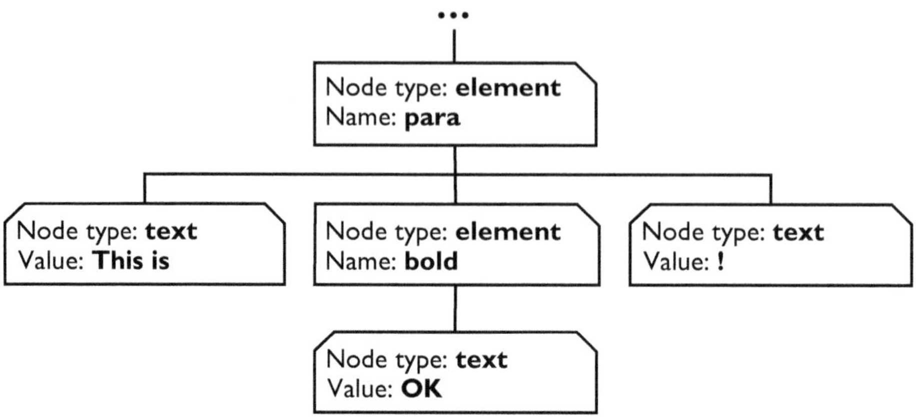

Figure A.4 – The XPath tree representation for Example A.4

It's simply a matter of following the content of the element from left to right:

- A piece of text becomes a text node.
- A nested element, like `<bold>` in Example A.4, becomes a sibling node of type element.
- If this nested element contains something (text, other elements), the tree gets an extra level to represent this.

And so on, and so forth. If there's another nested element, we simply dive deeper:

Example A.5 – An element containing more complex mixed contents (appearing somewhere in a document)

```
...
  <para>This is <bold>OK, <italic>yeah</italic></bold>!</para>
...
```

The tree representation for Example A.5 is shown in Figure A.5.

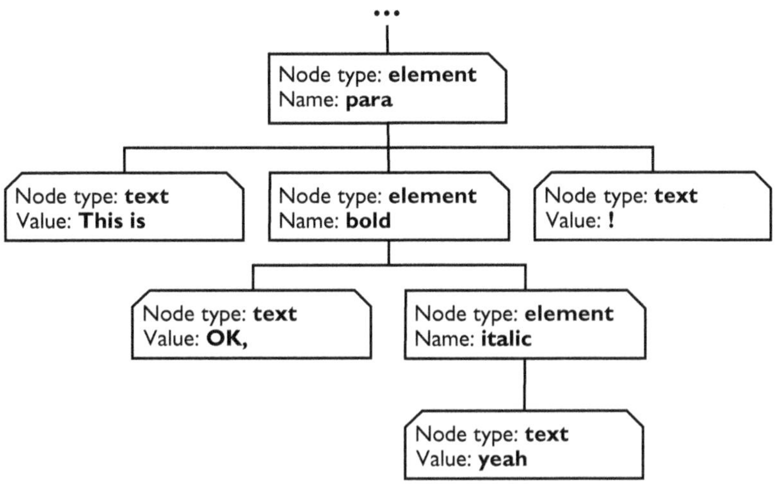

Figure A.5 – The XPath tree representation for Example A.5

Basic tree navigation

I hope that by now you have an idea of how you can view XML documents as abstract tree-shaped structures. But why do you need to know this and how are these structures useful?

Consider Example A.6. Suppose you have a document with messages in various languages (a variation on Example A.2). The document also specifies the color the messages should be displayed in (the `color` attribute) and that English is the default language (the `default` attribute).

Example A.6 – An XML document with human-readable messages (`schematron-book-code-2025/data/basic-messages.xml`)

```
<messages>
  <dutch color="red">
    <message>Hallo daar!</message>
  </dutch>
  <english color="yellow" default="true">
    <message>Hi there!</message>
  </english>
  <french color="purple">
    <message>Salut!</message>
  </french>
</messages>
```

The tree for this document looks like Figure A.6:

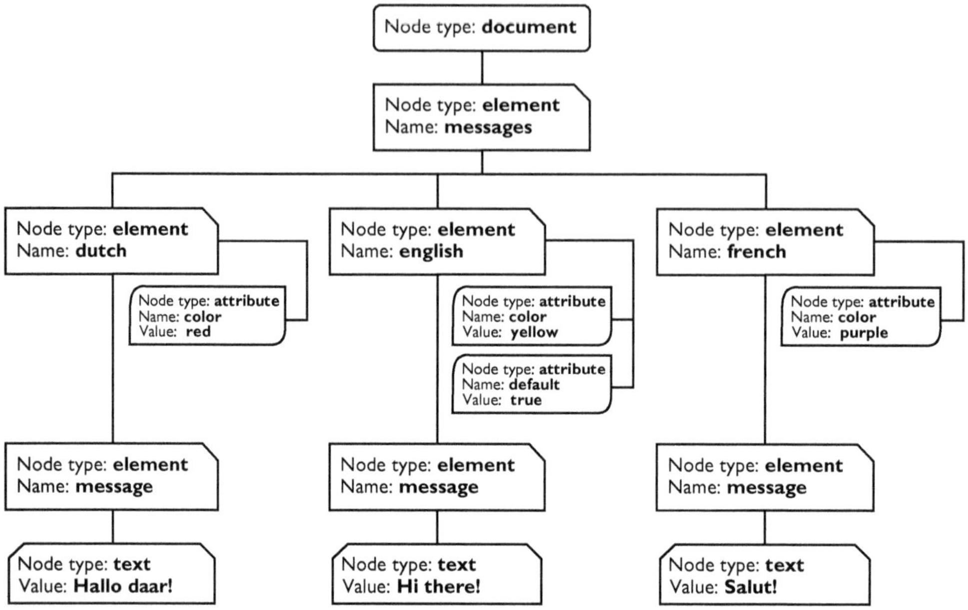

Figure A.6 – The XPath tree representation for Example A.6

Given this document, we want to find the French message. How do you do that using XPath?

Basic XPath tree navigation uses the element names as stepping stones and the slash character / as separator. Using this, the XPath navigation expression to select the French message becomes:

Example A.7 – XPath expression to select the French message in Example A.6)

```
/messages/french/message
```

- The first character is a /, which means we start our journey through this document at its top-level `document` node.
- It then uses the name of the first (root) element in the tree: `messages`.
- Separated by another / comes the language element we want to navigate to: `french`.
- And finally, separated again by a /, the name of the element that holds the actual message: `message`.

If we plot this in the document's tree, it looks like Figure A.7:

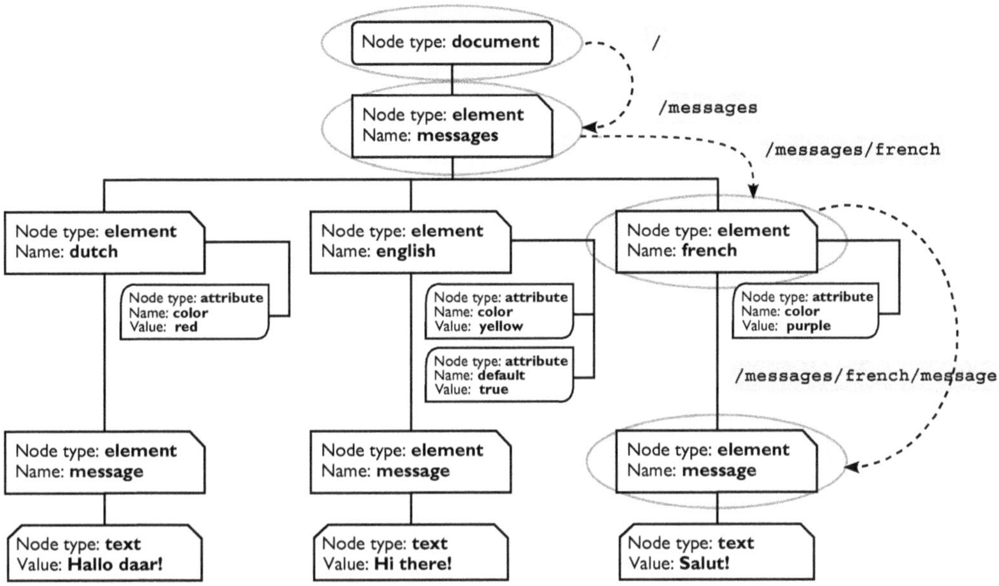

Figure A.7 – The XPath expression `/messages/french/message` shown as a document tree

Tree navigation and file systems...

You might notice a striking similarity with navigating/addressing files and directories in a file system, especially when you're used to Unix- or Linux-based systems with paths like `/home/erik/work/`.... I suppose some inspiration for the XPath design came from this convention.

File/directory paths on Windows look a bit different, using backslashes (\) and drive letters (for instance `C:\users\erik\work\`...), but the idea is the same.

Using navigation expressions

To further illustrate this, let's see how we can actually use these expressions. For example, assume you want to show the French message in an HTML page. In XSLT, a language that relies heavily on XPath, you could write something like Example A.8.

Example A.8 – Using an XPath tree navigation expression in XSLT

```
<p>
  <xsl:value-of select="/messages/french/message"/>
</p>
```

This would result in the HTML code `<p>Salut!</p>`.

Schematron also uses XPath navigation expressions. For instance, to check that the length of the French greeting is not too long you could write a test like that shown in Example A.9 (`lt` means less than).

Example A.9 – Using an XPath tree navigation expression in Schematron

```
<assert test="string-length(/messages/french/message) lt 15">
  French message too long
</assert>
```

The value of elements

Eh, wait a minute, there seems to be something not quite right here! Our XPath expression `/messages/french/message` navigates to an element node. The code in Example A.8 requests the value of this element node. But a node of type `element` does not have a `value` property. What you would think of as its "value" is in its children:

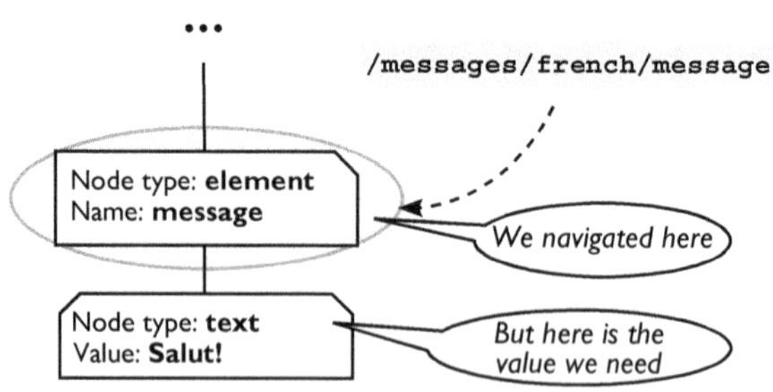

Figure A.8 – The value of a node of type `element`?

The answer to this riddle: if you request the value of an element node, XPath looks down for descendant text nodes and uses their values. Underneath `/message/french/message` is a single text node `Salut!`, so the value of `/message/french/message` is also `Salut!`.

A (useful) gotcha here is that XPath does not look only at the direct children, it looks all the way down in the tree. It searches for all descendant text nodes and concatenates them. This is helpful when you're working with mixed text.

For example, the value of `<para>Hello <b>there</b>!</para>` is, as you would expect, the concatenation of all text nodes: `Hello there!` (the `<b>` element has disappeared). But it can also easily lead to mistakes like accidentally asking for the value of `/messages`, which is the, not very helpful, `Hallo daar!Hi there!Salut!`.

Since XPath looks at all descendant text nodes when it computes the value of an element node, this means that, in our example, the value of `/messages/french` is the same as the value of `/messages/french/message`. However, it is good practice to navigate as close as possible to the node you're interested in. This prevents problems if the document changes (for example, consider what would happen if you used `/messages/french` and the `<french>` element gets another child element with text).

Basic navigation to attributes

Now, what if you want to retrieve an attribute value from our tree? For instance, how do you retrieve the value of the `color` attribute for the French language.

An attribute in XPath is addressed using the `@` sign, followed by the name of the attribute. So to get the color of the French message you could write:

```
/messages/french/@color
```

Multiple selections: sequences

An XPath navigation expression can return more than a single node. In fact, an expression may return multiple nodes or no nodes at all. For instance, consider Example A.10, which is a variation of Example A.6, and you apply this XPath expression: `/messages/message`:

Example A.10 – An XML document with human-readable messages (variation of Example A.6)

```
<messages>
  <message language="nl">Hallo daar!</message>
  <message language="en">Hi there!</message>
  <message language="fr">Salut!</message>
</messages>
```

Since XPath cannot guess which message you want, it addresses all three `<message>` elements in the document. If you use the original XPath expression, `/messages/french/message`, it addresses none, since `<messages>` has no child element named `<french>`.

That the answer to an expression can yield multiple (or no) results is actually an important XPath feature, called *sequences*. Every XPath expression always results in a sequence of answers, with none, one, or multiple results.

This is important because you can do lots of wonderful things with sequences. For instance: The XPath `count()` function returns the number of members in a sequence. So to check whether there are exactly three messages in Example A.10 with Schematron, you could write (`eq` means equal to):

Example A.11 – Checking how many members a sequence has in Schematron

```
<assert test="count(/messages/message) eq 3">
  There must be exactly three messages!
</assert>
```

Sequences and expressions on simple data

Expressions on simple data (see the section titled "Expressions on simple data" (p. 210)), such as numbers and strings, also work with sequences. For basic operations, you may not notice this. For instance, `1 + 2` has the (single) answer `3`, and concatenating two strings, like in `'XP' || 'ath'` yields the single answer `'XPath'`.

However, working with sequences is a useful tool to have in your toolbox. For instance, in Example A.11 suppose you want to check whether the value of a `language` attribute is one of Dutch, English, or French. You could express this in XPath as:

Example A.12 – An XPath expression that uses a sequence of strings in a comparison

```
@language = ('en', 'nl', 'fr')
```

The code `('nl', 'en', 'fr')` constructs a sequence of strings. The expression in Example A.12 asks whether the value of a `language` attribute is a member of this sequence. For all `language` attributes in Example A.11 this will return `true`.

Tree navigation and the context item

In the previous section we navigated the tree by starting at the top-level document node. Such a navigation expression always begins with the / character.

XPath also allows you to navigate the tree starting anywhere. Such a starting point within the tree is called the *context item*. Navigation expressions that start at the context item do not begin with the / character. This is a useful feature because it allows you to navigate the tree without having to know exactly where you are. Expressions become reusable.

The context item can be referenced or addressed using the dot operator . (see also the section titled "The context item single dot . operator" (p. 201)).

What determines the location of the context item in the tree? The answer to this lies not in XPath but in the language it's embedded in. As explained at the beginning of this appendix, XPath never stands on its own. It's always used as part of some other programming language. For instance, both XSLT and Schematron use XPath as the language for expressions and tree navigation. Each language has a different mechanism for determining the context item.

XSLT and the context item

XSLT's main mechanism for setting the context item is called *template matching*. Example A.13 shows a basic example.

Example A.13 – Example of setting and using the context item in XSLT

```
<xsl:template match="message">
  <p>
    <xsl:value-of select="."/>
  </p>
</xsl:template>
```

This piece of XSLT matches any `<message>` element in the document (because of the `match="message"` attribute). When your XSLT program encounters a `<message>` element, the code inside the `<xsl:template>` is executed. This will produce a `<p>` element containing the value of the context item. The context item itself is referenced with the dot character (`select="."`).

For instance, the result when the XSLT program encounters the French message is:
`<p>Salut!</p>`

To keep Example A.13 simple, I intentionally left-out the details of what the rest of the XSLT program looks like. XSLT template matching needs a careful program structure that is beyond the scope of this book.

Schematron and the context item

In Schematron, you set the context item using the `context` attribute of the `<rule>` element. Example A.14 checks whether all messages are less than 10 characters long (`lt` means less than).

Example A.14 – Basic usage of the context item in Schematron
(schematron-book-code-2025/examples/technology-primer/check-messages-1.sch)

```
<schema xmlns="http://purl.oclc.org/dsdl/schematron" schematronEdition="2025"
  queryBinding="xslt3">

  <pattern>

    <rule context="message">
      <assert test="string-length(.) lt 10">
        The message <value-of select="."/> is too long!
      </assert>
    </rule>

  </pattern>
</schema>
```

- The `<rule context="message">` element triggers on every `<message>` element in the document. So when validating Example A.6 it triggers three times.
- Every time it triggers, the `context="message"` attribute makes the `<message>` element it triggered on the context item.
- It then uses the context item dot operator to check the length of the message: `string-length(.) lt 10` (we'll get to strings and string-functions later on).
- It uses the context dot operator again to insert the value of the too long message into the result: `<value-of select=".">`.
- As a result, the Dutch message will be reported as failing this test: **`The message Hallo daar! is too long!`**.

The way Schematron works with context items shows their power. If this mechanism wasn't available, we would have to write a lot more code to make things happen and would be dependent on the structure of our input document. For example, consider Example A.15.

Example A.15 – Example A.14 implemented without using the context item

```
<?xml version="1.0" encoding="UTF-8"?>
<schema xmlns="http://purl.oclc.org/dsdl/schematron" queryBinding="xslt3">
  <pattern>

    <rule context="/messages/dutch/message">
      <assert test="string-length(/messages/dutch/message) lt 10">
        The message <value-of select="/messages/dutch/message"/> is too long!
      </assert>
    </rule>

    … rule repeated for all languages in the input document …

  </pattern>
</schema>
```

Think about what would happen to Example A.15 as more languages are added over time: every time you added a new language, you would need to add a new rule. This would quickly become an unmaintainable software nightmare!

Some special operators

Now that I've introduced the concepts of XPath navigation expressions, sequences, and the context item, it's time to introduce a few additional common XPath operators.

The context item single dot . operator

Both Example A.13 and Example A.14 already used the single dot . operator. This operator always refers to the context item. That's all there is to it.

Referring to children of the context item

Starting at the context item you can, of course, refer to its children. For instance, assume the context item is the element `<message color="red">`, and you want to get the value of the `color` attribute. How can you do that?

One approach is this: "This context item element can be referred with a dot. We want to get to one of its children, an attribute. So I have to write a dot, a slash and then an `@` followed by the name of the attribute" `./@color`. This is correct and it works.

However, XPath allows you to shorten expressions that start at the context item. Writing the starting `./` is optional. So in our example, `./@color` can be shortened to `@color`. This is also correct and it still works.

Not writing a leading `./` is very common. In the vast majority of cases it is omitted.

The parent double dot .. operator

The double dot `..` operator refers to the parent node. For example, assume the context item is the `type` attribute of the following XML element:

Example A.16 – An XML element to illustrate the parent double dot `..` operator on

```
<thing type="X23" code="123-456"/>
```

For this example, let's create a rule that says that a type element must start with the letter `C`. In the Schematron error message for this we want to display the value of the `code` attribute. The parent double dot `..` operator allows us to do this, as shown in Example A.17.

Example A.17 – Using the double dot `..` operator to get the value of another attribute

```
<rule context="@type">
  <assert test="starts-with(., 'C')">
    Invalid type for code <value-of select="../@code"/>: <value-of select="."/>
  </assert>
</rule>
```

- The `<rule context="@type">` element sets the context item to the `type` attribute.
- The `<assert test="starts-with(., 'C')>` tests whether this starts with a capital `C` (in Example A.16 it does not).
- The `<value-of select="../@code">` starts its tree traversal at the context item (the `type` attribute). So we could have written `./../@code`, but as explained in the section titled "The context item single dot `.` operator" (p. 201), the leading `./` is superfluous.
- Then it goes up to its parent, the `<thing>` element, using the double dot `..` operator.
- From there it goes down again to the `code` attribute.

The result of applying Example A.17 to Example A.16 is the error message:

```
Invalid type for code 123-456: X23
```

The `*` and `@*` wildcard operators

The wildcard `*` operator refers to any child element. Since a wildcard can return more than one result, it is a typical application of XPath sequences. Let's try this out on Example A.6, which is repeated below in Example A.18.

Example A.18 – Example A.6 repeated.
(`schematron-book-code-2025/data/basic-messages.xml`)

```
<messages>
  <dutch color="red">
    <message>Hallo daar!</message>
  </dutch>
  <english color="yellow" default="true">
    <message>Hi there!</message>
  </english>
  <french color="purple">
    <message>Salut!</message>
  </french>
</messages>
```

- The XPath expression `/messages/*` results in a sequence of three results: the elements `<dutch>`, `<english>`, and `<french>`.
- To access the underlying `<message>` elements, you could write `/messages/*/message`. This gives you three `<message>` elements, one for each language.

> **Addressing the root element as `/*`**
>
> XML prescribes that a document has exactly one root element (in Example A.18 this is `<messages>`). Being lazy, this means we could write the previous two examples as `/*/*` and `/*/*/message`.
>
> This may feel like a misuse of the wildcard operator. There's only one root element and its name is known, so why not write it in full. Well, since programmers tend to be stingy with keystrokes, you'll often see XPath expressions start with `/*` where the root element is meant.
>
> Another reason for using `/*` to address the root element is that some XML dialects have more than one root element with (roughly) the same type of contents. For instance, DocBook (a standard for writing texts) allows `<book>`, `<article>`, and several other elements to be root elements. Using `/*` let's you address any of them.

As you might have guessed there's also a wildcard operator for attributes: `@*`. For example, the expression `/messages/english/@*` returns two attributes: `color="yellow"` and `default="true"`.

Wildcard operators are often used in conjunction with predicates. You can find more information about this in the section titled "Predicates in tree navigation" (p. 205).

The "search" // operator

Although that's not its official name, the `//` operator acts like a search. For instance, `//english` will return the `<english>` element, no matter where it is in the document. So even when Example A.18 is embedded somewhere in a much larger XML structure, `//english` will return the right element.

That is to say… it works fine on Example A.18, but for other documents it could just as well return none or multiple `<english>` elements. Be careful what you wish for and know your document structure before using it.

Some important details:

- Starting an XPath expression with // always starts searching at the very beginning, at the document node.
- To start your search from the context item, you must start your expression with .//

  For instance, if the `<english>` element is the context item, writing `.//message` will return the underlying `<message>` element, even if, maybe in a future version of the document, it's no longer a direct child.
- You can also use the // operator in the middle of an XPath expression. For instance, to search for any `<english>` element that is not the root element, you could write `/messages//english` (or `/*//english`).
- It is also possible to search for attributes. As you might have guessed, writing //@ followed by the attribute's name does the trick.

Predicates in tree navigation

The last concept I want to introduce is *predicates*. Predicates are filters, applied during the tree traversal. To illustrate this, let's go back to Example A.6, repeated here in Example A.19.

Example A.19 – Example A.6 repeated.
(`schematron-book-code-2025/data/basic-messages.xml`)

```
<messages>
  <dutch color="red">
    <message>Hallo daar!</message>
  </dutch>
  <english color="yellow" default="true">
    <message>Hi there!</message>
  </english>
  <french color="purple">
    <message>Salut!</message>
  </french>
</messages>
```

Assume we need the message in the default language. We don't know which one that is, but we do know that this language's element has the attribute `default="true"`. Example A.20 is an XPath tree navigation expression that gives us the default language:

Example A.20 – Getting the default language in Example A.19 using a predicate

```
/messages/*[@default eq 'true']/message
```

The part between the square brackets, `[@default eq 'true']` is a predicate. The operator `eq` means equal to, so this predicate tests for an attribute named `default` with a value equal to `true`. Let's see what exactly is happening here:

- With what we already know about tree navigation expressions, the first part of Example A.20, `/messages/*`, holds no surprises. It returns a sequence of three elements: `<dutch>`, `<english>`, and `<french>` (Figure A.9).

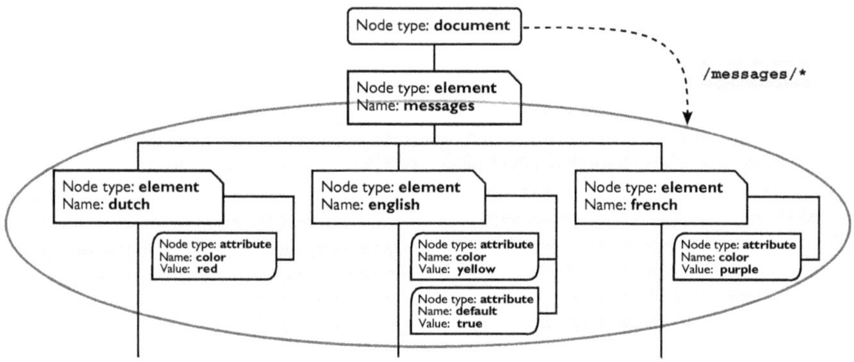

Figure A.9 – `/messages/*` applied to the (partial) tree representation of Example A.19

- Then the predicate `[@default eq 'true']` kicks in. This expression is held against all members of the sequence:
  - For `<dutch>` and `<french>` the result of this expression is `false`: these elements have no attribute `default="true"`. Because of this, these elements are dismissed.
  - However, for the `<english>` element the predicate is `true`: this element does have an attribute `default="true"`. So this element is kept.

  As a result, the sequence returned by `/messages/*` is reduced, only the `<english>` element remains. In other words: the predicate acted as a filter on what came before (Figure A.10).

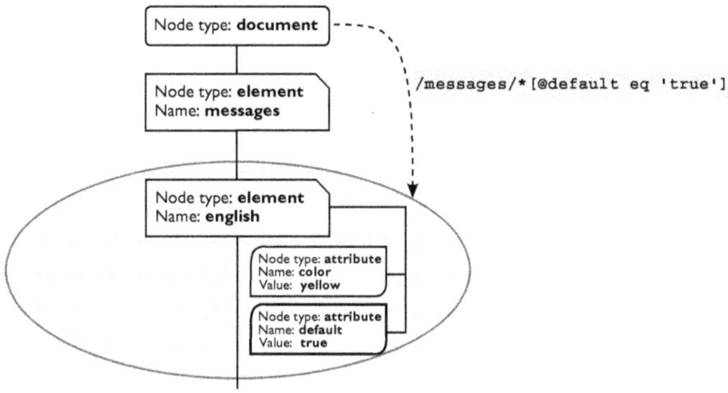

Figure A.10 – `/messages/*[@default eq 'true']` applied to the (partial) tree representation of Example A.19

- The final part of the original XPath expression in Example A.20, `/message` now only has to deal with this single remaining `<english>` element and returns the correct `<message>` element: `<message>Hi there!</message>` (Figure A.11).

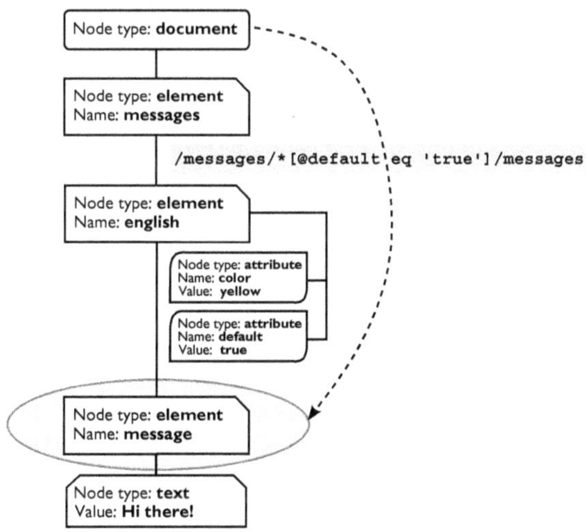

Figure A.11 – `/messages/*[@default eq 'true']/message` applied to the tree representation of Example A.19

A useful mnemonic when thinking about predicates is the words "for which," as in: Give me the elements `/messages/*` *for which* the expression `@default eq 'true'` holds.

Predicates and the context item

In the section titled "Tree navigation and the context item" (p. 199), I talked about the context item and how it allows You to write relative XPath navigation expressions (ones that do not start with a `/`).

Observant readers might already have noticed that this is also what we do in the predicate of Example A.20: `@default` is a relative XPath navigation expression: it selects the `default` attribute of the current context item.

What happens here is that, when a predicate is evaluated, the context item is always the node the predicate is applied on. So for our example, the context item will first be the `<dutch>` element, then `<english>`, and finally `<french>`.

A frequently used application of predicates is to get the nth element of a sequence. Assume you want the first message in Example A.19. This can be arranged as follows:

Example A.21 – Getting the first language in Example A.19 using a predicate

```
/messages/*[1]/message
```

The `[1]` predicate filters out all but the first element in the `/messages/*` sequence, leaving only the `<dutch>` element.

For more elaborate predicate filtering based on the position of nodes in a sequence you can use the functions `position()` and `last()`:

- The `position()` function returns the position of the node in the sequence. For the first node it returns `1`, for the second `2`, and so on.

  So, for instance, to get a sequence with the first two messages, you can write (`le` means less than or equal to):

  Example A.22 – Getting the first two messages in Example A.19 using a predicate

  ```
  /messages/*[position() le 2]/message
  ```

Positional syntactic sugar

Strictly speaking, Example A.21, which gets the first message, should be written as:

```
/messages/*[position() eq 1]/message
```

The simpler predicate notation `[1]` is called "syntactic sugar": an easier way of stating frequently occurring expressions. XPath silently rewrites this to `[position() eq 1]`. Using the shorter form shown in Example A.21 is so common that most people probably don't even realize its sugar level...

- The `last()` function returns the number of nodes in the sequence (which is also the position of the last one, therefore `last()`). So to get the last message of Example A.19:

  Example A.23 – Getting the last message in Example A.19 using a predicate with the `last()` function

  ```
  /messages/*[last()]/message
  ```

  Or (waiving the syntactic sugar):

  Example A.24 – Getting the last message in Example A.19 using a predicate with the `position()` and `last()` functions

  ```
  /messages/*[position() eq last()]/message
  ```

Predicates are enormously useful in navigating XML trees and you'll see and use them a lot. For instance, the Schematron fragment in Example A.25 uses the expression from Example A.20 to get to the message in the default language. After this, it checks whether this message is too long (`lt` means less than).

Example A.25 – A Schematron rule that uses a predicate

```
<rule context="/messages/*[@default eq 'true']/message">
  <assert test="string-length(.) lt 25">
    The default message is too long!
  </assert>
</rule>
```

To wrap up, here are a few questions you may still have about predicates:

- **What if a predicate filters out all nodes?** In that case the result of the predicate is an empty sequence and the result of the full XPath expression will also be empty. For instance, the following XPath expression tries to find a brown message, and since there's no such thing in Example A.19, the result of the expression will be empty:
  `/messages/*[@color eq 'brown']/message`
- **Can you use predicates on predicates?** Absolutely. For instance, suppose you need a single red message but aren't sure there is only one in the XML. In that case you could decide that the first one will do. The following XPath expression first selects all red messages and then selects the first red message by applying another predicate:
  `/messages/*[@color eq 'red'][1]/message`
- **How complex can predicates become?** Very. All tricks in the XPath book are allowed. For instance, it's entirely possible, and not uncommon, to use expressions with predicates inside a predicate. Because this is a primer, I won't go into any details, but the sky and your imagination are the limit.

Expressions on simple data

The previous sections of this technology primer explained how you can use XPath to navigate through an XML document. XPath tree navigation expressions are what most people think of as "doing XPath."

However, XPath can also handle more mundane programming jobs, such as working with text, numerical computations, or making comparisons. For example, if you want to calculate `2 + 3` or the sine of `3.14`, or you need the first three characters of a piece of text, XPath can handle it.

Once you get a little beyond the basics, you need at least some knowledge about these capabilities. Therefore, I end this technology primer with a discussion of how to work with data types like strings (text) and numbers. I also talk about performing comparisons (Boolean expressions).

At the end, in the section titled "Working with dates, times and durations" (p. 226), I describe how to work with dates, times, and durations. This is a bit more exotic, but Schematron schemas often deal with comparisons such as "is this date `n` days before that date," etc. If this isn't applicable to your schemas you can skip this, but in case you need it, it's there.

The XPath function library

XPath has an extensive library of functions. Functions can compute all kinds of things for you, from the length of a piece of text, `string-length(...)`, to rounding a number to the nearest integer, `round(...)`. Although the coming sections will cover some of these functions, it's impossible to discuss them all here. There are simply too many.

Here are two web pages I recommend for more information:

- **https://www.w3schools.com/xml/xsl_functions.asp** provides an overview with simple examples. Unfortunately, this page is for a previous version of XPath (2.0), and it doesn't contain the extensions introduced in newer versions (as of this writing, we're now at 3.1). Although incomplete, this page is a useful resource for the most commonly used functions.
- **https://www.w3.org/TR/xpath-functions-31/** covers XPath 3.1 and lists all of the functions. However, this is an official standards page, which contains a lot of information and uses formal language that might not make sense to a beginner. Please don't let this keep you from using this resource; it is a valuable source of information.

Both pages order the information by the kind of data the functions are working on. For example, you can find text (string) functions here: https://www.w3schools.com/xml/xsl_functions.asp#string and here: https://www.w3.org/TR/xpath-functions-31/#string-functions. If you're looking for something, go to the right section and look at the function names. Most likely that will be enough to help you find what you need.

What's the `fn:` doing in front of the function names?

Both information sources list the function names with an `fn:` prefix, for instance `fn:string-length`. What does this mean and why isn't this used in the examples throughout this book?

Let me reassure you first: you don't have to write the `fn:` prefix, it's entirely optional.

But then, what is it doing there? XPath functions must be in an XML namespace (namespaces are explained in Appendix B). For the standard XPath functions this namespace is `http://www.w3.org/2005/xpath-functions`, usually denoted by the prefix `fn:`. But this is also the default namespace for functions, so using a namespace prefix on a standard function is not necessary.

XPath data types

To handle data correctly, computer languages attach a *data type* to a piece of data. Computers need to know whether something is, for instance, a number, string, boolean, or date and, if it's a number, whether it's an integer or decimal number. The collection of data types a particular computer language works with is called its *type system.*

XPath has a rather elaborate type system:

- It works with XML, so it contains types like documents, elements, and attributes. These types are called *nodes*. Working with nodes is what the previous sections about navigating the tree were all about.
- It can handle "simple" data like numbers, strings, and booleans. The XPath type system calls these *atomic types*. The basics of these will be covered in the coming sections.
- It also has two more advanced data types, maps and arrays, which I do not cover here.

Data types galore

XPath has an astonishing number of atomic data types (over 40): numbers (in several flavors), strings, booleans, dates, times, durations, and more. In addition, some of these types have subtypes.

For instance, integers have subtypes for various number ranges. Floating point data types (numbers with decimals) come in several precisions. Strings have subtypes for things like names and URIs. Even durations (stretches of time) have two variants.

Fortunately, in practice, it is usually not that complicated. You only need a few. In most cases you don't even have to be aware that things like data types play a role.

Table A.1 describes the most common data types:

Table A.1 – XPath common data types

Name	Description	Example
`xs:string`	A string of characters, aka a piece of text.	`'Schematron rocks!'`
`xs:integer`	An integer number.	`16` `-267,801`

Name	Description	Example
xs:double	A floating point number (a number with decimals). Use this for numbers on a continuous scale (for example, weights, distances, or temperatures). It's possible to use exponential notation, using the E character: 1E3 is 1,000 and -2E-4 is -0.0002. Due to the way an xs:double is stored in computer memory, small rounding errors can occur. To avoid rounding errors use the less efficient but more precise data type: xs:decimal.	16.688999 -1.1E3
xs:decimal	A floating point number (a number with decimals) with accurate precision. With floating point numbers, such as xs:double, rounding sometimes causes minor decimal deviations. This does not happen for the xs:decimal data type. Therefore, use this type for discrete quantities, like sums of money.	16.23 1.00001
xs:date xs:time xs:dateTime	Dates, times, and the combination of these. See the section titled "Working with dates, times and durations" (p. 226).	2025-01-01 12:01:34.897 2025-01-17T09:59:36
xs:dayTimeDuration	A duration or period (stretch of time), expressed in days, hours, minutes, seconds, and fractions of a second. See the section titled "Working with dates, times and durations" (p. 226).	P3DT6M PT1M1.1S

What's this `xs:` in front of the type names?

XPath borrows its type system from the XML Schema language. The XML Schema language defines an XML namespace `http://www.w3.org/2001/XMLSchema`. This namespace is, in most cases, referenced with the prefix `xs:`. Therefore, XPath (atomic) type names are usually written using an `xs:` prefix.

Your Schematron processor may or may not pre-define this namespace prefix. If it doesn't, you'll get an error message about a missing namespace declaration when using type names like `xs:string` or `xs:boolean`.

To avoid this, explicitly add the namespace declaration for the `xs` namespace prefix to your schema:

```
<ns prefix="xs" uri="http://www.w3.org/2001/XMLSchema"/>
```

Some other XML programming languages, like XSLT, also require that you define the XML Schema namespace with the right prefix explicitly. So if you get error messages about an undeclared `xs:` prefix, add the following attribute to the root element:

```
xmlns:xs="http://www.w3.org/2001/XMLSchema"
```

For instance, for XSLT:

```
<xsl:stylesheet xmlns:xsl="http://www.w3.org/1999/XSL/Transform"
  xmlns:xs="http://www.w3.org/2001/XMLSchema" ...>
```

XML programming languages based on XPath differ in how they work with data types. For example, XSLT and XQuery allow you to specify data types explicitly when you declare a variable or parameter. Schematron, on the other hand, doesn't. When you create a variable using the `<let>` element, its data type is automatically inferred from its value, which is usually OK but not always. The next section explains the why and how of more precise data typing.

Explicit data typing and data type conversions

There are situations where you need to be explicit about the data type you're handling. For instance, assume an attribute has a numerical value:

Example A.26 – An attribute `count` with a numerical value

```
<things count="3">
```

Now assume we want to make sure there are exactly three things. A Schematron schema fragment that at first sight looks like it performs this check is:

Example A.27 – Comparing a numerical value in Schematron (incorrect)

```
<rule context="things">
  <assert test="@count eq 3">There must be 3 things!</assert>
</rule>
```

When you run this, an error message will pop-up saying: `Cannot compare xs:untypedAtomic to xs:integer`. XPath does not know what to make of the attribute's value and gives up. The solution is to tell XPath explicitly what type the attribute is supposed to be. This can easily be done: use the type's name as a function, as shown in Example A.28.

Example A.28 – Comparing a numerical value in Schematron (Example A.27 corrected)

```
<rule context="things">
  <assert test="xs:integer(@count) eq 3">There must be 3 things!</assert>
</rule>
```

There's an additional benefit here: by telling XPath it must consider a value to be an integer, values that we humans think of as 3, like `"03"`, `"000003"`, or `"   3"`, are all considered `3`.

The only data type XPath can compare directly in situations like this is string (`xs:string`). So you could rewrite Example A.28 as Example A.29.

Example A.29 – Comparing an attribute's value as a string

```
<rule context="things">
  <assert test="@count eq '3'">There must be 3 things!</assert>
</rule>
```

This will work for Example A.26, but it dismisses values written like `"03"` or `"  3"`. Therefore, if you use a value other than a string for a comparison or calculation, explicitly type the value using the data type's name as a function (as in Example A.28).

Numerical expressions

XPath has numerical expressions, just like other computer languages. They usually work as expected: `2+3` yields `5` and `12*5.1+7.3` yields `68.5`. However, here are a few things to know:

- The subtraction operator is the hyphen (`-`), as in most computer languages. But since a hyphen is a valid character in an XPath name (for instance, a variable, element, or attribute name), XPath doesn't always know what to do.

  For example, `30-2` works and yields `28`. However, if you have a variable `$a` with value `30`, `$a-2` will not work. XPath assumes you mean a variable named `$a-2`, which, even if such a variable exists, is probably not what you intended. To solve this, surround the hyphen with spaces and write `$a - 2` instead. This makes your code unambiguous.

- The usual division operator in most computer languages is the slash character `/`. However, in XPath the slash character is already used as an operator in XPath navigation expressions (like `/messages/dutch/@color`). Therefore, XPath uses the word `div` for division. For instance, `4 div 2` is `2` and `10 div 4` is `2.5`.

  XPath also has an integer division operator, written as `idiv`. This will throw away all decimals and always return an integer result. So `10 idiv 4` is `2` and `10 idiv 6` is `1`.

There are also functions that work on numerical data. For instance `round()` rounds a number to the nearest integer. Please refer to the section titled "The XPath function library" (p. 211) to learn how to find these functions.

String expressions

Strings are pieces of text, or sequences of characters if you prefer. As with most computer languages, a string constant is written between quotes, for example, `'XPath'` or `'John Doe'`. You can use single or double quotes, so `"XPath"` and `"John Doe"` are also correct.

However, XPath expressions, including string constants, are very often written as attribute values, and attribute values must be surrounded by quotes. This requires you to use quotes within quotes. For instance, setting a Schematron variable to a constant string value looks like Example A.30.

Example A.30 – A string constant as an XPath expression, using quotes within quotes.

```
<let name="firstname" value="'John'"/>
```

The double quotes in `value="'John'"` delineate the attribute value, the single quotes the string constant within.

Quoting the other way around

It's not very common, but you can use single quotes to delineate attribute values. With this, Example A.30 becomes:

Example A.31 – Writing Example A.30 with the quotes the other way around.

```
<let name='firstname' value='"John"'/>
```

To concatenate strings, use the "double pipe" operator `||`. For instance, assume you have two name variables, `$firstname` and `$lastname`, and you want to turn these into a full name in Schematron. Example A.32 shows how to do this.

Example A.32 – Concatenating strings using the `||` operator.

```
<let name="fullname" value="$firstname || ' ' || $lastname"/>
```

Concatenating strings for older versions of XPath

The `||` operator was introduced in version 3.0 of XPath. If you're using an older version, Example A.32 will not fly. Use the `concat()` function instead (Example A.33).

Example A.33 – Concatenating strings using the `concat()` function.

```
<let name="fullname" value="concat($firstname, ' ', $lastname)"/>
```

There are a lot of standard functions for working with strings (see the section titled "The XPath function library" (p. 211)). Here are a few noteworthy examples:

- The `substring()` function returns part of a string: `substring('abcdefg', 3, 2)` returns `'cd'`. The second argument, `3`, is the starting position and the third argument, `2`, the length of the required substring. If you omit the third argument you get the remainder of the string, so `substring('abcdefg', 3)` returns `'cdefg'`.

> Programmers, be aware that, unlike languages such as C and Java, indexing in XPath always starts at `1`, not at `0` (everywhere, not only here). So to get the first character of a string write `substring(..., 1, 1)`, not `substring(..., 0, 1)`.

- The `string-length()` function returns a string's length. So `string-length('abc')` returns `3`.
- the `upper-case()` and `lower-case()` functions convert the case of a string. For example, `upper-case('XPath')` returns `'XPATH'` and `lower-case('XPath')` returns `'xpath'`.
- The `normalize-space()` function, which is remarkably useful, takes a string and "normalizes" the whitespace characters (spaces, tabs, newlines, etc.). It removes all leading and trailing whitespace and replaces all sequences of whitespace characters inside the string with a single space. For example, `normalize-space('  XPath   3.0 ')` returns `'XPath 3.0'`.

  One reason this function is so useful is that it can make your code resilient against inadvertent but common typos. If you accidentally type `<code>XZY6 </code>` instead of `<code>XZY6</code>`, a comparison of this code value to `'XZY6'` will fail. Doing a `normalize-space()` on the code value makes comparisons more robust: `normalize-space(code) eq 'XZY6'` will work whether or not there are additional leading or trailing spaces.

  `normalize-space()` is also often handy to correct problems caused by the pretty-printing feature of XML editors. The pretty-print feature can break text into multiple lines, as shown in Example A.34.

  Example A.34 – A long value broken into multiple lines by the editor's pretty-printing feature.

```
<para>Something typed on a single line but broken
  into multiple lines by the pretty-printing feature of
  the editor.</para>
```

  Performing a `normalize-space()` on the value of the `<para>` element in Example A.34 removes all of the additional whitespace.

  Of course, be careful applying `normalize-space()`. Sometimes whitespace is important!

Regular expressions

XPath also contains functions for working with regular expressions, *regexps* for short. Regexps are strings that perform pattern matching on other strings. It's a complex technology, too complicated to fully cover here. For the curious there's an excellent Wikipedia page: https://en.wikipedia.org/wiki/Regular_expression.

Here's a simple example. The regexp `'[^0-9]'` matches all characters in a string that are not numbers. You can replace all non-numbers with hyphens using the XPath `replace()` function: `replace('88A|B99', '[^0-9]', '-')` yields `'88---99'`.

Boolean expressions and comparisons

Boolean expressions are all about making decisions in your code. As an example, let's look back at the <assert> element in Example A.14, repeated in Example A.35.

Example A.35 – A Schematron assert using a boolean expression

```
<assert test="string-length(.) lt 10">
  The message <value-of select="."/> is too long!
</assert>
```

The expression in the `test` attribute of the <assert> element, `string-length(.) lt 10`, tests whether the string length of the context item is less than 10 characters. The result is a boolean expression: either `true` or `false`.

Boolean expressions are commonly used to compare two values, as shown in Example A.35. The value comparison operators in XPath are shown in Table A.2.

Table A.2 – XPath value comparison operators

Operator	Meaning	Example
`eq`	Equal	`$code eq 'XQZ56'`
`ne`	Not equal	`$code ne 'XQZ56'`
`lt`	Less than	`string-length($code) lt 12`
`le`	Less than or equal to	`$number-of-references le 100`

Operator	Meaning	Example
gt	Greater than	$author-count gt 0
ge	Greater than or equal to	count(//message) ge 3

Where are > and the <?

If you have used other languages, you might expect comparison operators to be written using symbols: = for equal and > for greater than, etc. And if you try this in XPath expressions, it will work.... What's happening here?

XPath has a second set of comparison operators for so-called "general comparisons." These are =, !=, >, >=, < and <=. General comparisons are considerably more powerful than the value expressions in Table A.2. They can, for instance, compare sequences, while value comparisons can only compare single values.

That sounds like an advantage, but it has downsides, including the following:

- Comparing values using general comparisons is more expensive.
- Writing (and reading) them can be awkward, because < is a reserved character in XML and must be written as < For example, count(//messages) <= 3. Just typing/reading le instead of <= is much easier. Strictly speaking, the > character does not need to be written as >. However, this is often done also.
- The exact rules for general comparisons are complicated and can lead to situations where they don't provide the answer you expect. There are even circumstances where a = b is true and a != b is also true.... Therefore, to negate the outcome of a = b, always use not(a = b) and not a != b.

So, as general guidance, use the value comparisons from Table A.2 when comparing values, and use general comparisons only when sequences come into play.

If you want to know more about value versus general comparisons, I recommend reading the sections about comparisons in chapter 8 of the book *XSLT 2.0 and XPath 2.0: Programmer's Reference* by Michael Kay (Wiley, 2008). A more concise and technical description can be found in the XPath 3.1 standard.[2]

[2] https://www.w3.org/TR/xpath-31/#id-comparisons

Here are some additional things to know about comparisons and boolean expressions:

- You can combine boolean expressions with the operators `and` and `or`. Example A.36 tests whether some number (stored in the variable `$count`) is between `3` and `10`:

  Example A.36 – Testing whether some number is in between 3 and 10

  ```
  $count ge 3 and $count le 10
  ```

- To negate the value of a boolean expression (`true` becomes `false` and `false` becomes `true`), use the `not()` function. For instance, to negate the expression of Example A.36:

  Example A.37 – Testing whether some number is not in between 3 and 10

  ```
  not($count ge 3 and $count le 10)
  ```

- Boolean constants must also be written as functions. So it's not `true` but `true()` and not `false` but `false()`. For instance, to set a variable that determines whether some debug tests are enabled:

  Example A.38 – Setting a variable to a fixed boolean value

  ```
  <let name="enable-debug-tests" value="true()"/>
  ```

Testing sequences

As explained in the section titled "Multiple selections: sequences" (p. 197), every result in XPath is a sequence, with none, one, or many values. It's possible to perform tests on sequences directly: an empty sequence results in `false`, a non-empty one in `true`. For instance, Example A.39 checks whether there are any `<message>` elements in a document.

Example A.39 – Using a sequence directly to test for `<message>` elements

```
<rule context="/">
  <assert test="//message">There are no messages</assert>
</rule>
```

If there are any <message> elements in the document, the expression //message returns a sequence with one or more results. This then results in the value true. If there are no <message> elements, the expression returns the empty sequence, resulting in false.

This feature is useful in many ways, including the following:

- To test whether a particular attribute is there:

  Example A.40 – Testing for the presence of an attribute

```
<rule context="thing">
  <assert test="@code">The code attribute is missing</assert>
</rule>
```

- To test whether a particular attribute is not there:

  Example A.41 – Testing for the absence of an attribute

```
<rule context="order">
  <assert test="not(@tax-percentage)">Tax information not permitted</assert>
</rule>
```

- To test whether a certain child element is there:

  Example A.42 – Testing for the presence of a child element

```
<rule context="person">
  <assert test="address">Address information missing</assert>
</rule>
```

The `exists()` and `empty()` functions

XPath also contains two functions for testing sequences: exists() and empty(). As you would expect, exists(...) returns true when its argument is a non-empty sequence and empty(...) returns true when its argument is an empty sequence.

These functions are mainly present for cosmetic reasons: to make code more readable. For instance, Example A.43 rewrites Example A.40 using the `exists()` function.

Example A.43 – Testing for the presence of an attribute using `exists()`

```
<rule context="thing">
  <assert test="exists(@code)">The code attribute is missing</assert>
</rule>
```

And Example A.41 using the `empty()` function:

Example A.44 – Testing for the absence of an attribute using `empty()`

```
<rule context="order">
  <assert test="empty(@tax-percentage)">Tax information not permitted</assert>
</rule>
```

Whether you want to use these functions or not is up to you; they're cosmetic. But they can make your intention clearer. Judge for yourself.

Besides testing for being empty or not, you can also check the number of values in a sequence. The `count()` function does just that. Example A.45 rewrites Example A.39 to check whether there are more than three `<message>` elements.

Example A.45 – Testing for more than three message elements

```
<rule context="/">
  <assert test="count(//message) gt 3">There are not enough messages</assert>
</rule>
```

You could also rewrite Example A.40 using the `count()` function as Example A.46 shows.

Example A.46 – Testing for the presence of an attribute using the `count()` function

```
<rule context="thing">
  <assert test="count(@code) ne 0">The code attribute is missing</assert>
</rule>
```

Testing string values

Testing string values is very common. For instance, Example A.47 checks whether a `code` attribute contains the right value.

Example A.47 – Testing the string value of an attribute

```
<rule context="thing">
  <assert test="@code eq 'AB123'">The thing code is incorrect</assert>
</rule>
```

XPath string comparisons are case-sensitive. So `'XPath'` is not the same as `'xpath'`. And if the value of the `code` attribute in Example A.47 is `code="ab123"`, the assertion will fail.

The cheap and easy way to make string value comparisons case-insensitive is to use `upper-case()` or `lower-case()`. These functions convert a string to upper or lower case. Example A.48 modifies Example A.47 to use `upper-case()`.

Example A.48 – Testing the string value of an attribute, case-insensitive

```
<rule context="thing">
  <assert test="upper-case(@code) eq 'AB123'">The thing code is incorrect</assert>
</rule>
```

Collations

For more fine-grained control on string value comparisons, you can use *collations*. Using the right collation you can, for instance, test independent of diacritics, so `'ü'` tests equal to `'u'` and `'ç'` equal to `'c'`. There's also a collation for case-insensitive compares, which would make using the `upper-case()` or `lower-case()` function for comparisons no longer necessary.

Working with collations is an advanced subject that I do not cover here. For more information see: https://www.w3.org/TR/xpath-functions-31/#collations.

There are several useful functions for doing partial string value comparisons:

- The `starts-with()` and `ends-with()` functions check whether a string starts or ends with a certain substring. Example A.49 checks whether the value of `@code` ends with `'CQ'`:

  Example A.49 – Testing the end of a string value

  ```
  <rule context="thing">
    <assert test="ends-with(@code, 'CQ')">Codes must end with CQ</assert>
  </rule>
  ```

- The `contains()` function checks for the presence of a string somewhere in another string. Example A.50 checks whether a description contains the word `product`.

  Example A.50 – Testing for a string containing another string

  ```
  <rule context="description">
    <assert test="contains(., 'product')">
      Descriptions must contain the word product
    </assert>
  </rule>
  ```

These comparisons are also case-sensitive. The assert in Example A.50 will fail if you type `Product` instead of `product`. Example A.51 makes the comparison in Example A.50 case-insensitive.

Example A.51 – Testing for a string containing another string, case-insensitive

```
<rule context="description">
  <assert test="contains(lower-case(.), 'product')">
    Descriptions must contain the word product
  </assert>
</rule>
```

Comparing strings for greater than or less than

You can also compare strings using the `gt`, `ge`, `lt`, and `le` comparison operators. These comparisons are made based on the position of the individual characters in the *character set*, which is usually Unicode.

For simple strings this is straightforward: `'A'` is less than `'Z'`, `'9'` is greater than `'0'`, `'a'` is greater than `'A'`, etc. This is exactly what you would expect, as long as you are comparing strings that contain simple characters (western languages, non-accented, non-symbols, etc.).

However, when your strings get more complicated, value comparisons might not behave so well. So be careful and test thoroughly if you need this feature. You might even need to use a specific collation (see the note titled "Collations" (p. 224)).

Working with dates, times and durations

Schematron schemas often compare dates, times, and durations. For example, "this date must be more than 5 days before that date." XPath is great for working with these data types.

Let's start with how date, time, and duration values must officially be written. XPath uses the international standard ISO 8601 for this.[3]

Here are some highlights:

- A date must be written as `YYYY-MM-DD`, so use `2025-01-01` for January 1st 2025.
- A time must be written as `hh:mm:ss` using the 24 hour clock. So use `13:15:03` for fifteen minutes and three seconds past one in the afternoon.
  - If you need to be more precise you can use a decimal fraction with the seconds, for instance `13:15:03.125`, which means fifteen minutes, three seconds and 125 milliseconds past one in the afternoon.
  - A time can be followed by a *time zone designator*. For instance, for my location (The Netherlands) a time including a time zone designator is `11:24:29+01:00`. For us it's one hour later than the "Universal Time Coordinated" (UTC), also known as "Greenwich Mean Time" (GMT), therefore the `+01:00`.

[3] The Wikipedia article https://en.wikipedia.org/wiki/ISO_8601 has a good description of this standard.

As you can imagine, timezones can be crucial. One o'clock in the afternoon in New York (`13:00:00-05:00`) is 6 hours behind one o'clock in The Netherlands (`13:00:00+01:00`). If these timestamps are compared they should not come out as equal; they are 6 hours apart. If your timezone designators are correct, XPath will take care of this.

- To combine date and time values, separate the two values with a capital `T`, for instance `2025-02-02T13:15:03`.
- According to ISO 8601, a duration is specified as `P3Y6M4DT12H30M5S`, which represents three years, six months, four days, twelve hours, thirty minutes, and five seconds. A duration always starts with a capital `P`. You can leave out parts when zero. For instance, a duration of five days is simply `P5D` and five minutes `PT5M` (note that you still need the `T` separator).

  Durations can also be negative, for instance `-PT3H` for minus three hours.

XPath has many data types that you can use to work with dates, times, and durations. The major ones are listed in Table A.3. There are several others, like `xs:gYear` for a year and `xs:gMonthDay` for a month+day combination, that I don't cover in this book.

Table A.3 – XPath date, time and duration data types

Name	Description	Example
`xs:date`	A date.	`2025-01-01`

`xs:time`	A time.	`13:15:00`
		`13:15:00.125`
		`13:15:00.125-05:00`

`xs:dateTime`	A date and time combination.	`2025-01-01T13:15:00`
		`2025-01-01T13:15:00.125`
		`2025-01-01T13:15:00.125-05:00`

`xs:dayTimeDuration`	A duration.	`P3Y6M4DT12H30M5S`
		`P1D`
		`PT1H3M`

In calculations, these data types do exactly what you expect:

- Subtracting two dates/times results in a duration. For example, `2025-01-01T13:15:00` minus `2025-01-01T01:00:00` results in a duration of `PT12H15M`.
- Adding a duration to a date/time, or subtracting it, shifts this into the future or past. For example, `2025-01-01T13:15:00` minus `PT5M` becomes `2025-01-01T13:10:00`.

But how does XPath know it's dealing with this type of data? How does it know it needs to treat the value of some element, attribute, or variable as a date, time, date+time, or duration? XPath doesn't attempt to guess; you need to be explicit.

The section titled "Explicit data typing and data type conversions" (p. 214) describes how to use the type name as a function to tell XPath the type of some data. This trick also works here.

Let's illustrate this with some examples.

- Assume your data contains, somewhere, an element about a payment, like Example A.52.

  Example A.52 – An element with date/time information

  ```
  <payment timestamp="2025-02-01T23:11:59" due-timestamp="2025-01-31T12:00:00"/>
  ```

  In a Schematron schema you want to check whether the payment registered in Example A.52 was on time (it's not). This could be done as shown in Example A.52.

  Example A.53 – Schematron rule to check whether Example A.52 payment is on time

  ```
  <rule context="payment">
    <assert test="xs:dateTime(@timestamp) le xs:dateTime(@due-timestamp)">
      Payment too late
    </assert>
  </rule>
  ```

  The assertion's test explicitly tells XPath to treat the values of the `timestamp` and `due-timestamp` attributes as type `xs:dateTime` so the compare will be correct.

- Now assume your payment data is formatted differently. It has an order date and a payment term expressed in days.

Example A.54 – An element with date/time and payment term expressed in days

```
<payment timestamp="2025-02-01T23:11:59" order-timestamp="2025-02-11T12:00:00"
  payment-term="5"/>
```

To check whether the payment was on time you need to use a duration. However, the payment term is expressed as the number of days, `5`, not as a duration, `P5D`.

Here is how to handle this:

1. Convert the number of days into a string that is a valid duration: `'P' || @payment-term || 'D'`. For Example A.54 this will result in `'P5D'`.
2. Convert this into a duration using `xs:dayTimeDuration(…)`
3. Use this value in the assertion's test. Example A.55 shows the end result.

Example A.55 – Schematron fragment that checks whether the payment of Example A.54 was on time

```
<rule context="payment">
  <assert test="xs:dateTime(@timestamp) le
    xs:dateTime(@order-timestamp) + xs:dayTimeDuration('P' ||
      @payment-term || 'D')">
    Payment too late
  </assert>
</rule>
```

- As a final example, assume the payment term is a fixed 30 days. To make our schema more maintainable, we record this duration in a global variable:

Example A.56 – Creating a variable with a duration data type

```
<let name="payment-term" as="xs:dayTimeDuration"
value="xs:dayTimeDuration('P30D')"/>
```

Example A.57 shows how to use this variable.

Example A.57 – Schematron fragment that uses the variable declared in Example A.56 to check whether a payment was on time

```
<rule context="payment">
  <assert test="xs:dateTime(@timestamp) le
    xs:dateTime(@order-timestamp) + $payment-term">
    Payment too late
  </assert>
</rule>
```

Additional date, time, and duration functions

There are several additional functions for dates, times, and durations. Here are the most common ones. The section titled "The XPath function library" (p. 211) has details on how to find them all.

- The current date, time, or date+time can be retrieved with the functions `xs:current-date()`, `xs:current-time()` and `xs:current-dateTime()`. These functions have no parameters and return a value with the appropriate data type.

> **The times are not a-changing**
>
> You'll probably never notice, but during execution the values returned by these functions never change. So even if you have a lengthy validation that takes minutes or more, these functions return exactly the same value at the beginning as at the end: the day and/or time the execution started.

- Converting a date or time into text can be done with the functions `xs:format-date()`, `xs:format-time()`, and `xs:format-dateTime()`. These functions use a format string to specify what the date/time must look like. For instance, in The Netherlands we usually write dates as day-month-year. To format the current date in this format, you can use this:

  ```
  format-date(current-date(), '[D]-[M]-[Y]')
  ```

  On February 1st 2025 the result would be `1-2-2025`. The string that formats the output has many options. For instance you can format a month as a decimal number (`2`), Roman numeral (`II`), name (`February`), abbreviation (`Feb`), and several others. For a full list of options and examples, see https://www.w3.org/TR/xpath-functions-31/#rules-for-datetime-formatting.

APPENDIX B

An introduction to namespaces

XML namespaces are rather strange. In my humble opinion they're a great invention because they help keep XML dialects unambiguously apart. But their implementation leaves something to be desired, most importantly in comprehensibility. By that I mean not only comprehensibility for beginners but also comprehensibility when interpreting XML documents that use namespaces. Getting the namespace information you need can be like solving a puzzle.

However, don't let this discourage you. XML namespaces are here to stay, and even when you are writing a simple Schematron schema, you will run in to at least one: the Schematron namespace. So, let's take the bull by the horns.

Why namespaces?

The main reason for namespaces is to provide uniquely named elements and attributes for XML documents. A namespace is a collection of elements and attributes that, together, form a *vocabulary*.

Assume you have an XML document that contains a `<para>` element. When this document contains book contents, `<para>` probably means a paragraph. But what if this is an XML document about parachuting? It could mean something completely different.

Namespaces attach a not-directly-visible label to elements and attributes: a label that says "this is a piece of text" on the book `<para>` element and a label that says something different on the parachuting `<para>` element. What's on this label is the namespace name. What these names are and how to attach them is the subject of this chapter.

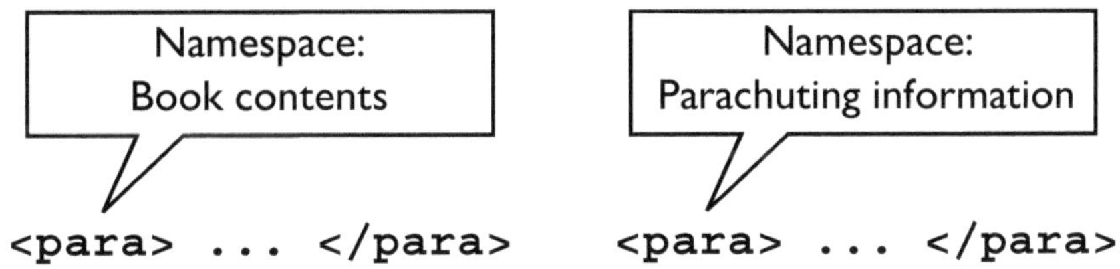

Figure B.1 – Namespaces as not-directly-visible labels

An application may be able to find out the meaning of a `<para>` element using the context. Book XML documents would probably start with a different root element than parachuting information, for instance `<book>` versus `<parachuting-info>`. And the application that processes the XML may assume it will receive XML in the right vocabulary.

However, sometimes it is difficult to determine the XML vocabulary of a document. For example, Schematron schemas start with a `<schema>` element, but so do W3C XML Schemas. They are two completely different languages with the same root element. And given that they both have to do with validation, it's not inconceivable to mix them up. A Schematron or XML Schema processor must know the schema it is working with. The processor can determine this by looking at the namespace.

Most XML standards use namespaces to define a vocabulary. For instance, DocBook is a standard for writing book content (used for the book you're reading now). DocBook contents must be in the DocBook namespace to be considered DocBook. Exactly the same XML in some other namespace wouldn't be DocBook.

Another reason for namespaces is to combine different XML vocabularies. For example, SVG (Scalable Vector Graphics) is an XML vocabulary for describing drawings. HTML is a completely different vocabulary used for web pages. Sometimes you want an SVG drawing on your web page. Using namespaces you can safely embed the SVG XML somewhere in the HTML. Because of the namespace labeling, the browser, or any XML-aware processor, can tell the vocabularies apart.

Bottom line: Namespaces add not-directly-visible labels, which contain the namespace name, to XML elements and attributes. These labels unambiguously tell you that a particular XML document, or part of a document, is in a certain vocabulary. The vocabulary determines the goal, the meaning of the XML.

Namespace names

Namespaces have a name. This name is what sets one namespace apart from the other, and therefore, it must unambiguous. To achieve this, the convention is to base namespace names on the web domain owned by the organization that issues them and format them as a URL (Uniform Resource Locator, the thing you see in the address bar of your browser).[1] Domain names must be claimed, and the organization behind them makes sure they are unique. Therefore, you can

[1] Officially a namespace name must be a valid URI (Uniform Resource Identifier). The definition of URIs is broader than that of URLs and includes, for instance, official identifiers like `urn:isbn:0-486-27557-4`. However, in most cases, URLs are used for namespace names.

be reasonably sure that a namespace name based on a domain that you own will not be used, invented, or issued by somebody else. Here are some examples of namespaces:

- The World Wide Web consortium (W3C) publishes the XHTML standard, which is used for describing the contents of web pages in XML. The namespace name for XHTML is: `http://www.w3.org/1999/xhtml`.
- The DocBook standard is widely used for book contents, including this book. The namespace name for DocBook is: `http://docbook.org/ns/docbook`.
- When you've registered a domain for your company, it's safe to use it to define your own namespace names. For instance: `http://my-own-company.com/ns/xml-vocab-1`.

Be aware that the convention of using a domain name you own for namespace names is just that, a convention. Nothing stops you from inventing something completely different. However, as soon as your XML becomes public and is used outside your organization, I strongly advise you to follow along. And why not stick to this convention anyway, even for non-public XML?

Local namespace names

One exception I usually make for the "use the organization domain for namespace names" convention is when it really doesn't matter.

For example: XPath functions must be in some namespace. Self-defined functions in a program (for instance an XSLT stylesheet) are usually just local and cannot be used outside of it. You can go through the hassle of creating a full URL-based namespace name, but that's hardly worthwhile. In these cases I simply use the namespace name `#local` or `#functions`. For an example of this in Schematron see the section titled "Using XSLT functions" (p. 133).

Newcomers to the XML (namespace) world often find this convention extremely confusing. The name looks like a URL, but it isn't one? But it even has the `http` or `https` protocol in front. Despite that, there's no guarantee whatsoever that using it in a browser will lead you to a web page. Sometimes it does, sometimes it doesn't. There's no other choice than to get used to it: namespace names look like URLs of web pages, but they're not.

XML elements and attributes that do not use a namespace are in the so-called *null namespace*. They have no label (or an empty label) attached. This happens automatically if you don't use a namespace declaration, as explained in the next section.

QNames

You might come across the term QName (Qualified Name) when working with namespaces. A QName is a data type with two components:

- The namespace of the element or attribute. For the null namespace this is empty.
- The local name of the element or attribute. This is what you would normally consider to be its name. For instance the local name of a `<para>` element is always `para`, regardless of the namespace.

XPath has several functions for working with QNames. See the section titled "The XPath function library" (p. 211) for more information.

Declaring namespaces

We now know that a namespace defines an XML vocabulary and attaches a not-directly-visible label, the namespace name, to elements and attributes. We also know that namespace names are formatted as URLs. With this knowledge we can redraw Figure B.1 as Figure B.2.

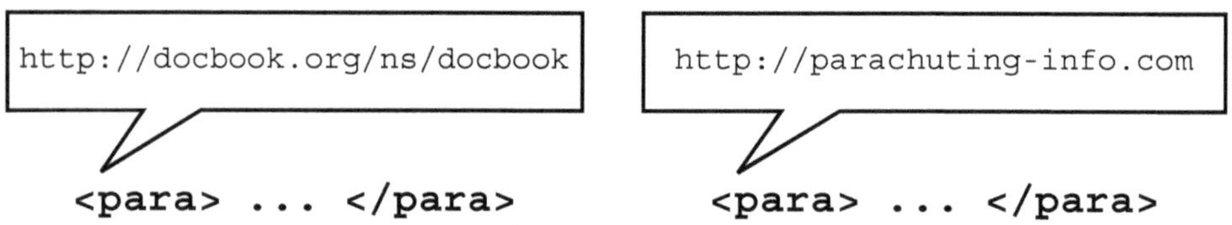

Figure B.2 – Namespaces names, using the URL convention, as not directly visible labels

What we don't know yet is how to attach labels to declare that some element or attribute is in a specific namespace. You can do this by: defining a default namespace or using a namespace prefix.

Defining a default namespace

A default namespace is a namespace that is declared on some element and stays in effect for its descendants (children, grandchildren, etc.) unless explicitly changed. You define a default namespace using the `xmlns` "attribute." This book has many examples, including Example B.1.

Example B.1 – Defining the Schematron namespace as default for a Schematron schema using the `xmlns` “attribute”.
(`schematron-book-code-2025/examples/basics/check-type-1.sch`)

```
<schema xmlns="http://purl.oclc.org/dsdl/schematron" schematronEdition="2025"
  queryBinding="xslt3">
  <pattern>
    <rule context="@type">
      <assert test="(. eq 'normal') or (. eq 'special')">
        The type must be normal or special
      </assert>
    </rule>
  </pattern>
</schema>
```

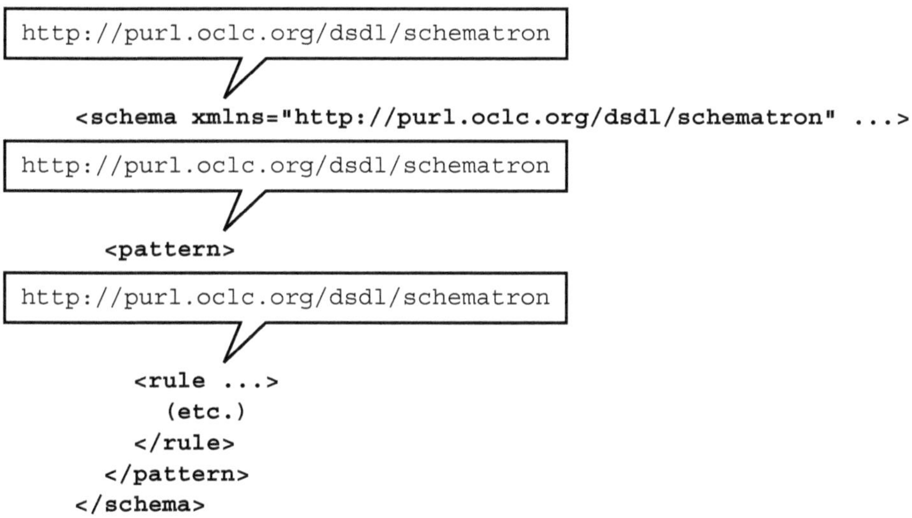

Figure B.3 – The Schematron namespace, declared as the default namespace

As shown in Figure B.3, the schema root element declares that it is in the Schematron namespace by specifying `xmlns="http://purl.oclc.org/dsdl/schematron"`. This stays in effect for its descendants, so the `<pattern>`, `<rule>`, and `<assert>` elements are in the Schematron namespace, too.

The reason I write `xmlns` "attribute" in quotes is that, although it looks like an attribute, it's not. It's a namespace declaration. `xmlns` is a reserved name in XML, and you cannot use it as a normal attribute name.

But what about attributes: are the attributes in Example B.1, like `context` and `test`, also in the Schematron namespace? The answer is no. Declaring a default namespace is for elements only. If you need to put attributes in a namespace, you have to use the namespace prefix mechanism, which is described in the next section.

A default namespace stays in effect until, on a child element, another default namespace declaration is encountered. For example, see Example B.2.

Example B.2 – Overriding a default namespace declaration

```
<A xmlns="http://my-own-company.com/ns/1">
  <B>
    <C xmlns="http://my-own-company.com/ns/2">
      <D/>
    </C>
  </B>
  <E/>
</A>
```

- The elements `<A>`, `<B>`, and `<E>` are in the `http://my-own-company.com/ns/1` namespace.
- The elements `<C>` and `<D>` are in the `http://my-own-company.com/ns/2` namespace.

To put the `<C>` and `<D>` elements in the null namespace you can define the namespace as being an empty string, as shown in Example B.3.

Example B.3 – Overriding a default namespace declaration with the null namespace

```
<A xmlns="http://my-own-company.com/ns/1">
  <B>
    <C xmlns="">
      <D/>
    </C>
  </B>
  <E/>
</A>
```

Defining and using namespace prefixes

Another mechanism for declaring namespaces is namespace prefixes. A namespace prefix is a short string that serves as stand-in for the, usually much longer, namespace name. Declaring a namespace prefix is done using an `xmlns:prefix` "attribute." For example, rewriting Example B.1 using namespace prefixes looks like Example B.4.

Example B.4 – Overriding a default namespace declaration with the null namespace

```
<sch:schema xmlns:sch="http://purl.oclc.org/dsdl/schematron" queryBinding="xslt3">
  <sch:pattern>
    <sch:rule context="@type">
      <sch:assert test="(. eq 'normal') or (. eq 'special')">
        Invalid type!
      </sch:assert>
    </sch:rule>
  </sch:pattern>
</sch:schema>
```

On the root element we declare a namespace prefix, `sch`, with the Schematron namespace name as its value, using the `xmlns:sch="http://purl.oclc.org/dsdl/schematron"` "attribute" (again it's officially not an attribute but a namespace declaration). We use the declared `sch` prefix on all elements that need to be in the Schematron namespace (for this example on all elements). This is done by prefixing the element's name with `sch:`.

Despite the obvious textual differences between Example B.4 and Example B.1, Example B.4 has the same meaning as Example B.1. All elements are in the Schematron namespace. You can feed it to a Schematron processor, which will accept the input and process it the same as it would process Example B.1.

A few details about namespace prefixes:

- A namespace prefix must be declared before it can be used.
- But you can declare as many namespace prefixes as you like, anywhere in your document. You don't have to use them. A namespace prefix declaration just creates a link between a prefix and a namespace name. It says nothing about how to use the namespace.
- A namespace prefix declaration is in effect on the element it's declared on and all its children, grandchildren, and so on.
- A namespace prefix stays defined until, on one of its descendant elements, another namespace prefix declaration is found with the same prefix.
- Namespace prefixes can be used to put an attribute in a namespace. To do this, prefix the attribute name with the namespace prefix.
- A namespace prefix must conform to the same rules as the name of an element or attribute.
- The default namespace and namespace prefix mechanisms can be mixed. It's not unusual to do this. For example, in Example 7.3, the Schematron XML is in the default namespace, and the XSLT key declaration uses the `xsl:` prefix, which puts it in the XSLT namespace (`http://www.w3.org/1999/XSL/Transform`).

Rewriting Example B.2 using namespace prefixes instead of the default namespace mechanism looks like Example B.5.

Example B.5 – Using the namespace prefix mechanism to create a semantically identical version of Example B.2

```
<ns1:A xmlns:ns1="http://my-own-company.com/ns/1"
    xmlns:ns2="http://my-own-company.com/ns/2">
  <ns1:B>
    <ns2:C>
      <ns2:D/>
    </ns2:C>
  </ns1:B>
  <ns1:E/>
</ns1:A>
```

Since it doesn't matter where you define the prefix (as long it's done before being used), you could also define the prefix as shown in Example B.6.

Example B.6 – Another way of using the namespace prefix mechanism to create a semantically identical version of Example B.2

```
<ns1:A xmlns:ns1="http://my-own-company.com/ns/1">
  <ns1:B>
    <ns2:C xmlns:ns2="http://my-own-company.com/ns/2">
      <ns2:D/>
    </ns2:C>
  </ns1:B>
  <ns1:E/>
</ns1:A>
```

And what if you want to use the prefix mechanism to create a semantically identical version of Example B.3? In that example there is, in the middle of elements-in-a-namespace, an "island" of elements (<C> and <D>) in the null namespace. Luckily that's easy to do. If you do not add a prefix, the namespace goes back to the default namespace. In Example B.7 no default namespace is defined, so those elements are in the null namespace. Thus, Example B.7 is semantically identical to Example B.3.

Example B.7 – Using the namespace prefix mechanism to create a semantically identical version of Example B.3

```
<ns1:A xmlns:ns1="http://my-own-company.com/ns/1">
  <ns1:B>
    <C>
      <D/>
    </C>
  </ns1:B>
  <ns1:E/>
</ns1:A>
```

The XML namespace

All namespace prefixes must be declared before use, but there's one exception: the prefix `xml` is reserved and always bound to the `http://www.w3.org/XML/1998/namespace` namespace. You're not allowed to re-declare it.

This namespace defines a number of special attributes, ready to be used in any document without having to declare the `xml` prefix. For instance, you can specify the natural language for an element containing text, using the `xml:lang` attribute (see Example B.8).

Example B.8 – Example of using the `xml:lang` attribute

```
<texts>
  <text xml:lang="nl">Hallo daar, gezellig dat je er bent!</text>
  <text xml:lang="en">Hi there, nice to have you here!</text>
  <text xml:lang="fr">Salut, ravi de vous avoir ici!</text>
</texts>
```

Of course, what actually happens with these language settings is still up to the application that processes the XML. But you now have a standardized way to specify the language.

Notice that the `xml` prefix is not declared explicitly. We could have done this (`xmlns:xml="http://www.w3.org/XML/1998/namespace"`) but it's unnecessary.

You can find more information about the XML namespace and all the attributes it defines at https://www.w3.org/XML/1998/namespace.

Namespaces in Schematron

The rules for declaring and using namespaces in Schematron are unfortunately a bit of a hybrid:

- For the XML elements in a Schematron schema, Schematron follows the rules described in the sections above. It must follow those rules, otherwise the XML wouldn't be well-formed and would, therefore, be unacceptable for XML parsers.
- Namespaces used in the XPath expressions in Schematron (which are in attributes such as `test`) must be defined using the Schematron `<ns>` element. This is explained in the section titled "Declaring namespaces" (p. 78).

The `<ns>` element mechanism in Schematron doesn't allow you to define a default namespace. You can find an example in the section titled "Handling a default namespace" (p. 164).

APPENDIX C

Schematron reference

This appendix contains a reference for Schematron 2025. It describes all elements and attributes.

Some elements and attributes appear over and over again. Their definitions are gathered in the last section of this appendix (the section titled "Standard attributes and elements" (p. 270)).

Implementation-defined?

The Schematron language has a lot of *implementation-defined* elements and attributes. What does that mean?

An implementation-defined element or attribute has a defined meaning in the standard, but what actually happens with it (if anything) is completely up to the Schematron processor.

For example, one of the elements marked as implementation defined is `<emph>`. As described in the section titled "Emphasis: `<emph>` " (p. 268), you can use this element to emphasize parts of your messages. Example C.1 emphasizes the word *important*.

Example C.1 – Message using the `<emph>` element

```
<assert test="…">This is <emph>important</emph>: wrong value!</assert>
```

However, how this markup is handled is implementation defined. The processor handling the SVRL has complete freedom as to whether it will recognize any markup passed through. If it does recognize the markup, how it chooses to render that markup is also implementation defined.

The bottom line is that all you can rely on with implementation-defined elements and attributes is that they are legal to insert into a Schematron schema.

XML structure overview notation

This appendix and Appendix D use a pseudo-code notation to define and explain XML structures. This notation looks like XML, but it's not well-formed! So don't copy/paste any of it into your code and expect it to work. For example, this is an XML structure for the fictitious `<some-element>` element:

```
<some-element attribute-1-optional? = (type)
              attribute-2-required = (type)
              attribute-3-fixed-values? = "value-1" | "value-2" >
  <elm-1-optional>?
  <elm-2-mandatory>
  <elm-3-multiple-optional>*
  <elm-4-multiple-mandatory>+
  ( <elm-in-group-1> |
    <elm-in-group-2> )*
</some-element>
```

After this structure summary/overview, the attributes are listed in a table:

Table C.1 – Attributes of the `<some-element>` element

<table>
<tr><th>Attribute</th><th>#</th><th>Type</th><th>Description</th></tr>
<tr><td><code>attribute-1-optional</code></td><td>?</td><td>(type)</td><td>Default: <code>some-default</code>

Optional attribute (there is a ? after its name in the structure overview and in the # column).</td></tr>
<tr><td><code>attribute-2-required</code></td><td>1</td><td>(type)</td><td>Required attribute (There is nothing after its name in the structure overview and a 1 in # column).</td></tr>
<tr><td><code>attribute-3-fixed-values</code></td><td>?</td><td>(type)</td><td>Default: <code>value-1</code>

Optional attribute that must have one of these values:

<table><tr><th>Value</th><th>Description</th></tr><tr><td><code>value-1</code></td><td>The first value you can use</td></tr><tr><td><code>value-2</code></td><td>The second value you can use</td></tr></table></td></tr>
</table>

Also the child elements are detailed in a table:

Table C.2 – Child elements of the `<some-element>` element

Child element	#	Description
`elm-1-optional`	?	This is an optional child element (there is a ? after its name in the structure example above and also in the occurrences column #).
`elm-2-mandatory`	1	This is a required child element (there is nothing after its name in the structure example above and a 1 in the occurrences column #).
`elm-3-multiple-optional`	*	This is an optional child element that can occur multiple times (there is a * after its name in the structure example above and also in the occurrences column #).
`elm-4-multiple-mandatory`	+	This is a required child element that can occur multiple times (there is a + after its name in the structure example above and also in the occurrences column #).
`elm-in-group-1`	*	An element in a group, see the explanation below
`elm-in-group-2`	*	Another element in a group, see the explanation below

- The # column says something about the occurrence of the attribute or element:

Nothing or 1	Exactly once (required, single)
?	Zero or once (optional, single)
*	Zero or more (optional, multiple)
+	One or more (required, multiple)

- Attributes are followed by a data type (for instance `xs:string` or `xs:boolean`) or by the list of values it can have (like for `attribute-3-fixed-values`).

- Sometimes child elements are in a group, like `<elm-in-group-1>` and `<elm-in-group-2>` in the example above. You can see this because the group is between parentheses and there's a pipe character (|) between the elements. This means you have a choice of elements and you can repeat this choice as often as the occurrence indicator on the group allows.

  In the example above this occurrence indicator is `*` (zero-or-more), so any combination of both elements would be valid, including none at all.

The Schematron namespace

All elements that make up the Schematron language are in the namespace:

```
http://purl.oclc.org/dsdl/schematron
```

Schematron attributes are not in a namespace.

Using other namespaces

Additional elements and attributes in another (non-Schematron) namespace are allowed (almost) anywhere. For instance, this is completely valid (but what it means is up to you):

Example C.2 – Use of a foreign namespace in Schematron

```
<assert test="…" xmlns:nsx="http://some.namespace.definition" nsx:special="true">
  Invalid value for <nsx:fieldname>date</nsx:fieldname> field
</assert>
```

Root element: `<schema>`

The root element of a Schematron schema is always `<schema>`, and it must be in the Schematron namespace (`http://purl.oclc.org/dsdl/schematron`). This means that a basic Schematron schema will usually look like this (using the default namespace construction):

Example C.3 – A basic Schematron schema using a default namespace construction

```
<schema xmlns="http://purl.oclc.org/dsdl/schematron" …>
  …
</schema>
```

If you choose, you can use a prefixed namespace construction, as shown in Example C.4. If you use a prefix, you are free to choose any prefix, but I suggest you use `sch` to avoid confusion.

Example C.4 – A basic Schematron schema using a prefixed namespace construction

```
<sch:schema xmlns:sch="http://purl.oclc.org/dsdl/schematron" ...>
  ...
</sch:schema>
```

The definition for the <schema> element is:

```
<schema defaultPhase? = xs:IDREF
        fpi? = xs:string
        icon? = xs:anyURI
        id? = xs:ID
        queryBinding? = xs:string
        schemaVersion? = xs:string
        schematronEdition? = xs:string
        see? = xs:anyURI
        xml:lang? = xs:language
        xml:space? = xs:string >
  ( <include> |
    <title> |
    <extends> |
    <ns> |
    <p> |
    <let> |
    <phase> |
    <pattern> |
    <group> |
    <diagnostics> |
    <properties> |
    <rules> |
    <param> )*
</schema>
```

Table C.3 – Attributes of the <schema> element

Attribute	#	Type	Description
`defaultPhase`	?	`xs:IDREF`	Reference to the default phase for this schema. See the section titled "Selecting what checks are active: <phase> " (p. 89).
`fpi`	?	`xs:string`	A formal public identifier for this element. See the section titled "The `fpi` attribute" (p. 270).

Attribute	#	Type	Description
icon	?	xs:anyURI	Location of an appropriate graphics file for this element. See the section titled "The icon attribute" (p. 270).
id	?	xs:ID	An identifier for this schema. The Schematron standard says nothing about this attribute, so its meaning and usage are implementation-defined.
queryBinding	?	xs:string	Default: xslt The query binding for this schema. See Chapter 7.
schemaVersion	?	xs:string	The version of this schema. The value is not restricted (as long as it's non-empty). Its use is implementation-defined, but it's usually copied to the SVRL (as an attribute with the same name on the root element). Don't confuse this with the Schematron version. It's meant to be the version of this particular schema, not the Schematron version used.
schematronEdition	?	xs:string	The Schematron edition this schema is for. For Schematron edition 2025, its value must be 2025. This attribute was introduced in the 2025 edition. For older editions it should be omitted.
see	?	xs:anyURI	A URI pointing to external information for this element. See the section titled "The see attribute" (p. 271).
xml:lang	?	xs:language	The default natural language for this element (and its children). See the section titled "The xml:lang attribute" (p. 271).
xml:space	?	xs:string	How whitespace must be handled for this element. See the section titled "The xml:space attribute" (p. 272).

Table C.4 – Child elements of the <schema> element

Child element	#	Description
include	*	Includes a document. See the section titled "The <include> element" (p. 274).
title	*	Some title, usually meant for documenting (this part of) the schema. See the section titled "The <title> element" (p. 274).
extends	*	Extend this schema with code from a Schematron library. See the section titled "Referencing a library or an abstract rule: <extends> " (p. 262).
ns	*	A namespace declaration for use in this schema. See the section titled "Declaring a namespace: <ns> " (p. 250).
p	*	A paragraph of text, usually meant for documenting (this part of) the schema. See the section titled "The <p> element" (p. 273).
let	*	A (top-level) variable declaration. See the section titled "The <let> element" (p. 272).
phase	*	Defines a validation phase for this schema. See the section titled "Defining validation phases: <phase> " (p. 251).
pattern	*	Defines a pattern for this schema. See the section titled "Grouping validation rules: <pattern> and <group> " (p. 254).
group	*	Defines a group for this schema. See the section titled "Grouping validation rules: <pattern> and <group> " (p. 254).
diagnostics	*	Container element for diagnostics in this schema. See the section titled "Defining diagnostic messages: <diagnostics> " (p. 263). Officially only a single <diagnostics> element is allowed, but most Schematron processors accept multiple occurrences.

Child element	#	Description
properties	*	Container element for properties for the asserts and reports in this schema. See the section titled "Defining additional properties: <properties> " (p. 265). Officially only a single <properties> element is allowed, but most Schematron processors accept multiple occurrences.
rules	*	Container element for global abstract rules. See the section titled "Global abstract rules" (p. 104).
param	*	Defines a global schema parameter. See the section titled "Defining parameters: <param> " (p. 262).

Root element: <library>

The <library> element is used as the root element of a document containing a partial Schematron schema. Its contents can be imported in a full Schematron schema or in another library. See the section titled "Using libraries: <library> and <extends> " (p. 122) for more information.

```
<library fpi? = xs:string
         icon? = xs:anyURI
         id? = xs:ID
         see? = xs:anyURI
         xml:lang? = xs:language
         xml:space? = xs:string >
  ( <include> |
    <title> |
    <extends> |
    <p> |
    <let> |
    <pattern> |
    <group> |
    <diagnostics> |
    <properties> |
    <rules> |
    <param> )*
</library>
```

Table C.5 – Attributes of the `<library>` element

Attribute	#	Type	Description
fpi	?	xs:string	A formal public identifier for this element. See the section titled "The fpi attribute" (p. 270).
icon	?	xs:anyURI	Location of an appropriate graphics file for this element. See the section titled "The icon attribute" (p. 270).
id	?	xs:ID	An identifier for this library. The Schematron standard says nothing about this attribute, so its meaning and usage are implementation-defined.
see	?	xs:anyURI	A URI pointing to external information for this element. See the section titled "The see attribute" (p. 271).
xml:lang	?	xs:language	The default natural language for this element (and its children). See the section titled "The xml:lang attribute" (p. 271).
xml:space	?	xs:string	How whitespace must be handled for this element. See the section titled "The xml:space attribute" (p. 272).

Table C.6 – Child elements of the `<library>` element

Child element	#	Description
include	*	Includes a document. See the section titled "The <include> element" (p. 274).
title	*	Some title, usually meant for documenting (this part of) the schema. See the section titled "The <title> element" (p. 274).
extends	*	Extend this schema with code from a Schematron library. See the section titled "Referencing a library or an abstract rule: <extends> " (p. 262).
p	*	A paragraph of text, usually meant for documenting (this part of) the schema. See the section titled "The <p> element" (p. 273).

Child element	#	Description
let	*	A (top-level) variable declaration. See the section titled "The <let> element" (p. 272).
pattern	*	Defines a pattern for this schema. See the section titled "Grouping validation rules: <pattern> and <group> " (p. 254).
group	*	Defines a group for this schema. See the section titled "Grouping validation rules: <pattern> and <group> " (p. 254).
diagnostics	*	Container element for diagnostics in this schema. See the section titled "Defining diagnostic messages: <diagnostics> " (p. 263). Officially only a single <diagnostics> element is allowed, but most Schematron processors accept multiple occurrences.
properties	*	Container element for properties for the asserts and reports in this schema. See the section titled "Defining additional properties: <properties> " (p. 265). Officially only a single <properties> element is allowed, but most Schematron processors accept multiple occurrences.
rules	*	Container element for global abstract rules. See the section titled "Global abstract rules" (p. 104).
param	*	Defines a global schema parameter. See the section titled "Defining parameters: <param> " (p. 262).

Declaring a namespace: `<ns>`

The `<ns>` element defines a namespace and its prefix for use in the expressions in the schema, for instance in the `select` and `context` attributes. See the section titled "Declaring namespaces" (p. 78) for more information.

```
<ns prefix = xs:NCName
    uri = xs:anyURI />
```

Table C.7 – Attributes of the <ns> element

Attribute	#	Type	Description
prefix	1	xs:NCName	The prefix to use for this namespace.
uri	1	xs:anyURI	The namespace's URI.

You might expect to define namespaces (and their prefixes) for this with the usual xmlns "attribute" notation. You can, but these namespace declarations will not be used for namespaces in expressions. For these you have to use <ns> elements.

However, if your schema has elements and/or attributes in another namespace (for instance <xsl:key>), you *must* declare this namespace the usual way, using the xmlns "attribute" notation. If you didn't, your XML wouldn't be well-formed. The <ns> element is for namespaces in expressions only.

Defining validation phases: <phase>

A phase is a set of patterns that belong together. When you fire a Schematron validation containing phases you can specify which phase(s) should be active. Only patterns in active phases are checked (see the section titled "Selecting what checks are active: <phase> " (p. 89)).

```
<phase fpi? = xs:string
       from? = XPath expression
       icon? = xs:anyURI
       id = xs:ID
       see? = xs:anyURI
       when? = XPath expression
       xml:lang? = xs:language
       xml:space? = xs:string >
  ( <include> |
    <p> |
    <let> |
    <active> )*
</phase>
```

Table C.8 – Attributes of the <phase> element

Attribute	#	Type	Description
fpi	?	xs:string	A formal public identifier for this element. See the section titled "The fpi attribute" (p. 270).
from	?	XPath expression	An XPath expression that matches parts of the document being validated. When this attribute is present on an active phase, only the parts selected will be validated. See the section titled "Partial document validation using phases" (p. 100).
icon	?	xs:anyURI	Location of an appropriate graphics file for this element. See the section titled "The icon attribute" (p. 270).
id	1	xs:ID	The identifier (name) of this phase.
see	?	xs:anyURI	A URI pointing to external information for this element. See the section titled "The see attribute" (p. 271).
when	?	XPath expression	An XPath expression that can be cast to a boolean. It is used for dynamic phase selection. See the section titled "Dynamic phase selection" (p. 96).
xml:lang	?	xs:language	The default natural language for this element (and its children). See the section titled "The xml:lang attribute" (p. 271).
xml:space	?	xs:string	How whitespace must be handled for this element. See the section titled "The xml:space attribute" (p. 272).

Table C.9 – Child elements of the <phase> element

Child element	#	Description
include	*	Includes a document. See the section titled "The <include> element" (p. 274).

Child element	#	Description
p	*	A paragraph of text, usually meant for documenting (this part of) the schema. See the section titled "The <p> element" (p. 273).
let	*	A variable declaration, in-scope for this phase. See the section titled "The <let> element" (p. 272).
active	*	Reference to a pattern that belongs to this validation phase. See the section titled "Attaching a single pattern to a phase: <active> " (p. 253).

Attaching a single pattern to a phase: <active>

The <active> element, which can occur only as child of <phase>, attaches a single pattern to its parent. The pattern is referenced by the value of its id attribute.

```
<active pattern = xs:IDREF >
  Mixed contents, can contain:
  <dir>*
  <emph>*
  <span>*
</active>
```

Table C.10 – Attributes of the <active> element

Attribute	#	Type	Description
pattern	1	xs:IDREF	The identifier of the referenced pattern or group (<pattern> or <group> element, id attribute. See the section titled "Grouping validation rules: <pattern> and <group> " (p. 254)).

Table C.11 – Child elements of the <active> element

Child element	#	Description
dir	*	Text writing direction. See the section titled "Writing direction: <dir> " (p. 267).

Child element	#	Description
emph	*	Emphasize this text. See the section titled "Emphasis: <emph> " (p. 268).
span	*	Text span. See the section titled "Spanning text: <span> " (p. 268).

The text contents of an <active> element are for documentation purposes only.

Grouping validation rules: <pattern> and <group>

The <pattern> and <group> elements are container elements for grouping Schematron validation rules. See the section titled "Patterns, groups, rules, assertions, and reports" (p. 53) for more information.

The <group> element has the same definition as the <pattern> element described below. The difference is in their processing of the rules enclosed:

- In a pattern, for every node in the document being validated, only the first rule that matches is processed.
- In a group all rules are processed.

```
<pattern abstract? = xs:boolean
         documents? = XPath expression
         fpi? = xs:string
         icon? = xs:anyURI
         id? = xs:ID
         is-a? = xs:IDREF
         role? = xs:string
         see? = xs:anyURI
         xml:lang? = xs:language
         xml:space? = xs:string >
  ( <include> |
    <title> |
    <p> |
    <let> |
    <rule> |
    <param> )*
</pattern>
```

Table C.12 – Attributes of the `<pattern>` element

Attribute	#	Type	Description
`abstract`	?	`xs:boolean`	Default: `false` Whether this is an abstract or a concrete pattern. See the section titled "Reusing patterns and groups: Abstract patterns and groups" (p. 106).
`documents`	?	`XPath expression`	XPath expression that must result in one or more references to documents (URIs/IRIs). If specified, the rules in this pattern will be applied to these documents and not the currently active document. See the section titled "Validating documents referenced by XInclude" (p. 151).
`fpi`	?	`xs:string`	A formal public identifier for this element. See the section titled "The `fpi` attribute" (p. 270).
`icon`	?	`xs:anyURI`	Location of an appropriate graphics file for this element. See the section titled "The `icon` attribute" (p. 270).
`id`	?	`xs:ID`	The identifier of this pattern. ■ An abstract pattern (`abstract="true"`) must have an identifier. ■ If you want to use this pattern as part of a phase (see the section titled "Defining validation phases: `<phase>` " (p. 251)), you must specify an identifier as well.
`is-a`	?	`xs:IDREF`	Specifies that this pattern is an instance of the abstract pattern as referenced by this attribute. See the section titled "Reusing patterns and groups: Abstract patterns and groups" (p. 106). Abstract patterns (`abstract="true"`) must not specify the `is-a` attribute.

Attribute	#	Type	Description
role	?	xs:string	A name for the default role of assertions or context items in this pattern. See the section titled "The role attribute" (p. 270).
see	?	xs:anyURI	A URI pointing to external information for this element. See the section titled "The see attribute" (p. 271).
xml:lang	?	xs:language	The default natural language for this element (and its children). See the section titled "The xml:lang attribute" (p. 271).
xml:space	?	xs:string	How whitespace must be handled for this element. See the section titled "The xml:space attribute" (p. 272).

Table C.13 – Child elements of the <pattern> element

Child element	#	Description
include	*	Includes a document. See the section titled "The <include> element" (p. 274).
title	*	Some title, usually meant for documenting (this part of) the schema. See the section titled "The <title> element" (p. 274).
p	*	A paragraph of text, usually meant for documenting (this part of) the schema. See the section titled "The <p> element" (p. 273).
let	*	A variable declaration, in-scope for this pattern. See the section titled "The <let> element" (p. 272).
rule	*	A rule within a validation pattern, see the section titled "Validation rules: <rule> " (p. 257).
param	*	Specifies a parameter for an abstract pattern. See the section titled "Defining parameters: <param> " (p. 262). Use only when this pattern is an instance of an abstract pattern (has an is-a attribute).

Validation rules: `<rule>`

A `<rule>` element specifies a validation rule in a pattern or group. See the section titled "Patterns, groups, rules, assertions, and reports" (p. 53) for more information.

```
<rule abstract? = xs:boolean
      context? = Match expression
      flag? = xs:string
      fpi? = xs:string
      icon? = xs:anyURI
      id? = xs:ID
      role? = xs:string
      see? = xs:anyURI
      subject? = XPath expression
      visit-each? = XPath expression
      xml:lang? = xs:language
      xml:space? = xs:string >
  ( <include> |
    <p> |
    <let> |
    <assert> |
    <report> |
    <extends> )*
</rule>
```

Table C.14 – Attributes of the `<rule>` element

Attribute	#	Type	Description
`abstract`	?	`xs:boolean`	Default: `false` Whether this is an abstract or a concrete rule. See the section titled "Reusing rules: abstract rules" (p. 101)
`context`	?	`Match expression`	Match expression that identifies on which node(s) this rule fires. Subsequently its assertions and reports are checked. When this is an abstract rule (`abstract="true"`), the `context` attribute must be absent. Otherwise it is required.
`flag`	?	`xs:string`	Name of a flag to be set to `true` when this element fires. See the section titled "The `flag` attribute" (p. 270).
`fpi`	?	`xs:string`	A formal public identifier for this element. See the section titled "The `fpi` attribute" (p. 270).

Attribute	#	Type	Description
icon	?	xs:anyURI	Location of an appropriate graphics file for this element. See the section titled "The icon attribute" (p. 270).
id	?	xs:ID	The identifier of this rule.
role	?	xs:string	A name for the role of an assertion or context item. See the section titled "The role attribute" (p. 270).
see	?	xs:anyURI	A URI pointing to external information for this element. See the section titled "The see attribute" (p. 271).
subject	?	XPath expression	A path expression that allows a more precise specification of the node a rule, assert or report is about. See the section titled "The subject attribute" (p. 271).
visit-each	?	XPath expression	An XPath expression that selects items, based on what was selected by the rule's context attribute. Each resulting item is validated against the assertions and reports of the rule. See the section titled "Detailing rules: visit-each" (p. 113).
xml:lang	?	xs:language	The default natural language for this element (and its children). See the section titled "The xml:lang attribute" (p. 271).
xml:space	?	xs:string	How whitespace must be handled for this element. See the section titled "The xml:space attribute" (p. 272).

Table C.15 – Child elements of the <rule> element

Child element	#	Description
include	*	Includes a document. See the section titled "The <include> element" (p. 274).
p	*	A paragraph of text, usually meant for documenting (this part of) the schema. See the section titled "The <p> element" (p. 273).

Child element	#	Description
let	*	A variable declaration, in-scope for this rule. See the section titled "The <let> element" (p. 272).
assert	*	An assertion to check when this rule is active. See the section titled "Defining assertions and reports: <assert> and <report> " (p. 259).
report	*	A report to check when this rule is active. See the section titled "Defining assertions and reports: <assert> and <report> " (p. 259).
extends	*	Specifies that this rule is an extension of the abstract rule specified by the <extends> element's rule attribute. See the section titled "Referencing a library or an abstract rule: <extends> " (p. 262).

Defining assertions and reports: <assert> and <report>

The <assert> and <report> elements define assertions and reports to check when the encompassing rule fires. See the section titled "Patterns, groups, rules, assertions, and reports" (p. 53) for more information.

The <report> element has the same definition as the <assert> element described below. The difference is in their usage of the test attribute.

```
<assert diagnostics? = xs:IDREFS
        flag? = xs:string
        fpi? = xs:string
        icon? = xs:anyURI
        id? = xs:ID
        properties? = xs:IDREFS
        role? = xs:string
        see? = xs:anyURI
        severity? = xs:string
        subject? = XPath expression
        test = XPath expression
        xml:lang? = xs:language
        xml:space? = xs:string >
  Mixed contents, can contain:
  <dir>*
  <emph>*
  <span>*
  <value-of>*
```

```
  <name>*
</assert>
```

Table C.16 – Attributes of the <assert> element

Attribute	#	Type	Description
diagnostics	?	xs:IDREFS	Whitespace-separated list of identifiers of diagnostics. See the section titled "Defining diagnostic messages: <diagnostics> " (p. 263).
flag	?	xs:string	Name of a flag to be set to `true` when this element fires. See the section titled "The `flag` attribute" (p. 270).
fpi	?	xs:string	A formal public identifier for this element. See the section titled "The `fpi` attribute" (p. 270).
icon	?	xs:anyURI	Location of an appropriate graphics file for this element. See the section titled "The `icon` attribute" (p. 270).
id	?	xs:ID	The identifier of this assertion.
properties	?	xs:IDREFS	Whitespace separated list of identifiers of properties. See the section titled "Defining additional properties: <properties> " (p. 265).
role	?	xs:string	A name for the role of an assertion or context item. See the section titled "The `role` attribute" (p. 270).
see	?	xs:anyURI	A URI pointing to external information for this element. See the section titled "The `see` attribute" (p. 271).
severity	?	xs:string	An indication of the severity of the assert or report. See the section titled "Specifying a severity: the `severity` attribute" (p. 155). The standard reserves the following values without further definition: `fatal`, `error`, `warning`, and `info`.

Attribute	#	Type	Description
`subject`	?	`XPath expression`	A path expression that allows a more precise specification of the node a rule, assert or report is about. See the section titled "The `subject` attribute" (p. 271).
`test`	1	`XPath expression`	The test to perform. ■ For assertions: when the effective boolean value is `false` the assertion fires. ■ For reports: when the effective boolean value is `true` the report fires.
`xml:lang`	?	`xs:language`	The default natural language for this element (and its children). See the section titled "The `xml:lang` attribute" (p. 271).
`xml:space`	?	`xs:string`	How whitespace must be handled for this element. See the section titled "The `xml:space` attribute" (p. 272).

Table C.17 – Child elements of the `<assert>` element

Child element	#	Description
`dir`	*	Text writing direction. See the section titled "Writing direction: `<dir>` " (p. 267).
`emph`	*	Emphasize this text. See the section titled "Emphasis: `<emph>` " (p. 268).
`span`	*	Text span. See the section titled "Spanning text: `<span>` " (p. 268).
`value-of`	*	Inserts the result(s) of an expression in the text. See the section titled "Value of an XPath expression: `<value-of>` " (p. 269).
`name`	*	Inserts the name of (usually) the context item in the text. See the section titled "Retrieving the name of a node: `<name>` " (p. 268).

Referencing a library or an abstract rule: `<extends>`

The `<extends>` element is used for two different situations:

- As child of the root `<schema>` or `<library>` elements: to include a library. For more information see the section titled "Using libraries: `<library>` and `<extends>` " (p. 122).
- As child of a `<rule>` element: reference an abstract rule. For more information see the section titled "Reusing rules: abstract rules" (p. 101).

```
<extends href? = xs:anyURI
         rule? = xs:IDREF />
```

Table C.18 – Attributes of the `<extends>` element

Attribute	#	Type	Description
`href`	?	`xs:anyURI`	Reference to an external file that contains a Schematron library or an abstract rule definition.
`rule`	?	`xs:IDREF`	Reference by identifier to an abstract rule. See the section titled "Validation rules: `<rule>` " (p. 257).

- If `<extends>` references a library: `href` must be present and `rule` is ignored.
- If `<extends>` references an abstract rule: use either a `rule` or an `href` attribute, not both.

Defining parameters: `<param>`

The `<param>` element defines a parameter. It can be used in the following circumstances:

- As child of a root `<schema>` or `<library>` element: defines a global schema parameter. See the section titled "Global schema parameters: `<param>` " (p. 111).
- As child of a `<pattern>` or `<group>` element that defines an abstract pattern (has an `abstract="true"` attribute): define a parameter for this abstract pattern or group. See the section titled "Reusing patterns and groups: Abstract patterns and groups" (p. 106).
- As child of a `<pattern>` or `<group>` element that instantiates an abstract pattern/group (has an `is-a` attribute): sets a parameter value for the abstract pattern/group instantiation. See the section titled "Reusing patterns and groups: Abstract patterns and groups" (p. 106).

```
<param name? = xs:string
       value? = xs:string />
```

Table C.19 – Attributes of the <param> element

Attribute	#	Type	Description
name	?	xs:string	Name of the parameter.
value	?	xs:string	Value of the parameter.

The <param> element has no as attribute to define its data type. However, some Schematron processors accept (and use) an as attribute for global parameter definitions.

Defining diagnostic messages: <diagnostics>

The <diagnostics> element is a container for zero or more <diagnostic> elements.

```
<diagnostics>
  ( <diagnostic> |
    <include> )*
</diagnostics>
```

Table C.20 – Child elements of the <diagnostics> element

Child element	#	Description
diagnostic	*	A single diagnostic message. See the section titled "Diagnostic message: <diagnostic> " (p. 263).
include	*	Includes a document. See the section titled "The <include> element" (p. 274).

Officially only a single <diagnostics> element is allowed in a Schematron schema, but most Schematron processors accept multiple occurrences.

Diagnostic message: <diagnostic>

A <diagnostic> element holds a generic, re-usable, diagnostic message. A diagnostic message can be attached to an assert or report, based on its identifier. When the assert or report fires, the diagnostic message will be issued. For more information see the section titled "Providing multiple messages: <diagnostics> " (p. 81).

```
<diagnostic fpi? = xs:string
            icon? = xs:anyURI
            id = xs:ID
            role? = xs:string
            see? = xs:anyURI
            xml:lang? = xs:language
            xml:space? = xs:string >
  Mixed contents, can contain:
  <dir>*
  <emph>*
  <span>*
  <value-of>*
  <name>*
</diagnostic>
```

Table C.21 – Attributes of the <diagnostic> element

Attribute	#	Type	Description
fpi	?	xs:string	A formal public identifier for this element. See the section titled "The fpi attribute" (p. 270).
icon	?	xs:anyURI	Location of an appropriate graphics file for this element. See the section titled "The icon attribute" (p. 270).
id	1	xs:ID	The identifier of this diagnostic message.
role	?	xs:string	The role of this diagnostic. Typical values are warning, caution or note. See the section titled "Specifying a role: the role attribute" (p. 154).
see	?	xs:anyURI	A URI pointing to external information for this element. See the section titled "The see attribute" (p. 271).
xml:lang	?	xs:language	The default natural language for this element (and its children). See the section titled "The xml:lang attribute" (p. 271).
xml:space	?	xs:string	How whitespace must be handled for this element. See the section titled "The xml:space attribute" (p. 272).

Table C.22 – Child elements of the <diagnostic> element

Child element	#	Description
dir	*	Text writing direction. See the section titled "Writing direction: <dir> " (p. 267).
emph	*	Emphasize this text. See the section titled "Emphasis: <emph> " (p. 268).
span	*	Text span. See the section titled "Spanning text: <span> " (p. 268).
value-of	*	Inserts the result(s) of an expression in the text. See the section titled "Value of an XPath expression: <value-of> " (p. 269).
name	*	Inserts the name of (usually) the context item in the text. See the section titled "Retrieving the name of a node: <name> " (p. 268).

Defining additional properties: <properties>

The <properties> element is a container for zero or more <property> elements.

```
<properties>
  <property>*
</properties>
```

Table C.23 – Child elements of the <properties> element

Child element	#	Description
property	*	A single property. See the section titled "Defining a property: <property> " (p. 266).

Officially only a single <properties> element is allowed in a Schematron schema, but most Schematron processors accept multiple occurrences.

Defining a property: `<property>`

A property is an additional outcome of an assert or report. It allows you to attach arbitrary information when an assert or report fires. For more, see the section titled "Properties" (p. 144).

```
<property id = xs:ID
          role? = xs:string
          scheme? = xs:string >
  Mixed contents, can contain:
  <dir>*
  <emph>*
  <span>*
  <value-of>*
  <name>*
</property>
```

Table C.24 – Attributes of the `<property>` element

Attribute	#	Type	Description
`id`	1	`xs:ID`	The identifier of this property.
`role`	?	`xs:string`	The role of this property.
`scheme`	?	`xs:string`	An IRI or other public identifier that specifies the notation used for its value.

Table C.25 – Child elements of the `<property>` element

Child element	#	Description
`dir`	*	Text writing direction. See the section titled "Writing direction: `<dir>` " (p. 267).
`emph`	*	Emphasize this text. See the section titled "Emphasis: `<emph>` " (p. 268).
`span`	*	Text span. See the section titled "Spanning text: `<span>` " (p. 268).
`value-of`	*	Inserts the result(s) of an expression in the text. See the section titled "Value of an XPath expression: `<value-of>` " (p. 269).
`name`	*	Inserts the name of (usually) the context item in the text. See the section titled "Retrieving the name of a node: `<name>` " (p. 268).

Message markup: mixed contents

There are several elements in Schematron that can be used to markup messages, resulting in mixed contents: text and markup elements mingled. See the section titled "Messages with markup: `<emph>`, `<span>`, and `<dir>` " (p. 141) for more information.

Writing direction: `<dir>`

The `<dir>` element specifies the reading direction of the enclosed text. For more information see the section titled "Messages with markup: `<emph>`, `<span>`, and `<dir>` " (p. 141).

```
<dir value? = "ltr" | "rtl" >
  Mixed contents, can contain:
  <value-of>*
  <name>*
</dir>
```

Table C.26 – Attributes of the `<dir>` element

<table>
<tr><th>Attribute</th><th>#</th><th>Type</th><th>Description</th></tr>
<tr><td>value</td><td>?</td><td>xs:string</td><td>Specify the reading direction for the text inside the element.
<table>
<tr><th>Value</th><th>Description</th></tr>
<tr><td>ltr</td><td>Left-to-right</td></tr>
<tr><td>rtl</td><td>Right-to-left</td></tr>
</table>
</td></tr>
</table>

Table C.27 – Child elements of the `<dir>` element

Child element	#	Description
value-of	*	Inserts the result(s) of an expression in the text. See the section titled "Value of an XPath expression: `<value-of>` " (p. 269).
name	*	Inserts the name of (usually) the context item in the text. See the section titled "Retrieving the name of a node: `<name>` " (p. 268).

Emphasis: `<emph>`

The <emph> element specifies that the enclosed text should be rendered with emphasis. For more information see the section titled "Messages with markup: <emph>, <span>, and <dir> " (p. 141).

```
<emph>
  Mixed contents, can contain:
  <value-of>*
  <name>*
</emph>
```

Table C.28 – Child elements of the <emph> element

Child element	#	Description
`value-of`	*	Inserts the result(s) of an expression in the text. See the section titled "Value of an XPath expression: <value-of> " (p. 269).
`name`	*	Inserts the name of (usually) the context item in the text. See the section titled "Retrieving the name of a node: <name> " (p. 268).

Retrieving the name of a node: `<name>`

The <name> element inserts the name of a node (usually the context item) in messages produced by <assert>, <report>, and <property> elements. See the section titled "The <name> element" (p. 158) for more information.

```
<name path? = XPath expression />
```

Table C.29 – Attributes of the <name> element

Attribute	#	Type	Description
`path`	?	`XPath expression`	Default: . XPath expression that leads to the node you want to retrieve the name of.

Spanning text: `<span>`

The <span> element indicates that the enclosed text should be rendered as indicated by the (required) `class` attribute. It could for instance refer to a definition in some external CSS file.

Whether and how this mechanism works is implementation-defined. For more information see the section titled "Messages with markup: <emph>, <span>, and <dir> " (p. 141).

```
<span class = xs:string >
  Mixed contents, can contain:
  <value-of>*
  <name>*
</span>
```

Table C.30 – Attributes of the <span> element

Attribute	#	Type	Description
class	1	xs:string	Rendering class information for the enclosed text.

Table C.31 – Child elements of the <span> element

Child element	#	Description
value-of	*	Inserts the result(s) of an expression in the text. See the section titled "Value of an XPath expression: <value-of> " (p. 269).
name	*	Inserts the name of (usually) the context item in the text. See the section titled "Retrieving the name of a node: <name> " (p. 268).

Value of an XPath expression: <value-of>

The <value-of> element inserts the result of an XPath expression in messages produced by <assert>, <report>, <diagnostic> and <property> elements. For more information see the section titled "More meaningful messages: inserting values" (p. 65).

```
<value-of select = XPath expression />
```

Table C.32 – Attributes of the <value-of> element

Attribute	#	Type	Description
select	1	XPath expression	XPath expression to be evaluated.

Standard attributes and elements

Some attributes and elements are used in multiple places in the Schematron specification. Their definitions are gathered here.

The `flag` attribute

Data type: `xs:string`

The `flag` attribute contains the name of a flag. The Schematron specification states that the initial value of such a flag is `false` and that it becomes `true` when a `<rule>`, `<assert>`, or `<report>` with that flag fires. How it's handled is implementation-defined. See the section titled "Flags" (p. 142) for more information.

This attribute can be dynamically evaluated. See the section titled "Dynamic flags" (p. 143) for more information.

The `fpi` attribute

Data type: `xs:string`

The `fpi` (formal public identifier) attribute is meant to associate a public (globally unique) identifier with the element it's on. How it's handled is implementation-defined. For more information see the section titled "The `icon`, `see`, and `fpi` attributes" (p. 159).

The `icon` attribute

Data type: `xs:anyURI`

The `icon` attribute associates some graphics file with the element it's on. How it's handled is implementation-defined. For more information see the section titled "The `icon`, `see`, and `fpi` attributes" (p. 159).

The `role` attribute

Data type: `xs:string`

The `role` attribute allows you to say something about the role of an assertion, report or property. How it's handled is implementation-defined. See the section titled "Specifying a role: the `role` attribute" (p. 154) for more information.

This attribute can be dynamically evaluated. See the section titled "Dynamic flags" (p. 143) for an example on how to do this, based on the `flag` attribute.

The `severity` attribute

Data type: `xs:string`

The `severity` attribute can allows you to say something about the severity of an assertion or report. How it's handled is implementation-defined. See the section titled "Specifying a severity: the `severity` attribute" (p. 155) for more information.

This attribute can be dynamically evaluated. See the section titled "Dynamic flags" (p. 143) for an example on how to do this, based on the `flag` attribute.

The `subject` attribute

Data type: `XPath expression`

The `subject` attribute allows you to specify an alternate location in the XML for the subject of an assert or report. See the section titled "Specify a different location: the `subject` attribute" (p. 155) for more information.

The `see` attribute

Data type: `xs:anyURI`

The `see` attribute contains some URI to additional information regarding the element it's on. How it's handled is implementation-defined. For more information see the section titled "The `icon`, `see`, and `fpi` attributes" (p. 159).

The `xml:lang` attribute

Data type: `xs:language`

The `xml:lang` attribute sets the natural (human) language for the children of the element it's on. How it's handled is implementation-defined.

Setting a language is often done in conjunction with using diagnostics (the section titled "Providing multiple messages: `<diagnostics>`" (p. 81)).

The `xml:space` attribute

Data type: `xs:string`. Allowed values: `default`, `preserve`.

The `xml:space` attribute defines how to handle whitespace for the element it's on. Allowed values are `default` (as you might guess, its default value) and `preserve` only. How it's handled is implementation-defined.

A reason outside of Schematron to use `xml:space="preserve"` is to stop the pretty-print function of an XML editor from formatting your carefully manually indented text contents. However, your editor may not recognize and respect `xml:space="preserve"`.

The `<let>` element

The `<let>` element declares a variable for use in the schema. See the section titled "Declaring and using variables: `<let>`" (p. 70) for more information.

```
<let as? = XPath type
     name = QName
     value = XPath expression />
```

Table C.33 – Attributes of the `<let>` element

Attribute	#	Type	Description
`as`	?	`XPath type`	The data type for this variable.
`name`	1	`QName`	The name of the variable.
`value`	1	`XPath expression`	The XPath expression that provides the value for this variable.

The <p> element

The <p> element represents, according to the standard, "a paragraph of natural language text containing maintainer and user information about the parent element." How it's handled is implementation-defined. For more information see the section titled "Adding structured comments: <title> and <p> " (p. 149).

```
<p class? = xs:string
   icon? = xs:anyURI
   id? = xs:ID >
  Mixed contents, can contain:
  <dir>*
  <emph>*
  <span>*
</p>
```

Table C.34 – Attributes of the <p> element

Attribute	#	Type	Description
class	?	xs:string	A class to signify that this paragraph of text should be rendered in a specific way.
icon	?	xs:anyURI	Location of an appropriate graphics file for this element. See the section titled "The icon attribute" (p. 270).
id	?	xs:ID	Some identifier for this paragraph.

Table C.35 – Child elements of the <p> element

Child element	#	Description
dir	*	Text writing direction. See the section titled "Writing direction: <dir> " (p. 267).
emph	*	Emphasize this text. See the section titled "Emphasis: <emph> " (p. 268).
span	*	Text span. See the section titled "Spanning text: <span> " (p. 268).

The <title> element

The <title> element contains, according to the standard, "a summary of the purpose or role of the schema, pattern or rule for the purpose of documentation or a rich user interface." How it's handled is implementation-defined. For more information see the section titled "Adding structured comments: <title> and <p> " (p. 149).

```
<title>
  Mixed contents, can contain:
  <dir>*
</title>
```

Table C.36 – Child elements of the <title> element

Child element	#	Description
dir	*	Text writing direction. See the section titled "Writing direction: <dir> " (p. 267).

The <include> element

The <include> element includes the contents of an external XML document. For more information see the section titled "Including documents: <include> " (p. 118).

```
<include href = xs:anyURI />
```

Table C.37 – Attributes of the <include> element

Attribute	#	Type	Description
href	1	xs:anyURI	The location of the XML document to include.

APPENDIX D

SVRL reference

This appendix provides a reference for the SVRL vocabulary. SVRL stands for Schematron Validation Reporting Language. SVRL documents are produced by a Schematron processor as the result of a validation. See also the section titled "SVRL" (p. 43).

The SVRL produced by the processor might be hidden from you. For instance, when you run a Schematron validation inside an IDE, you usually don't see any SVRL. Instead you get a nicely formatted list of messages and red squiggly lines. However, SVRL is used behind the scenes.

Producing the SVRL

When you perform a Schematron validation, SVRL is generated. SVRL is an XML language of its own, with its own namespace, structure, elements, and attributes. To get a result that is Schematron processor-independent and consistent, rules are needed. Rules that describe what actions of the Schematron processor result in what SVRL.

The Schematron specification devotes some three pages in Appendix D, full of detailed tables and a lot of footnotes, to this subject. This is a huge improvement over the previous Schematron version, which did not address this topic.

This kind of information in a specification is necessarily rather formal and detailed. So, instead of repeating it here, I've tried to incorporate this information in the language description below. This, I hope, makes it more accessible and easier to grasp. However, such a translation comes with a cost: some of the finer details will be lost. If you're in the business of writing a Schematron processor and producing SVRL, you'll need the original information in the specification!

Notation

The SVRL description in this appendix uses the same notation as the description of the Schematron language in Appendix C. See the section titled "XML structure overview notation" (p. 242) for more information.

To distinguish the SVRL XML from the Schematron XML that produced it, all elements from the producing Schematron schema are prefixed with the namespace prefix `sch:`.

The SVRL namespace

The elements that make up an SVRL message are in the namespace:

```
http://purl.oclc.org/dsdl/svrl
```

The attributes are not in a namespace. Some elements, most notably <text>, let you use attributes and elements in other namespaces.

Root element: <schematron-output>

The root element for an SVRL document is always <schematron-output>:

```
<schematron-output phase? = xs:NMTOKEN
                   schemaVersion? = xs:string
                   schematronEdition? = xs:string
                   title? = xs:string >
  <error>*
  <text>*
  <ns-prefix-in-attribute-values>*
  ( <active-pattern> |
    <active-group> |
    <fired-rule> |
    <failed-assert> |
    <successful-report> )*
</schematron-output>
```

Table D.1 – Attributes of the <schematron-output> element

Attribute	#	Type	Description
phase	?	xs:NMTOKEN	The Schematron phase that this SVRL is a result of. See the section titled "Selecting what checks are active: <phase> " (p. 89).
schemaVersion	?	xs:string	A copy of the sch:schema/@schemaVersion attribute (see the section titled "Root element: <schema> " (p. 244)).
schematronEdition	?	xs:string	Unspecified in the standard. Most probably a copy of the sch:schema/@schematronEdition attribute (see the section titled "Root element: <schema> " (p. 244)).

Attribute	#	Type	Description
title	?	xs:string	The contents of the optional sch:schema/sch:title element, turned into a string.

Table D.2 – Child elements of the <schematron-output> element

Child element	#	Description
error	*	An error that occurred during processing. See the section titled "Errors during processing: <error> " (p. 286).
text	*	Unspecified in the standard. Most probably: some text about the schema and/or validation. See the section titled "Mixed text: <text> " (p. 284).
ns-prefix-in-attribute-values	*	A namespace and prefix declaration, as declared with <ns> in the schema. See the section titled "Namespace declarations: <ns-prefix-in-attribute-values> " (p. 278).
active-pattern	*	Indicates that this pattern (<sch:pattern>) was active. See the section titled "Active patterns and groups: <active-pattern> and <active-group> " (p. 278).
active-group	*	Indicates that this group (<sch:group>) was active. See the section titled "Active patterns and groups: <active-pattern> and <active-group> " (p. 278).
fired-rule	*	Indicates that a rule (<sch:rule>) fired. See the section titled "Fired rules: <fired-rule> " (p. 280).
failed-assert	*	Indicates a failed assert (<sch:assert>). See the section titled "Failed asserts: <failed-assert> " (p. 281).
successful-report	*	Indicates a successful report (<sch:report>). See the section titled "Successful reports: <successful-report> " (p. 283).

A <schematron-output> element is not allowed to be empty. If things go wrong it must at least contain an <error> element.

Namespace declarations: <ns-prefix-in-attribute-values>

The <ns-prefix-in-attribute-values> element is the counterpart of the <ns> element in the original schema (see the section titled "Declaring a namespace: <ns> " (p. 250)). It defines a namespace and corresponding prefix for use in expressions.

```
<ns-prefix-in-attribute-values prefix = xs:NMTOKEN
                               uri = xs:string />
```

Table D.3 – Attributes of the <ns-prefix-in-attribute-values> element

Attribute	#	Type	Description
prefix	1	xs:NMTOKEN	The prefix to use for this namespace.
uri	1	xs:string	The namespace's URI.

Data type inconsistencies

The prefix attribute here is an example of some data type inconsistencies in the SVRL definition. Schematron defines the prefix attribute on the <ns> element as data type xs:NCName. And that's correct: a namespace prefix can't contain a colon, which is the constraint the xs:NCName data type provides.

In contrast, the prefix attribute of the SVRL <ns-prefix-in-attribute-values> element is defined as having the data type xs:NMTOKEN, which is way too broad, since it allow characters, including colon, that are not allowed in a namespace prefix.

Active patterns and groups: <active-pattern> and <active-group>

The <active-pattern> and <active-group> elements indicate which patterns/groups were active. For more, see the section titled "Patterns, groups, rules, assertions, and reports" (p. 53).

The <active-pattern> element is described below. The <active-group> element has the same definition.

```
<active-pattern documents? = xs:string
                id? = xs:NCName
                name? = xs:string
                role? = xs:string >
  <error>*
</active-pattern>
```

Table D.4 – Attributes of the <active-pattern> element

Attribute	#	Type	Description
documents	?	xs:string	The documents on which this pattern was active. This can be the primary document the schema validated or the documents specified in the documents attribute of the <pattern> element (see the section titled "Validating documents referenced by XInclude" (p. 151)).
id	?	xs:NCName	The identifier for the pattern (copy of the sch:pattern/@id attribute).
name	?	xs:string	The contents of the optional sch:pattern/sch:title element, turned into a string.
role	?	xs:string	Copy of the sch:pattern/@role attribute.

Table D.5 – Child elements of the <active-pattern> element

Child element	#	Description
error	*	An error that occurred during processing. See the section titled "Errors during processing: <error> " (p. 286).

If the <pattern> element of an active pattern in the schema has no id attribute, the only thing you'll see in the SVRL is:

```
<active-pattern documents="..."/>
```

This is not very informative because it doesn't tell you which pattern was active. So if you're processing the SVRL and want to infer something useful from the list of active patterns, make sure to provide each pattern with an identifier (`@id` attribute).

Fired rules: `<fired-rule>`

The `<fired-rule>` element indicates that a rule has fired: that a node in the document was found for which the `context` attribute of the `<rule>` element in the schema matches. See the section titled "Patterns, groups, rules, assertions, and reports" (p. 53).

```
<fired-rule context = xs:string
            document? = xs:anyURI
            flag? = list of xs:token
            id? = xs:NCName
            name? = xs:string
            role? = xs:string />
```

Table D.6 – Attributes of the `<fired-rule>` element

Attribute	#	Type	Description
`context`	1	`xs:string`	The context for this rule (copy of the `sch:rule/@context` attribute).
`document`	?	`xs:anyURI`	The base URI of the document where the rule fired, as derived by evaluating the `documents` attribute of the parent `<pattern>` element.
`flag`	?	`list of xs:token`	The flags that were set to `true` when this rule fired (copy of the `sch:rule/@flag` attribute).
`id`	?	`xs:NCName`	The identifier for the rule (copy of the `<sch:rule/@id>` attribute).
`name`	?	`xs:string`	The contents of the rule's `<title>` element (if any).
`role`	?	`xs:string`	The role for this rule (copy of the `sch:rule/@role` attribute).

Failed asserts: <failed-assert>

The <failed-assert> element indicates that an assert has failed: the expression in the schema <assert> element's test attribute evaluated to false.

```
<failed-assert flag? = xs:string
               id? = xs:NCName
               location = xs:string
               role? = xs:string
               test = xs:string >
  <text>
  <diagnostic-reference>*
  <property-reference>*
</failed-assert>
```

Table D.7 – Attributes of the <failed-assert> element

Attribute	#	Type	Description
flag	?	xs:string	The flags that were set to true when this assert failed (copy of the sch:assert/@flag attribute).
id	?	xs:NCName	The identifier for the assert/report (copy of the sch:assert/@id attribute).
location	1	xs:string	The location of the node in the document (as an XPath expression) where the assert/report failed on.
role	?	xs:string	The role for this assert/report (copy of the sch:assert/@role attribute).
test	1	xs:string	The test expression for this assert/report (copy of the sch:assert/@test attribute).

Table D.8 – Child elements of the <failed-assert> element

Child element	#	Description
text	1	The resulting text (with optional markup) for this assert/report. See the section titled "Mixed text: <text> " (p. 284).

Child element	#	Description
diagnostic-reference	*	A diagnostic message that was linked to this assert/report. See the section titled "Diagnostic reference: <diagnostic-reference> " (p. 282).
property-reference	*	A property that was linked to this assert/report. See the section titled "Property reference: <property-reference> " (p. 283).

Diagnostic reference: <diagnostic-reference>

The <diagnostic-reference> element references a diagnostic connected to the assert/report. See the section titled "Providing multiple messages: <diagnostics> " (p. 81).

```
<diagnostic-reference diagnostic = xs:NMToken
                      role? = xs:string >
  <text>
</diagnostic-reference>
```

Table D.9 – Attributes of the <diagnostic-reference> element

Attribute	#	Type	Description
diagnostic	1	xs:NMToken	The identifier of the diagnostic (copy of the sch:diagnostic/@id attribute).
role	?	xs:string	The role for this assert/report (copy of the sch:diagnostic/@role attribute).

Table D.10 – Child elements of the <diagnostic-reference> element

Child element	#	Description
text	1	The resulting text (with optional markup) for this diagnostic. See the section titled "Mixed text: <text> " (p. 284).

Property reference: `<property-reference>`

The <property-reference> element references a property connected to the assert/report. See the section titled "Properties" (p. 144).

```
<property-reference property = xs:NCName
                    role? = xs:string
                    scheme? = xs:string >
  <text>
</property-reference>
```

Table D.11 – Attributes of the <property-reference> element

Attribute	#	Type	Description
property	1	xs:NCName	The identifier of the property (copy of the sch:property/@id attribute).
role	?	xs:string	The role for this property (copy of the sch:property/@role attribute).
scheme	?	xs:string	The scheme for this property (copy of the sch:property/@scheme attribute).

Table D.12 – Child elements of the <property-reference> element

Child element	#	Description
text	1	The resulting text (with optional markup) for this property. See the section titled "Mixed text: <text> " (p. 284).

Successful reports: `<successful-report>`

The <successful-report> element indicates that a report was successful: the expression in the schema <report> test attribute evaluated to true. Its attributes and child elements are exactly the same as for the <failed-assert> element. Therefore please refer to the section titled "Failed asserts: <failed-assert> " (p. 281) for details.

Mixed text: <text>

A <text> element contains the resulting text of an assert, report, diagnostic, or property. The term *mixed* means that text and certain markup elements can be intermingled. See the section titled "Message markup: mixed contents" (p. 267) for more information.

The main difference between Schematron and SVRL is that SVRL does not have the <value-of> and <name> elements. These schema elements are to be replaced by the evaluated expression or node name.

```
<text fpi? = xs:string
      icon? = xs:string
      see? = xs:string
      xml:lang? = xs:language
      xml:space? = xs:string >
  Mixed contents, can contain:
  <dir>*
  <span>*
  <emph>*
</text>
```

Table D.13 – Attributes of the <text> element

Attribute	#	Type	Description
fpi	?	xs:string	A formal public identifier for this element (copy of the @fpi attribute).
icon	?	xs:string	Location of an appropriate graphics file for this element (copy of the @icon attribute).
see	?	xs:string	A URI pointing to some external information for this element (copy of the @see attribute).
xml:lang	?	xs:language	The default natural language for this element (copy of the @xml:lang attribute).
xml:space	?	xs:string	How whitespace must be handled for this element (copy of the @xml:space attribute).

Table D.14 – Child elements of the `<text>` element

Child element	#	Description
dir	*	Text writing direction. See the section titled "Writing direction: <dir> " (p. 285).
span	*	Generic span for text markup. See the section titled "Spanning text: <span> " (p. 286).
emph	*	Emphasize this text. See the section titled "Emphasis: <emph> " (p. 286).

Writing direction: `<dir>`

The `<dir>` element specifies the reading direction of the enclosed text.

```
<dir class? = xs:string
     dir? = "ltr" | "rtl" >
  (text only)
</dir>
```

Table D.15 – Attributes of the `<dir>` element

<table>
<tr><th>Attribute</th><th>#</th><th>Type</th><th>Description</th></tr>
<tr><td>class</td><td>?</td><td>xs:string</td><td>Unspecified. Most probably rendering class information for the enclosed text. An <sch:dir> element has no class attribute.</td></tr>
<tr><td>dir</td><td>?</td><td>xs:string</td><td>Specify the reading direction for the text inside the element (copy of the sch:dir/@value attribute).
<table>
<tr><th>Value</th><th>Description</th></tr>
<tr><td>ltr</td><td>Left-to-right</td></tr>
<tr><td>rtl</td><td>Right-to-left</td></tr>
</table>
</td></tr>
</table>

Emphasis: `<emph>`

The <emph> element specifies that the enclosed text should be rendered with emphasis.

```
<emph class? = (unspecified) >
  (text only)
</emph>
```

Table D.16 – Attributes of the <emph> element

Attribute	#	Type	Description
class	?	(unspecified)	Unspecified. Most probably rendering class information for the enclosed text. An <sch:emph> element has no class attribute.

Spanning text: `<span>`

The <span> element indicates that the enclosed text should be rendered as indicated by the (required) class attribute. It could for instance refer to a definition in some external CSS file, but whether and how this mechanism works is completely implementation-defined.

```
<span class = xs:string >
  (text only)
</span>
```

Table D.17 – Attributes of the <span> element

Attribute	#	Type	Description
class	1	xs:string	Rendering class information for the enclosed text (copy of the sch:span/@class attribute).

Errors during processing: `<error>`

If an error occurs during processing of a Schematron schema, the Schematron processor can react in one of two ways. What will actually happen is implementation-defined:

- It can stop and raise an error.
- It can still produce SVRL and insert an <error> element at the appropriate location.

The <error> element is defined as follows:

```
<error code? = xs:string
       document = xs:anyURI
       location = xs:string >
  Mixed contents, can contain:
  <dir>*
  <span>*
  <emph>*
</error>
```

Table D.18 – Attributes of the <error> element

Attribute	#	Type	Description
code	?	xs:string	Implementation-defined code associated with the error.
document	1	xs:anyURI	URI of the document where the error was encountered.
location	1	xs:string	Location of the error in the document. What is reported here is implementation defined, for instance a line number or an XPath location.

Table D.19 – Child elements of the <error> element

Child element	#	Description
dir	*	Text writing direction. See the section titled "Writing direction: <dir> " (p. 285).
span	*	Generic span for text markup. See the section titled "Spanning text: <span> " (p. 286).
emph	*	Emphasize this text. See the section titled "Emphasis: <emph> " (p. 286).

APPENDIX E

Schematron QuickFix (SQF)

> This appendix provides an example of Schematron QuickFix using the oXygen IDE for Schematron *2020*. Since this book was published before oXygen released its Schematron 2025 support, I'm not completely sure how this will turn out, but most likely oXygen will support SQF for Schematron 2025 as well.

At the XML Prague conference in 2016, Nico Kutscherauer (data2type) and Octavian Nadolu (Syncro Soft, the company that develops the oXygen IDE) introduced an extension to Schematron: Schematron QuickFix or SQF. This extension allows you to embed so-called QuickFixes in Schematron schemas. SQF-enabled user interfaces can pick up these fixes and offer them to the user. For instance, when an element seems to be missing, an SQF QuickFix can tell the user interface to offer an "insert … element" option. SQF is based on the idea that a Schematron validation should not only tell the user what is wrong, it should also offer a solution.

SQF is a promising and useful standard, but support is limited:

- There is a W3C draft specification[1] from 2015.
- A nearly complete implementation is available in the oXygen IDE.
- Another implementation is Escali,[2] but as of this writing (early 2026) development seems to be stalled at version 0.2, last updated in 2019.

More information and examples can be found on the SQF website[3] or in the oXygen IDE help pages (search for SQF). Let's start by validating the document shown in Example E.1.

Example E.1 – XML document to use for demonstrating the QuickFix capabilities (`schematron-book-code-2025/data/things-for-sqf.xml`)

```
<things>
  <thing name="thing 1" type="normal"/>
  <thing name="thing 2" type="outstanding"/>
  <thing name="thing 3" type="special"/>
  <thing type="normal"/>
</things>
```

1 http://schematron-quickfix.github.io/sqf/publishing-snapshots/April2015Draft/spec/SQFSpec.html
2 https://github.com/schematron-quickfix/escali-package
3 https://schematron-quickfix.com/

The rules for this document are:

- The value of the type attribute on <thing> must be either normal or special.
- The <thing> element must have a name attribute.

As you can see, the second and fourth <thing> elements violate the rules. Example E.2 validates this document and offers users ways to resolve the issues.

Example E.2 – Schematron schema with QuickFixes
(schematron-book-code-2025/examples/sqf/check-things-for-sqf.sch)

```
<!-- 1 - Define the QuickFix namespace: -->
<schema xmlns="http://purl.oclc.org/dsdl/schematron" queryBinding="xslt3"
  xmlns:sqf="http://www.schematron-quickfix.com/validator/process">

  <pattern>
    <rule context="thing">

      <!-- 2 - Check that things have a correct type: -->
      <assert test="@type eq 'normal' or @type eq 'special'"
        sqf:fix="change-type delete-thing">
        Type must be normal or special
      </assert>

      <!-- 3 - Check that things have a name: -->
      <assert test="@name" sqf:fix="add-name delete-thing">
        A thing must have a name
      </assert>

      <!-- 4 - Define a QuickFix to delete a thing:-->
      <sqf:fix id="delete-thing">
        <sqf:description>
          <sqf:title>Remove thing</sqf:title>
          <sqf:p>Remove this thing from the list</sqf:p>
        </sqf:description>
        <sqf:delete/>
      </sqf:fix>

      <!-- 5 - Define a QuickFix to change the type of a thing: -->
      <sqf:fix id="change-type" use-for-each="('normal', 'special')">
        <sqf:description>
          <sqf:title>
            Set the thing's type to <value-of select="$sqf:current"/>
          </sqf:title>
        </sqf:description>
        <sqf:replace match="@type" node-type="attribute" target="type"
          select="$sqf:current"/>
      </sqf:fix>
```

```
    <!-- 6 - Define a QuickFix to add a name: -->
    <sqf:fix id="add-name">
      <sqf:description>
        <sqf:title>Add a name</sqf:title>
      </sqf:description>
      <sqf:user-entry name="newname">
        <sqf:description>
          <sqf:title>What is the name of the thing?</sqf:title>
        </sqf:description>
      </sqf:user-entry>
      <sqf:add node-type="attribute" target="name" select="$newname"/>
    </sqf:fix>

  </rule>
 </pattern>

</schema>
```

1. Define the SQF namespace with the prefix `sqf`. The namespace URL is `http://www.schematron-quickfix.com/validator/process`.
2. Define a Schematron assertion that checks the value of the `type` attribute.

   Link this assertion, using the `sqf:fix` attribute, with two SQF fixes: `change-type` and `delete-thing`. These identifiers refer to the QuickFixes described in point 4 and 5 below.
3. Define a Schematron assertion that checks for the presence of the `name` attribute.

   Link this assertion, using the `sqf:fix` attribute, with two SQF fixes: `add-name` and `delete-thing`. These identifiers refer to the QuickFixes described in point 4 and 6 below.
4. Define an SQF QuickFix that deletes a `<thing>` and give it the identifier `delete-thing`. This identifier is used in the `sqf:fix` attributes on the `<assert>` elements to reference this QuickFix.

   The QuickFix contains a description (`<sqf:description>`) that the processor displays in the user interface.

   Finally, it references the SQF action `<sqf:delete>`, which deletes the context item (the `<thing>` element that failed the test) from the document.
5. Define an SQF QuickFix that changes the type of a thing and give it the identifier `change-type`. This identifier is used to reference it from assert 2 in its `sqf:fix` attribute.

   This QuickFix gets repeated because of its `use-for-each` element. It creates two actions the user can select: one changes the type to `normal` and one changes it to `special`.

The QuickFix contains a description (`<sqf:description>`) that the processor displays in the user interface. This description references the internal variable `$sqf:current` that takes its value from the `use-for-each` attribute.

Finally, it references the SQF action `<sqf:replaces>`, which replaces the value of the `type` attribute of the context item (the `<thing>` element that failed the test) with the correct value chosen by the user.

6. Define an SQF QuickFix that adds a name to a thing and give it the identifier `add-name`. This identifier is used to reference it from assert 3 in its `sqf:fix` attribute.

   The QuickFix contains a description (`<sqf:description>`) that the processor displays in the user interface.

   It then defines a user-entry interaction using the `<sqf:user-entry>` element. This causes a message box with a text entry field to pop up for the user. The user's entry will be stored in the `$newname` variable.

   Finally, it references the SQF action `<sqf:add>`, which adds the `name` attribute to the context item (the `<thing>` element that failed the test), with the value entered by the user.

The following screenshots show how this looks in the oXygen version 24.0 user interface. After being validated against Example E.2, Example E.1 looks like Figure E.1.

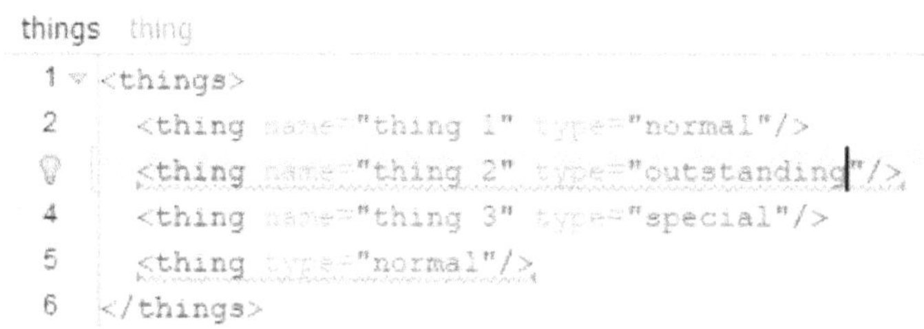

Figure E.1 – Example E.1 after validation with Example E.2.

When the cursor is placed on the second, invalid, thing a light bulb appears in the left margin. When you click on this, the following appears (Figure E.2):

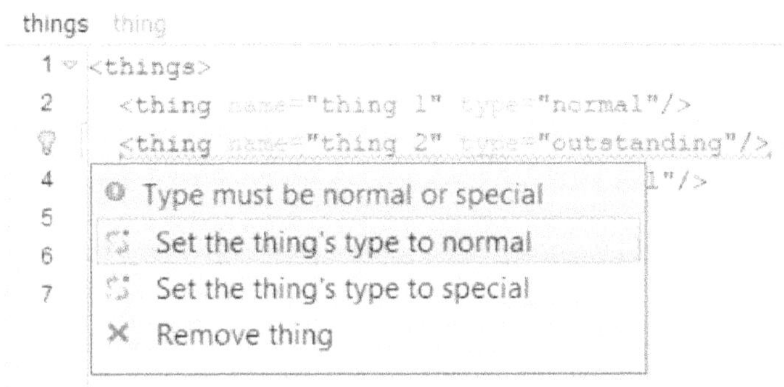

Figure E.2 – Figure E.1 after clicking on the light bulb.

This dropdown menu shown in Figure E.2 has four entries:

- The first entry is the Schematron schema error message, as defined in assert 2 of Example E.2.
- The second entry allows the user to set the type to `normal`. This comes from the QuickFix 5 `change-type` fix.
- The third entry allows the user to set the type to `special`. This also comes from the QuickFix 5 `change-type` fix.
- The fourth entry, which comes from the QuickFix 6, `delete-thing` fix allows the user to delete the `<thing>` element.

If you hover the mouse over the last entry you see an additional message pop-up (see Figure E.3). This message is defined in the `<sqf:p>` element, which is a child of `<sqf:description>` in this QuickFix in Example E.2.

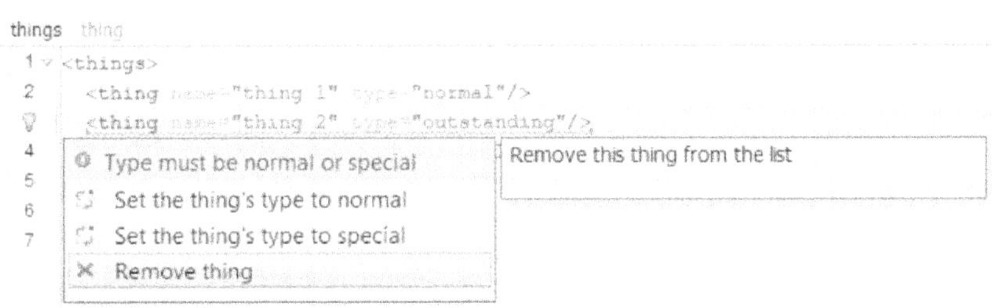

Figure E.3 – Figure E.2 after selecting the last menu entry.

Clicking one of the menu entries executes the associated action.

When you click on the light bulb for the fourth thing, which lacks a `name` attribute, you get a different menu because a different assertion was triggered (Figure E.4).

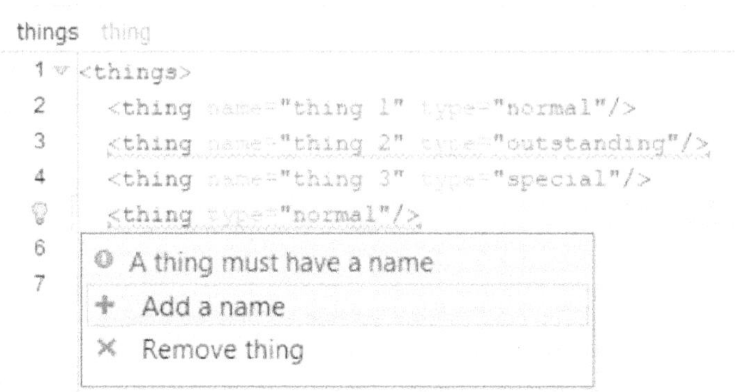

Figure E.4 – The QuickFix menu after selecting the fourth thing

Clicking the `Add a name` entry pops up a message box that lets you enter a name for the thing

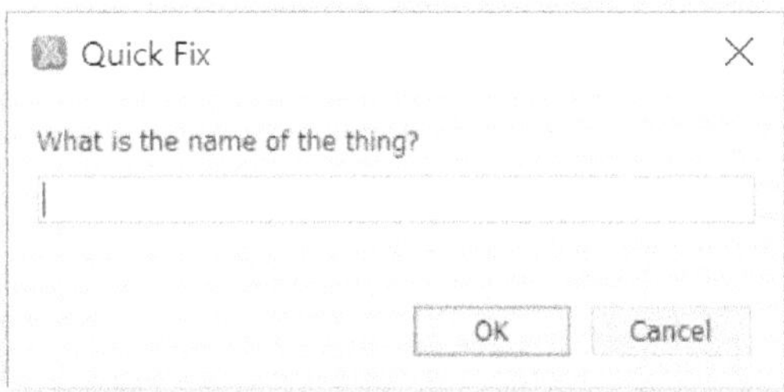

Figure E.5 – The QuickFix message box for entering a name

Since this is just an SQF appetizer, don't worry if you don't immediately grasp all the details. But I hope you agree that SQF is a valuable addition to Schematron. A schema designer can now offer users an automated way to fix validation problems. SQF currently (early 2026) works only with oXygen, but if you are using oXygen, it can make it easier for users to create valid documents.

APPENDIX F

Additional resources

This appendix contains suggestions for additional information resources. It's compiled using the personal preferences of the author, combined with suggestions from others. Although incomplete and biased, it's nevertheless a good place to start exploring.

> ⓘ As of this writing (mid 2026), XPath, XQuery, XSLT, and related standards are being updated to version 4 (under the name of the "XPath NG" initiative).

Schematron

- ***Schematron - A Language for Validating XML* by Erik Siegel (XML Press, 2022)**

  This is the predecessor of the book you're reading. It describes the previous (2020) version of the language.

- ***Schematron* by Eric van der Vlist (O'Reilly, 2007)**

  A short book (around 50 pages), describing an older version of the Schematron standard.

- **Schematron website: https://schematron.com/**

  A website about Schematron, maintained by the original designer of the language, Rick Jelliffe.

- **Awesome Schematron: https://github.com/Schematron/awesome-schematron**

  As it says itself: "A curated list of awesome Schematron tools and applications." Contains links to (all versions of) the specification, interesting articles, and more.

- **Andrew Sales website: https://andrewsales.com**

  Andrew Sales is the editor of the previous (2020) and the current (2025) edition of the Schematron standard. His personal website contains various resources about Schematron, among which links to presentations and an extensive list with the 2025 updates (of which the author of this book has gratefully made use).

XPath

XPath is the underlying technology for many XML-related languages, including Schematron. Given its importance, there's a whole appendix in this book (Appendix A) devoted to this subject.

There are, as far as I know, no books that cover just XPath. However, it does feature prominently in some books about other subjects, including the following:

- ***XSLT 2.0 and XPath 2.0: Programmer's Reference* by Michael Kay (Wiley, 2008)**

  Although outdated (it covers XSLT and XPath version 2.0, but in 2025 we're up to XSLT version 3.0 and XPath version 3.1, with versions 4 under development), it's still a valuable introduction to XPath. It doesn't cover the latest features, but it does teach the fundamentals of the language in a way I still haven't seen equaled anywhere else.

- ***XQuery: Search Across a Variety of XML Data* by Priscilla Walmsley (O'Reilly, 2016)**

  This book about XQuery covers the XPath 3.1 standard. It provides a function overview and has separate sections about advanced topics such as maps, arrays, JSON, and higher-order functions. Unfortunately, it doesn't clearly distinguish XQuery and XPath from each other.

Besides the information in these books, there are also the official standards:

- **XML Path Language (XPath) 3.1: https://www.w3.org/TR/xpath-31/**

  The official language W3C recommendation dated 21 March 2017.

- **XPath and XQuery Functions and Operators 3.1: https://www.w3.org/TR/-xpath-functions-31/**

  The XPath functions and operators W3C recommendation dated 21 March 2017. This resource is especially useful if you are looking for information about a specific function.

XML Schema

XML Schema is a schema language for validating XML documents. You can find an example in the section titled "W3C XML Schema" (p. 27).

- ***Definitive XML Schema* by Priscilla Walmsley (Prentice Hall, 2012)**

  Covers XML Schema in detail. Includes information on the 1.1 version.

RELAX NG

RELAX NG is a schema language for validating XML documents. You can find an example in the section titled "RELAX NG" (p. 31).

- ***RELAX NG* by Eric van der Vlist (O'Reilly, 2003)**

  Covers RELAX NG in detail.

- **RELAX NG website: https://relaxng.org/**

  Contains links to the standard itself and other related information.

XSLT

The programming language XSLT is mentioned a few times in this book. It's a language for transforming XML documents.

- ***XSLT 2.0 and XPath 2.0: Programmer's Reference* by Michael Kay (Wiley, 2008)**

  Although outdated (it covers XSLT and XPath version 2.0, but in 2025 we're up to XSLT version 3.0 and XPath version 3.1, with versions 4 under development), it is still an excellent resource when programming XSLT. It is also a good place to start when you need information on XPath.

- ***XSLT, 2nd Edition* by Doug Tidwell (O'Reilly, 2008)**

  A good book to learn and explore XSLT. Like Michael Kay's book, listed above, it's a bit outdated but can still be used to study the basics.

- ***XSLT Cookbook* by Sal Mangano (O'Reilly, 2006)**

  A cookbook with solutions for various XSLT programming problems. Like the preceding two books, it's outdated with regards to the current version of XSLT, but it is still useful.

- **The XSLT 3.0 standard: https://www.w3.org/TR/xslt-30/**

  This is a standard and, therefore, sometimes hard to follow for mere mortals. However, since there are not many information sources (yet) on XSLT 3.0, you need to look here if you want to learn about the more advanced features, such as streaming, or interesting new instructions such as `<xsl:iterate>` and `<xsl:where-populated>`.

XQuery

XQuery is a programming language designed for querying XML resources (like XML databases), but it can also be used as a general-purpose programming language.

- ***XQuery: Search Across a Variety of XML Data* by Priscilla Walmsley (O'Reilly, 2016)**

  Considered the authoritative resource for XQuery, this book is also a good place to start for information on the XPath standard. It is up-to-date with the most recent XPath standard.

- ***XQuery for Humanists* by Clifford B. Anderson and Joseph C. Wicentowski (Texas A&M University Press, 2020)**

  This book focuses on text processing, assuming the reader has no programming background. It also covers setting up XQuery processing environments such as BaseX and eXist.

XProc

The programming language XProc is mentioned a few times in this book. It's a language for transforming XML (and other) documents using a sequence of separate smaller steps: a pipeline.

- ***XProc 3.0 Programmer Reference* by Erik Siegel (XML Press, 2020)**

  This book describes the 3.0 version of the XProc standard. If you like this Schematron book, you will probably also enjoy this one, by the same author ;)

- **XProc website: https://xproc.org/**

  Site with links to information about XProc, including the standard and learning materials.

Other information

- **W3C: https://www.w3.org**

  The W3C is the body that manages, among other things, the XML standards.

- **xml.com: https://www.xml.com/**

  xml.com is a website with articles and news about XML and related technologies.

- **W3 Schools: https://www.w3schools.com**

  W3Schools is a site containing tutorials and references on web development languages.[1]

[1] W3Schools is controversial within the XML community. It has a history of errors and is infamous for its heavy advertising. Nonetheless, I consult it regularly and find the information useful and well-presented. Judge for yourself.

APPENDIX G
Changes in Schematron 2025

This appendix summarizes the changes in Schematron and SVRL between the 2020 and 2025 editions. Use this if you already know the 2020 edition and want to quickly see what's changed.

Schematron 2025 changes

This section describes the most important changes in Schematron 2025 from the 2020 version.

Specifying the Schematron edition

The root element for schemas `<schema>` has a new attribute called `schematronEdition`. This attribute specifies the version of Schematron this particular schema conforms to.

For Schematron 2025 version, its value should be `2025`:

Example G.1 – Example of using the `schematronEdition` attribute

```
<schema xmlns="http://purl.oclc.org/dsdl/schematron" schematronEdition="2025" …>
  …
</schema>
```

This attribute is optional to preserve backwards compatibility. This ensures that older Schematron schemas are still valid according to the 2025 specification. However, you should use this attribute for Schematron 2025 schemas.

For more information see the section titled "Setting up a Schematron schema" (p. 51).

Grouping of rules so all are evaluated

Schematron's assertions and reports are grouped within `<rule>` elements. For Schematron 2020, the only way to group `<rule>` elements was a `<pattern>` element.

A `<pattern>` element acts like an if-then-else statement: for every node in the document being validated, only the *first* rule (in schema document order) that matches the `context` attribute fires. See Example G.2 for an example that uses the `<pattern>` element.

Example G.2 – Example of using the `<pattern>` element

```
<pattern>
  <rule context="book">
    … (asserts and reports for book elements)
  </rule>
  <rule context="*">
    … (asserts and reports for other elements)
  </rule>
</pattern>
```

For <book> elements, the assertions and reports in the first rule are evaluated, for all other elements the assertions and reports in the second rule.

Schematron 2025 adds the <group> element for grouping <rule> elements. For a <group> element, the if-then-else behavior of evaluating rules does not apply: it simply evaluates *all* rules contained. For instance:

Example G.3 – Example of using the `<group>` element

```
<group>
  <rule context="book">
    … (asserts and reports for book elements)
  </rule>
  <rule context="*">
    … (asserts and reports for other elements)
  </rule>
</group>
```

For <book> elements the assertions and reports in the first *and* second rule are evaluated, for all other elements only the assertions and reports in the second rule.

For more information: the section titled "Patterns, groups, rules, assertions, and reports" (p. 53).

Specifying the severity of assertions and reports

Schematron 2025 introduces an additional attribute, `severity`, for <assert> and <report> elements to express their relative importance. Example G.4 illustrates the `severity` attribute.

Example G.4 – Example of using the `severity` attribute

```
<assert test="starts-with(@code, 'X')" severity="error">Invalid code</assert>
```

The standard does not mandate values for this attribute. However, it reserves, without further definition, three values: `fatal`, `error`, `warning`, and `info`. This means that you are advised, but not obliged, to use these values.

The value for the `severity` attribute can be dynamically evaluated.

For more information: the section titled "Specifying a severity: the `severity` attribute" (p. 155).

Dynamic evaluation of the `flag`, `role`, and `severity` attributes

The `<assert>` and `<report>` elements can contain `flag`, `role`, and/or `severity` attributes. Schematron 2025 allows the value of these attributes to be a variable reference. The value of this variable is then used as the value of the attribute. For instance, see Example G.5

Example G.5 – Example of dynamic evaluation of attributes

```
<let name="standard-severity" value="'error'"/>
...
<pattern>
  <rule context="@amount">
    <assert test="starts-with(@code, 'X')"
      severity="$standard-severity">Invalid code</assert>
  </rule>
</pattern>
```

A construction like shown in Example G.5 allows you to use the same, centrally defined, severity value in multiple asserts and reports.

For more information:

- the section titled "Dynamic flags" (p. 143).
- the section titled "Specifying a role: the `role` attribute" (p. 154).
- the section titled "Specifying a severity: the `severity` attribute" (p. 155).

Typed variables

Schematron 2025 now allows you to specify the data type of a variable, using the `as` attribute on the `<let>` element. For instance:

Example G.6 – Example of specifying the datatype for a variable using the `as` attribute

```
<let name="standard-severity" as="xs:string" value="'error'"/>
```

Strictly speaking, the allowed values of the `as` attribute (and their interpretation) depend on the query language binding (see Chapter 7) of the Schematron schema. In practice, however, these will be the data types that XPath defines, as in XSLT, XQuery, XProc and other languages that use XPath.

> ⓘ An XPath data type often uses the namespace prefix `xs`, which must be bound to the `http://www.w3.org/2001/XMLSchema` namespace. Whether your Schematron processor pre-defines this namespace prefix or not is implementation defined. If it doesn't, you'll get an error message about a missing namespace declaration when using type names like `xs:string` or `xs:boolean`.
>
> To avoid this, explicitly add the namespace declaration for the `xs` namespace prefix to your schema:
>
> ```
> <ns prefix="xs" uri="http://www.w3.org/2001/XMLSchema"/>
> ```
>
> For more, see the section titled "Declaring and using variables: `<let>` " (p. 70).

Grouping abstract rules

Abstract rules are a mechanism for defining and reusing rules within a pattern or group. Schematron 2025 introduces the top-level `<rules>` element, which allows you to define global abstract rules in your schema that can be reused in multiple patterns or groups. For instance, see Example G.7

Example G.7 – Example of using the <rules> element

```
<schema xmlns="http://purl.oclc.org/dsdl/schematron" schematronEdition="2025">

  <rules>
    <rule abstract="true" id="abstract-rule">
      …
    </rule>
    <rule abstract="true" id="abstract-rule-2">
      …
    </rule>
  </rules>

  <group>
    <rule context="book">
      <extends rule="abstract-rule"/>
    </rule>
    <rule context="*">
      <extends rule="abstract-rule-2"/>
    </rule>
  </group>

  <pattern>
    <rule context="magazine">
      <extends rule="abstract-rule"/>
    </rule>
  </pattern>

</schema>
```

For more information, see the section titled “Global abstract rules” (p. 104).

Libraries

Schematron 2025 introduces a new mechanism for reusing Schematron schema declarations: *libraries*. A library is a separate document with a `<library>` root element. It may contain the same kind of content as a schema. However, it is not directly executable.

The contents of a library can be imported into another schema (or another library) using the top-level `<extends>` element. This element has an `href` attribute that references the library to include.

For example, assume we have the following library, called `codelib.sch`, that checks the validity of code attributes (see Example G.8).

Example G.8 – Example of a Schematron library

```
<library xmlns="http://purl.oclc.org/dsdl/schematron">
  <let name="code-start" value="'X'"/>
  <pattern>
    <rule context="@code">
      <assert test="starts-with(., $code-start)">
        A code must start with an <value-of select="$code-start"/>
      </assert>
    </rule>
  </pattern>
</library>
```

If we want to use these declarations in a schema, we have to reference the library using the `<extends>` element:

Example G.9 – Example of using a Schematron library with the `<extends>` element

```
<schema xmlns="http://purl.oclc.org/dsdl/schematron" schematronEdition="2025">

  <extends href=".../codelib.sch"/>

  ...

</schema>
```

The net result is that the declarations in the library, excluding the `<library>` root element, are inserted at the location of the `<extends>` element:

Example G.10 – Result of using a Schematron library with the `<extends>` element

```
<schema xmlns="http://purl.oclc.org/dsdl/schematron" schematronEdition="2025">

  <let name="code-start" value="'X'"/>
  <pattern>
    <rule context="@code">
      <assert test="starts-with(., $code-start)">
        A code must start with an <value-of select="$code-start"/>
      </assert>
    </rule>
  </pattern>

  ...

</schema>
```

For more information: the section titled “Using libraries: <library> and <extends> ” (p. 122).

External schema parameters

Schematron 2025 introduces external parameters: An external parameter is similar to a top-level variable, but its value can be changed when invoking the schema.

To add an external parameter, use the <param> element as a direct child of the root element. Its definition is similar to defining a variable: it has a required `name` and optional `value` attribute, with the same definition and semantics as for the <let> element. For example:

Example G.11 – Example of using an external parameter

```
<schema xmlns="http://purl.oclc.org/dsdl/schematron" schematronEdition="2025">

  <param name="code-start" value="'X'"/>

  <pattern>
    <rule context="@code">
      <assert test="starts-with(., $code-start)">
        A code must start with an {$code-start}
      </assert>
    </rule>
  </pattern>

</schema>
```

In Example G.11, the external parameter `code-start` gets the default value `X`. When invoking the schema you can change this value. How to do this is processor dependent.

Unfortunately, the <param> element has no `as` attribute to specify its data type.

For more information, see the section titled “Global schema parameters: <param> ” (p. 111).

Defining parameters for abstract patterns and groups

Abstract patterns and groups allow you to re-use patterns and groups in your schema that contain structures that look alike but differ in things such as element names or other details.

Instantiating an abstract pattern or group happens using a <pattern> or <group> element with an `is-a` attribute. Values for the various parameters in the abstract pattern or group are passed using <param> elements, as shown in Example G.12.

Example G.12 – Example of instantiating an abstract pattern

```
<pattern is-a="table-pattern">
  <param name="table" value="table"/>
  <param name="row" value="tr"/>
  <param name="entry" value="td"/>
</pattern>
```

Abstract patterns for Schematron 2025 must define the parameters they expect. This is also done using `<param>` elements as the first children of the `<pattern>` or `<group>` element:

Example G.13 – Example of defining an abstract pattern with parameters

```
<pattern abstract="true" id="table-pattern">

  <param name="table"/>
  <param name="row"/>
  <param name="entry"/>

  <rule context="$table">
    ...
  </rule>
  <rule context="$table/$row">
    ...
  </rule>

</pattern>
```

Any `<param>` element in Example G.13 could also have had a `value` attribute. This would define the default value for the parameter.

For more information: the section titled "Reusing patterns and groups: Abstract patterns and groups" (p. 106).

Changes to phase handling

Phases, specified using `<phase>` elements, are a mechanism to let you selectively enable/disable patterns and groups in a schema. Schematron 2025 introduces two changes for this mechanism: dynamic phase selection and partial document validation.

Dynamic phase selection

Dynamic phase selection is a mechanism to select which phase becomes active, based on the contents of the document that is validated. Two things have been added to the standard for this:

- The mechanism for selecting the phase to use has been extended with the special value `#ANY`. Specifying this triggers dynamic phase selection. How to pass such a value to the Schematron processor is implementation-defined.
- An optional attribute called `when` was added to the `<phase>` element. Its value must be an expression that can be evaluated/cast to a Boolean value.

Now, if dynamic phase selection is active (the `#ANY` value was used), the expressions in the `when` attributes are evaluated. The first phase, in document order, where this attribute evaluates to `true` will become the active phase.

If no `when` attribute evaluates to `true`, all phases become active. This is the same as what happens when passing the value `#ALL` instead of `#ANY`.

For more information, see the section titled "Dynamic phase selection" (p. 96).

Partial document validation

Partial document validation is a mechanism to restrict validation to subsets of the document, based on the active phase.

For this feature, Schematron 2025 adds an optional attribute `from` to the `<phase>` element. Its value must be an expression that selects parts of the document being validated. When this attribute is present on an active phase, only the parts selected will be validated.

For more information, see the section titled "Partial document validation using phases" (p. 100).

Additional `visit-each` attribute for `<rules>` elements

Schematron 2025 adds an optional attribute `visit-each` to the `<rule>` element. Its value must be an XPath expression that selects items, based on what was selected by the rule's `context` attribute. Each resulting item is validated against the assertions and reports of the rule.

For more information, see the section titled "Detailing rules: `visit-each` " (p. 113).

Base URI fixup handling

Base URI fixup is something users normally don't need to be aware of and can take for granted. Its formal definition can be found in the XInclude 1.0 standard, section 4.5.5 Base URI Fixup: https://www.w3.org/TR/xinclude/#base.

Its most important effect for Schematron is correctly handling relative document references, even if these are in included documents. For example, if you have a relative document reference such as `<extends href="include/extra.sch"/>`, it must always get de-referenced from the document it's *in*, even if this is in an included document. Schematron 2020 did not define this and processors often got it wrong.

language fixup

Language fixup deals with the treatment of `xml:lang` attributes, which specify the natural language used in Schematron messages. Its formal definition can be found in the XInclude 1.0 standard, section 4.5.6 Language Fixup: https://www.w3.org/TR/xinclude/#language

To find the natural language for the text in some element, the processor searches for the nearest `xml:lang` attribute, starting from the current element and going up to the root of the document, following the XPath `ancestor-or-self::` axis.

Query Language Binding changes

The rules for the various query language bindings in Schematron have changed quite extensively in Schematron 2025. This section lists the major changes. A full description of query language bindings can be found in Chapter 7.

The query language bindings for EXSLT (`exslt`) and STX (`stx`) were removed from the ISO specification for Schematron 2025.

Default query language binding `xslt`

The default query language binding `xslt` has changed as follows:

- The XSLT elements `<xsl:import>` and `<xsl:include>` are now allowed (before the first `<pattern>` or `<group>` element in the Schematron schema). This means you can now use any XSLT code in your Schematron schema, as long as it's in an external document.

- You can use attribute-value-templates (AVTs, XPath expressions between curly braces: `{…}`) for dynamic evaluation of the `flag`, `role`, and `severity` attributes. For instance: `severity="{if ($bad) then 'error' else 'warning'}"`

Query language binding `xslt2`

The query language binding `xslt2` has changed as follows:

- All changes listed for the default `xslt` query language binding (see the section titled "Default query language binding `xslt` " (p. 308)).
- The XSLT element `<xsl:import-schema>` is now allowed (before the first `<pattern>` or `<group>` element in the Schematron schema).

Query language binding `xslt3`

The query language binding `xslt3` has changed as follows:

- All changes listed for the `xslt2` query language binding (see the section titled "Query language binding `xslt2` " (p. 309)).
- Text value templates (TVTs, XPath expressions between curly braces: `{…}`) may be used as an alternative for `<value-of>` elements in messages. Whether and how this is supported is implementation-defined.

Query language binding `xpath31`

The query language binding `xpath31` is new in Schematron 2025. It is the same as the existing, unchanged query language binding `xpath3`, except that XPath 3.1 is used instead of XPath 3.

Query language bindings `xquery3` and `xquery31`

The query language bindings `xquery3` and `xquery31` are new in Schematron 2025. You can find a full description in Chapter 7. Here is a summary:

- XPath 3 (binding `xquery3` or XPath 3.1 (binding `xquery31`) is used for all expressions.
- You can use anything allowed in an XQuery prolog in your Schematron schema (the prolog is the part before the XQuery FLWOR expressions, where all statements end with a semicolon).

SVRL 2025 changes

SVRL (the Schematron Validation Reporting Language) in itself has not changed (much), but its definition and description in the standard has changed significantly:

- Where in Schematron 2020 SVRL and its production were rather under-specified, there is now a full-blown description (in annex D of the specification) of how it should be produced given a Schematron schema execution.
- Small differences between the Schematron and SVRL definitions, for instance the data types of attributes, were fixed.
- A new attribute `schematronEdition` was introduced for the SVRL root element `<svrl:schematron-output>`. Its value must be the same as the `schematronEdition` attribute of the schema.
- An `<svrl:error>` element was added for reporting a dynamic error during Schematron validation. For instance, a missing include file, a query language syntax error, etc.

All in all, your SVRL should look largely the same, with just a few minor changes here and there. Of course, the devil is in the details, so be careful when your tool chain relies on SVRL…

Colophon

About the Author

Erik Siegel is a content engineer and XML specialist who runs Xatapult[1] consultancy in the Netherlands. He specializes in content design and conversions, XML Schemas and transformations, eXist and XProc applications, and XML-related training.

Since 2017, he has been part of the XProc 3.0 editorial team.

About XML Press

XML Press (https://xmlpress.net) was founded in 2008 to publish content that helps technical communicators be more effective. Our publications support managers, social media practitioners, technical communicators, and content strategists and the engineers who support their efforts.

Our publications are available through most retailers, and discounted pricing is available for volume purchases for business, educational, or promotional use. For more information, send email to orders@xmlpress.net or call us at (970) 231-3624.

1 https://xatapult.nl/en/

www.ingramcontent.com/pod-product-compliance
Ingram Content Group UK Ltd.
Pitfield, Milton Keynes, MK11 3LW, UK
UKHW051447290926
15471UKWH00008B/1070

9 781937 434939